I0131175

The added value of auditing in a non-mandatory environment

Promotor: Prof. dr. Ph. Wallage RA
Copromotor: Prof. dr. M. Willekens (Katholieke Universiteit Leuven)

Overige leden: Prof. dr. P.W.A. Eimers RA (Vrije Universiteit Amsterdam)
                 Prof. J.C.A. Gortemaker RA (Erasmus Universiteit Rotterdam)
                 Prof. dr. W.R. Knechel CPA (University of Florida)
                 Prof. dr. H.P.A.J. Langendijk
                 Prof. dr. J.J.A. Leenaars RA
                 Prof. dr. B.G.D. O'Dwyer

Faculteit: Economie en Bedrijfskunde

The added value of auditing in a non-mandatory environment

ACADEMISCH PROEFSCHRIFT

ter verkrijging van de graad van doctor
aan de Universiteit van Amsterdam
op gezag van de Rector Magnificus
prof. dr. D.C. van den Boom
ten overstaan van een door het college voor promoties ingestelde
commissie, in het openbaar te verdedigen in de Agnietenkapel
op woensdag 13 juni 2012, te 14.00 uur
door Hendrik Bernard Duits
geboren te Nijkerk

Routledge
Taylor & Francis Group
LONDON AND NEW YORK

The publication of this book is made possible by a grant from the University of Applied Sciences Utrecht (HU).

First published in 2012 by Amsterdam University Press Ltd.

Published 2025 by Routledge
4 Park Square, Milton Park, Abingdon, Oxon OX14 4RN
605 Third Avenue, New York, NY 10158

Routledge is an imprint of the Taylor & Francis Group, an informa business

© H.B. Duits / Taylor & Francis Group 2012

All rights reserved. No part of this book may be reprinted or reproduced or utilised in any form or by any electronic, mechanical, or other means, now known or hereafter invented, including photocopying and recording, or in any information storage or retrieval system, without permission in writing from the publishers.

Trademark notice: Product or corporate names may be trademarks or registered trademarks, and are used only for identification and explanation without intent to infringe.

ISBN: 9789056297114 (pbk)
ISBN: 9781003705055 (ebk)
NUR   780 / 786

Cover design: René Staelenberg, Amsterdam

For Product Safety Concerns and Information please contact our EU representative: GPSR@taylorandfrancis.com
Taylor & Francis Verlag GmbH, Kaufingerstraße 24, 80331 München, Germany

For my girls Maxime and Laura:
Dare to dream, think & do!

Acknowledgements

Being confronted one time too many by a close friend how often I talked about having a dream of writing a dissertation, I started picturing myself becoming an old man still 'stuck' in the phase of only dreaming of writing a dissertation. Not wanting to end up in that situation, I decided some years ago to live up to that dream and actually start doing it! Although I knew that writing a dissertation is not a short term project, it turned out to be hard to imagine the barriers you have to overcome during the process. But I was fortunate to be surrounded by a supportive environment which largely contributed to the realization of this dissertation. First, I would like to thank KPMG for giving me the opportunity and the support to start working on my phd-project. Also, I owe an immense debt to my promoters, Philip Wallage and Marleen Willekens for their continuous support, ideas, encouragement and remarks on the various drafts of this dissertation. Besides my promoters, I thank the members of the dissertation committee, Peter Eimers, Hans Gortemaker, Robert Knechel, Henk Langendijk, Hans Leenaars and Brendan O'Dwyer, for their interest in the research and the promptly evaluation and approval of the manuscript. I am also indebted to Hans van der Heijden and my brother Barend for their efforts to read parts of the manuscript of this dissertation with care and to offer me with helpful criticism and suggestions. I am also very grateful to my colleagues of KPMG, both at the Department of Professional Practice and KPMG SME Advisors. Especially I like to sincerely thank my KPMG-colleagues Pieter Hoogerbrugge, Huib Maas and Jan Willem Kuypers for their support and confidence in a successful completion of this dissertation and a shared belief in the bright future of SME auditing. Thanks are also due to the colleagues at the Faculty of Business and Management at the University of Applied Science Utrecht, especially Jan Klingen, the managing director of the Research Centre for Innovation & Business. Also I want to thank my family and friends for their 'mental' support in times when the 'phd-road was bumpy' and the path to phd-finalization showed signs of a 'fata morgana': they accepted periods of both mental as well as a physical absence on my part during the writing process of this dissertation. Finally, I want to express my sincere gratitude to my wife Astrid, her belief, support and back-up has motivated me to persevere through the tough times. And my two lovely girls, Maxime and Laura, for enduring a father who is 'writing a book', but who also wants to challenge them to dare to live the life of their dreams.

Hans Duits
Baarn, April 2012

Contents

Appendices

Chapter 1. Introduction

"The Auditors' Report is trust.
I trade in trust"
(free translated after W. Duisenberg:
"Money is trust. I trade in trust")

1.1   Preface

"Auditors exist by the grace of the legislator"[1]. This quote, of the managing director of the Netherlands Authority for the Financial Markets, the independent supervisory body of auditors, does not do justice to the history of auditing. On the contrary, this quote reflects todays' sentiment of a number of users regarding the added value of auditing. According to these users, the demand for audits would not be there if the legislator had not made it mandatory.

It has been this perception which, partly, has been the driver for this study. Combined with recent political discussions[2] whether or not the current mandatory audit regimes (e.g. Europe) for SME companies should be further alleviated, a scientific need arises to investigate whether the already known drivers for the demand for audit still hold in a contemporary non-mandatory environment. To understand where we are and how the future most likely will look like, largely depends on our history[3]. Therefore, this introduction starts with a brief sketch of the history of auditing before the subject of this study, the research question and the further outline are discussed.

Auditing has had a long history. There are signs that auditing already existed in Athens, in 500 BC (Costouros, 1978) and that since the start of the first business corporations in the Middle Ages, audits have been applied (Watts and Zimmerman, 1983). However, modern auditing[4], as we know it, emerged from the rise of the modern corporation. The modern corporation arose approximately 150 years ago[5]. The most distinctive element in this type of corporation is the separation of ownership and control. "The separation of ownership from control produces a condition where the interests of owner and of ultimate manager may,

---

[1] Translation of the Dutch quote "Accountants leven bij de gratie van de wetgever". This quote was made by Mr. Paul Koster on September 16, 2005 in the Dutch newspaper NRC.
[2] For example: Greenbook – Audit Policy: Lessons of the crisis of the European Commission (2010)
[3] In sociological literature this phenomenon is called 'path dependence'.
[4] The phrase "Modern Auditing" is deliberately used to describe the relationship with the developments in a time frame of society which is labelled within sociology as "Modernity".
[5] The 'birth' and existence of the modern corporation is commonly directly related to the 'industrial revolution' (Berle and Means, 1932; De Vries, 1985)

and often do, diverge, and where many of the checks which formerly operated to limit the use of power disappear" (Berle and Means, 1932: 7). Created by the concentration of economic power of these corporations and control which tended to move away from ownership to management as a result of the dispersion of stock ownership, with the large modern corporations new issues arose, such as: the concept of property, the concept of who are entitled to the wealth profits of the corporation and the consequences of a great concentration of power. As Berle and Means (1932) stated in their seminal work on the modern corporation, "(t)he depersonalization of ownership, the objectification of enterprise, the detachment of property from the possessor, leads to a point where the enterprise becomes transformed into an institution which resembles the state in character" (Berle and Means, 1932: 309). In the further theoretical developments regarding corporations/firms, auditing emerged as one of the control mechanisms to reduce problems arising from the separation of ownership and control (Jensen and Meckling, 1976).

With the rise of the corporations and financial markets also economic scandals appeared. Mostly in cases where control mechanisms, meant to reduce the problems arising from the separation of ownership and control, were not adequately implemented (or even not in place) and not effective. As the impact of modern corporations on economic and social life increased, also the impact of the scandals grew. This urged governments to implement a mechanism to ensure the effective functioning of capital markets. Already in the early 20th century, legislators considered independent auditing as a crucial mechanism to reduce uncertainty of market participants. Therefore in a number of countries, legislators forced corporations to have their financial statements audited in order to ensure the effective functioning of capital markets[6]. Auditing is defined as "(t)he primary purpose of the independent audit is to enhance the efficiency of capital markets and help protect the investing public by providing reasonable assurance concerning the integrity of the financial statements and related disclosures" (Campel and Parker, 1992: 297; cited in Wallace, 2004: 285). Also in reaction to corporate scandals, such as Enron, Parmalat and Ahold, national governments emphasised the importance of auditing as an essential control mechanism in order to restore confidence in financial markets and even tightened the control[7] regarding the auditor. From the perspective of the legislator auditing, as an

---

[6] Although in the UK the audit requirement was already incorporated in the company law of 1844, auditing became first mandatory in many countries, like the US and Germany, in the aftermath of the crisis of the 1920's. However, in the Netherlands it took until 1970 before the audit requirement for public companies was incorporated in the company law.
[7] Susan Shapiro (1987) describes this phenomenon of solving a trust problem with additional layers of control in her paper "The social control of impersonal trust", American Journal of Sociology, 93: 623-58.

additional layer of control, plays an important role. Auditing is seen as a mechanism to strengthen trust of participants in (financial) economic markets. Therefore, trust in the auditing profession is of the utmost importance (Explanation implementation WTA, 2005).

Why has auditing become such an important 'safeguard' in society? According to Michael Power (1997) our society has turned into an audit society which created an audit explosion. Power suggests that the main reason for this phenomenon is the growing accounting dimension in society, the need to measure performance (accountability). Audits are nowadays in many respects a substitute for democracy rather than its aid[8]. Within this constellation, auditing has become (or 'forced' by institutional forces, HBD) an even more proceduralized 'regulatory compliance' product (formal control mechanism, HBD), as each new crisis pushes it in this direction.

It is against this background that the image has come about that 'auditors exist by the grace of the legislator'. At the same time, this audit 'explosion' and the confiscation of auditing by national governments, is possibly one of the reasons that in present literature, researchers have given only limited attention to the drivers for the demand (postulates) for auditing. In the past decades, the audit profession has been faced with a demand regulation for auditing services which, also due to existing entry barriers, has been beneficial for the suppliers of auditing services (Maijoor, 1991). The latter could possible also explain the limited attention to the drivers for the demand for audit and the resulting image that the demand for auditing has been more or less 'taken for granted'.

However, it is essential to acknowledge the importance of auditing. Auditing, as a social control mechanism, is a part of an organizational order *in society* which itself is constantly changing. Throughout history, the changes in society and the changing demands of society regarding auditing have always influenced the place and position of the audit profession (Limperg, 1932; Mautz and Sharaf, 1961; Flint, 1988; Power, 1997). The audit profession has to reflect on the (changing) demands of society. If the profession does not constantly reflect the changes in society regarding the demand for auditing or if the profession acts defensively,

---

[8] Power (1997: 127) explained this view by phrasing Day and Klein (1987: 249): 'the emphasis of public policy has been to respond to complexity by setting up new institutions of accountability ... this may, in turn, bring about excessive complexity in the machinery of accountability and at the same time create dead ends. So why not concentrate less on formal links or institutions and engage more in a civic dialogue to recreate at least something of the high visibility and directness of the face to face accountability'. This resembles the phenomenon Shapiro (1987) identifies in her paper 'The social control of impersonal trust'.

there is a risk that auditing will become redundant or will even be marginalized ! (Power, 1997; Strikwerda, 2007).

1.2   Research subject

Why is there a demand for auditing? The answer can be found within the scientific audit discipline in both the analytical theoretical and the empirical research stream (Senkow et al., 2001).

Various explanatory theories have been brought on by researchers in order to clarify the drivers for the demand for auditing. The so-called 'policeman theory' was a generally accepted theory explaining the demand for audits until the 1940s (Porter, 1990). However, with the development of modern corporations and related theory development of the 'Chicago school' in particular, it can be stated that since the beginning of the eighties, the agency theory has become the dominant explanatory theory and a paradigm within the scientific field of auditing (Wallace, 1980; De Angelo, 1981; Dassen, 1989). With the existence of a paradigm, according to Kuhn (1962), the maturity of a scientific discipline has been proven.

Agency theory in its most simple form (Jensen and Meckling, 1976), assumes a principal-agent relation and information asymmetry between them. In the principal-agent relation, the principal hires an agent to act on his behalf. The principal-agent problem arises when the principal compensates an agent to perform certain activities which are useful for the principal and which requires an effort from the agent. Because the agent has a motivation to maximise self-interest, the principal needs to motivate or monitor that the agent acts in accordance with the interests of the principal. This can be done by creating incentives for the agent, like executive compensation based on financial measure of the delivered performance, contractual limitations on the power of managers (agents) to allocate firm resources and installing monitoring devices. Jensen and Meckling (1976) explicitly mention auditing as an example of a monitoring mechanism (see chapter 2 for a more comprehensive elucidation of agency theory).

The agency theory meets the standard of logical positivism. According to this philosophy, general theoretical statements are to be supported by empirical data. Empirical research has been performed by Chow (1982) and Buijink (1992), by formulating a number of hypotheses from the agency framework. These hypotheses have been empirically tested in order to validate the theory why firms would voluntarily engage in an audit. A major problem they encountered was that auditing in a lot of countries had already been 'confiscated' by national governments and laws had been implemented making auditing mandatory for corporations. When having mandatory auditing, empirical research on the drivers for demand for audits becomes complicated. Possible other factors influencing the demand for auditing are less clear in a mandatory audit environment. In order to solve this problem, both studies used the year 1926 because at that time auditing was voluntary[9]. Besides these studies, only a few studies have been identified which used the demand for audit as a dependent variable. The lack of empirical research on this topic can be explained by the difficulty of examining voluntary audits when governmental regulation requires the majority of firms to engage in mandatory audit of financial statements and the limited availability of data regarding the characteristic influencing the demand for audit in cases when auditing is not mandatory (Senkow et al., 2001; Willekens, 2008).

The other stream of empirical research regarding the demand for auditing follows the hypothetical-deductive science concept, whereby hypotheses are formulated on the basis of problems or events which are assumed to express a relation with the demand for audit. Empirical research is subsequently performed in order to determine whether hypotheses can be falsified. By applying this type of research, it is possible to use the demand for auditing not as a dependent variable but as an independent variable. Variables are then identified, such as loss of control, cost of debt finance, financial health and quality of financial information which could be expected to have an influence on the demand for audit also (Abdel-khalik, 1993; Willekens, 2008).

Although this second scientific movement has identified variables which are not covered by agency theory and scientists also acknowledge that auditing may be valuable for other reasons (Knechel et al., 2008), the latter has not (yet) caused a Kuhnian paradigm crisis. Nowadays, within the scientific community, there is still consensus that agency theory is the existing paradigm for explaining the demand for audit.

---

[9] Chow (1982) explained the choice of data collecting for the year 1926 by: "since the hypotheses related to the firms' voluntary hiring of external auditing, it is necessary to select a time period when there were no externally imposed audit requirement. At the same time, data must be available on the variables of interest. The year 1926 was judged to satisfy both requirement reasonably well". Buijink (1992) explained his choice of data collection for the year of 1926 also by the fact that as of 1926 the Amsterdam Stock Exchange required that limited liability companies with stocks or bonds listed, should provide an annual balance sheet and profit and loss account accompanied by the directors' annual report. It was not until 1929 (published 1928) before the Dutch company law first mentioned the possibility of engaging an external auditor. "Therefore a year before 1929, 1926, was chosen ... This is the year also used in Chow (1982)" (Buijink, 1992: 94).

However, a number of assumptions underlying agency theory (like rational behaviour), are challenged by other scientific disciplines. In the analysis of recent corporate scandals as well as the 2008 financial crisis, scientists criticize[10] some of the so-called existing economic models and assumptions (Clarke, 2004; Fukuyama, 2004; Folmer and Lindenberg, 2011). One of these criticism is that the science of economy, in an attempt to strengthen its status, has largely followed the procedures of natural science (like physics) in the past decades. By following physics, the development and use of economic models was strongly emphasized (Simon, 1982). To develop general theories and economic models, assumptions have to be used, such as rational expectations, self-interest, tending to market equilibrium and perfect information. The financial crises made it clear that the underlying assumptions in the economic models are not undisputable[11]. Therefore various fields of economic science conduct critical research regarding the development of existing paradigms as well as the search for new, competing, theories by using (more than in the past) knowledge from other disciplines like for example sociology, psychology in order to establish progress within their own scientific field[12]. Added to that, there also seems (however prudent) a reconsideration regarding the place of economy within science. Economics is the science which studies human behaviour as a relation between scarce means having alternative uses (Robbins, 1935). Therefore economic science is rooted in the domain of social science.

Viewing the development of science as an organic and social occurrence (Kuhn, 1962) research activity within a discipline normally can be considered as a 'puzzle-solving-activity' in order to achieve progress and growth of scientific knowledge. Thereby it can be fruitful to use social research science in economics (Simon, 1982). Thinking outside the boundaries of a theoretical framework increases the likelihood of enlarging our scientific knowledge. Auditing is part of a social order in society which itself is constantly changing. This constantly changing society necessitates researchers in the field of auditing to periodically (re-)investigate the sustainability of existing theories. This study therefore will not only focus on the existing relevant auditing literature but also take into

---

[10] Long before the recent corporate scandals and the financial crisis the underlying assumptions of agency theory, and other neo classical economic theories have already been criticized by a number of scholars, e.g. Herbert Simon and Daniel Kahneman. However, possible due to impact of the recent corporate scandals and financial crisis on society at large, the criticism on the assumptions underlying agency theory has become more mainstream recently.

[11] The failure of Long-Term Capital Management in 1998 is probably one of the most well-known examples that neo classical assumptions (e.g. rational behaviour and efficient market hypothesis) underlying the model used by the company could turn out to be wrong in real life.

[12] An example of this in a closely to agency theory related discipline is transaction cost economy theory. Williamson (2002), by taking into account critics but also another view on the theory of the firm made changes in transaction cost economy theory.

16

account recent criticism on agency theory and theoretical developments in other fields to determine if there are variables omitted, or newly identified, which can contribute in the clarification of the drivers for demand for audit in contemporary society.

1.3   Research objective and research question

Historically, the demand for audit has been affected by changes in social, economic and political thinking (Maijoor, 1991). In response to the world-wide corporate scandals in the early 21st century, regulators have imposed more layers of control on corporations and the audit profession in order to restore the trust of the public in financial markets. But also, especially in Europe, the beliefs about the added value of auditing and pressure from companies to lessen the administrative burden of auditing on companies will probably affect the demand for audit (European Commission, 2007a; Rietschoten, 2007; European Commission ('Green Paper – Audit Policy : lessons from the crisis'), 2010).

It is postulated in this study that auditing is a social control mechanism for securing accountability. Auditing is a wholly utilitarian function and it only satisfies the social need if the benefit it provides is greater than the sacrifice made to obtain it (Flint, 1988). Therefore the audit profession has to deal with the changes in society which (possibly) will affect the demand for audits, the way the audit is performed and requirements which have to be met by the auditor and audit organizations. Audit research can contribute to this in explaining more effectively our current understanding of the audit function. To stress the importance of audit research and further theory development Wallace (2004) retrieves the call made by Williamson (2002) as she concludes: "A comprehensive predictive theory for when certain forms of governance, controls, auditing, and varied contractual mechanisms will be used – particularly in multiple-party settings – merits development and testing" (Wallace, 2004: 287).

Of all the changes in society affecting auditing, the influence of government actions (regulations) historically has had the greatest impact. This influence is partially explained by the fact that one of the generally accepted functions of government (state) is its ability to provide order, security, law and property rights. Within society, government has also the legitimate power of enforcement (Fukuyama, 2005) But government is also "a product of society at a particular stage of development; it is the admission that this society has involved itself in insoluble self-contradiction and is cleft into irreconcilable antagonisms which it is powerless to exorcise" (Engels, 1942: 179-80). The state is a human community and the legitimacy of its scope and strength is given by the people living within the given territory of the state (Fukuyama, 2005). Therefore, although it looks like a dualism, it is possible that the European Parliament demanded more layers of control a few years ago (European Commission, 2003) as a response to the corporate scandals but at the same time also responding to the pressure from citizens and corporations to lessen the burden of 'installed' administrative obligations.

As an example of the latter, the European Commission is currently considering[13], and has started a consultation process in the member states, if the level of the audit exemption[14] for private companies in Europe should be raised to lessen the administrative burden of corporations. When a government reacts to the demand to lessen the administrative burden, and in a response raises the current audit exemptions, an opportunity for the research of the demand for audit is being created (Senkow et al., 2001). In the Netherlands discussion about the administrative burden already led to a deregulation in 2006 by adopting a change in European Law regarding the size criteria for the classification of companies. Due to this deregulation, data has become available of a group of companies facing a possible non- mandatory audit. Creating the opportunity to examine (direct) variables that may to some extent explain why a company would voluntarily engage in audits, was offered. It is therefore the purpose of this study to research the demand for audit in a non-mandatory environment. The research question of this study is:

What are drivers for the demand for audit in a non-mandatory environment?

To answer this question the study will consist of a literature review of the theory for the demand for auditing followed by empirical research. This study contributes to existing literature as it ought to:

---

[13] In 2007 the EC released a preliminary discussion paper about further simplification. After receiving responses the EC started a consultation process in 2008 in the member states. As a result European Commisionar for Internal Market, Mr. Barnier, launched a 'Greenbook – Audit Policy : lessons from the crisis in 2010'. At the time of this dissertation this process of consultation and legislation is not fully completed yet.

[14] In installing mandatory audit regimes, the function and role of the state in a given country has influenced the current existing different audit regimes in the world. Depending on this function and role (to which extent is the state 'allowed' by its citizens to interfere in (to regulate) society?) it occurs that governments, although installing a mandatory audit regimes, allowed on forehand defined group of companies to be exempted of this mandatory regime. As a consequence different audit regimes in the world exist. Also in the European Union, member states still have different audit regimes, although the European Union has installed a mandatory audit regime for companies (member states are allowed to follow a stricter regime, not a lighter regime).

- fill in the calls for a greater integration of literature in order to effectively predict and explain the demand for audit (Williamson, 2002; Wallace, 2004);
- fill in the calls for future empirical research to observe actual choices of directors confronted with a non-mandatory audit setting (Wallace, 2004; Collis, 2004); and
- use some direct variables besides general previous used 'proxy' variables[15] (Senkow et al., 2001; Knechel et al., 2008).

The results of this study can possibly contribute to the ongoing discussion in Europe between politicians, academics and audit firms whether or not a certain level of further audit deregulation is desirable and feasible.

1.4   Methodology

The study consists of a literature review and empirical research. The purpose of the literature review is providing the theoretical foundation for the existence of the demand for audit and an overview of previous empirical research regarding the drivers for the demand. The empirical research will be quantitative in nature and the dependent variable will be the demand for audit (DVA).

The applied dataset has been collected from the Dutch Chamber of Commerce and consists of all 2005 medium sized Dutch companies which were classified as small companies in 2006. The REACH database and Company.info are used to gather publicly available financial data of these companies. Also a questionnaire was sent to managing directors of all companies included in the dataset, to collect additional private data of the company and to further analyze the companies' decisions regarding the audit. In analyzing the empirical data and testing the developed research model various statistical techniques have been used such as uni- and bivariate analyses, multi collinearity checks, factor analysis and logistic regression.

1.5   Structure of the study

This study is organized in seven chapters. The structure can be presented as follows.

---

[15] Previous empirical studies used 'proxy' variables to test the causal relationship with the demand for audit. However the, sometimes, mixed results of these 'proxy' variables suggest that these may not reflect the important aspects of the causal relationships.

Research Question
(Chapter 1)

Literature Review
(Chapter 2)

Relationships explaining
Demand for Audit
(Chapter 3)

Research Model
(Chapter 3)

Empirical Results I
Individual hypotheses
(Chapter 5)

Data Description
(Chapter 4)

Empirical Results II
Regression analyses
(Chapter 6)

Conclusions and
Discussion
(Chapter 7)

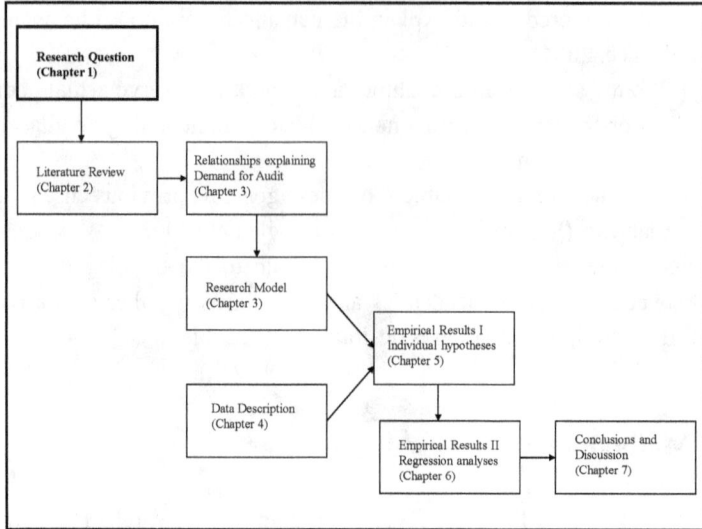

Figure 1.1: Overview of the structure of this study

In chapter two the theoretical foundations regarding the demand for audit are extensively discussed. The first part of that chapter reflects on the evolution of the current paradigm explaining the demand for audit and previous empirical research regarding the demand for audit based on the existing paradigm, the agency theory. The second part of the chapter focuses on (recent) criticisms brought forward against the underlying assumptions of agency theory and elaborates the possible impact of these criticisms. Chapter three starts with a comprehensive review of identified relationships affecting the demand for audit in previous empirical research. Elaborating on this review and the theoretical foundations as set out in chapter two, hypotheses and explanatory variables have been defined related to the demand for audit. The chapter concludes with the conceptual framework to be used in the empirical part of this study. In chapter four the dataset is presented and the results of the study are presented in chapter five and chapter six. Conclusions are addressed in chapter seven, including suggestions for future research.

Chapter 2.   The demand for audit - evolution of a theory

*"Was für eine Philosophie man wähle,
hängt sonach davon ab, was man für ein
Mensch ist: Denn ein philosophisches
System ist nicht ein todler Hausrath, den
man ablegen oder annehmen könnte, wie es
uns beliebte, sondern es ist beseelt durch
die Seele des Menschen, der es hat."*

(Johann G. Fichte, 1797)

2.1   Introduction

In chapter one the research question of this study was formulated: *what are drivers for the demand for audit in a non-mandatory environment?* As illustrated in figure 2.1, this chapter will provide the theoretical foundation for the existence of a demand for audit. The purpose of this chapter is, using a 'Kuhnian'-view on science development, to elucidate the theoretical construct that will be used as 'reference point' in this study to search for further enrichment of scientific knowledge of the drivers for the demand for audit.

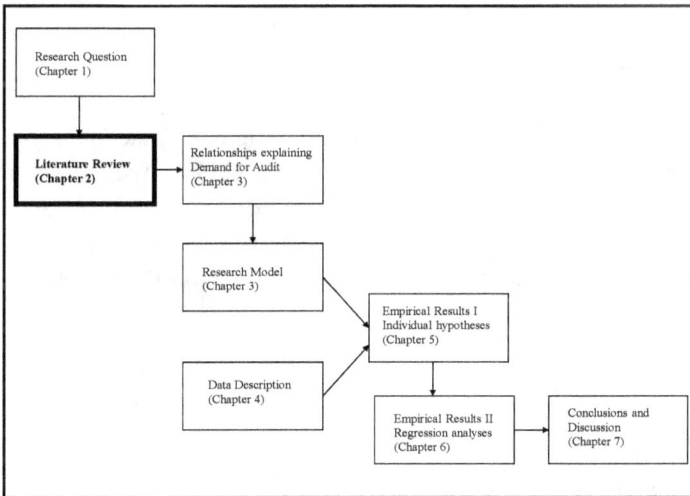

Figure 2.1: Overview of the structure of this study

The chapter starts in section 2.2 with a brief historical sketch of the search for a 'capable' theory of the demand for (an independent) audit, describes how agency theory became the current paradigm and presents an analysis of empirical studies regarding the demand for audit within the current paradigm. A number of criticisms and challenges brought forward by scholars against the current paradigm are presented in section 2.3. Followed, in section 2.4, by an analysis of possible implications of these criticisms for the science development regarding the demand for audit. Section 2.5 presents the conclusions of this chapter.

2.2 How agency theory became the paradigm in explaining the demand for audit

2.2.1 The search for a theory for the demand for audit

Modern auditing 'arised as a phoenix from the ashes' on the back of the first corporate scandals in modern corporations in the 19th century. In the aftermath of detected fraud cases by management, outside shareholders demanded independent auditing as an oversight mechanism to ensure the credibility of the presented financial information by the delegated managers. It is this demand which created a new profession of auditors (De Vries, 1985; Power, 1997).

Thus, the audit profession developed itself in a response to the needs of society. When the independent contours of the profession became visible, the search for an explanatory theory of auditing[16] began. However, at that time in a number of countries the demand for audit was already mandatory, leading to an 'inelastic' demand for audit.

Given the origin of the demand it is not surprising that in the initial period the 'policeman theory' was the widely held theory on auditing. Auditing was focused on arithmetical accuracy and on prevention and detection of fraud. But as over time auditing shifts to 'verification of truth and fairness of the financial statements' this theory lost much of its explanatory power (Porter, 1990 cited by Hayes et al., 1999).

---

[16] The development of auditing theory in the Anglo-Saxon countries first started after the audit had been made (partly) mandatory. In the UK the first mandatory audit was introduced in 1844 (Watts and Zimmerman, 1983), in the USA the mandatory audit for public companies was introduced in 1933. Mautz and Sharaf (1961:1) claimed in their seminal work on the philosophy of auditing: "*Present Status of Auditing Theory*. Currently, there is very little available in the professional literature that can be described as auditing theory".

In the Netherlands it took until the 1970s before the audit requirement for corporations was incorporated in the company law. However, also in the Netherlands the audit profession emerged in the beginning of the 20th century. In the absence of a mandatory demand for auditing the profession in the Netherlands (probably) had more reasons than professions in other countries to explain its right to existence. Under the leadership of professor Theodore Limperg discussions about a theory of auditing were conducted already in the 1920s[17]. These sometimes fierce discussions between scholars in the Netherlands (De Vries, 1985), ultimately led to the "Theory of Inspired Confidence"[18] as set out by Limperg in the early 1930s. It is this theory which greatly influenced the development of auditing in the Netherlands until the 1980s, when as a result of the globalization of the profession (driven by the mergers of several audit firms in the 1980s and 1990s) specific Dutch elements of auditing disappeared (Wallage, 1991).

The theory of inspired confidence requires auditors to perform their task in such a way that they do not betray expectation (general auditing norm) of a 'rational outsider', while on the other hand they should not arouse greater expectations than their audit justifies. The theory connects the social needs for reliable financial statements with the technical possibilities of auditing to meet these needs; it also takes into account the changes in needs over time (Blokdijk et al., 1995:23). In his analysis of the theory of inspired confidence and agency theory, Dassen (1989) concludes that the principles of the demand and supply side of both theories show similarities and therefore, taking into account the paradigmic evolution of agency theory, the theory of inspired confidence can be considered as a premature exponent of agency theory.

Also other attempts have been made to explain the demand for auditing using theories such as: the lending credibility theory, the moderator of claimants theory and the quasi-judicial theory, but merely these attempts were the results of fragmented scientific research. When finally auditing internationally emerged as an individual scientific discipline within the field of economics, economic scientific thinking was already dominated by the 'Chicago School'.

---

[17] Although these discussions mainly were conducted between scholars and practitioners in the Netherlands, Limperg also presented his views on a theory of auditing at an International Auditing Congres in 1926. However it is not clear from history to which extent this has influenced theory development outside the Netherlands. To my knowledge the first reference outside the Netherlands to the theory of 'inspired confidence' has been made in 1988 in the "Philosophy and Principles of Auditing" by David Flint.

[18] Based on the translation of the Limperg Instiuut. The originally Dutch title is: "De Leer van het Gewekte Vertrouwen". It is still discussed in the Netherlands if the translation by the Limperg Instituut is the most desirable (weblog Jules Muis, November 13, 2009, www.nivra.nl). Blokdijk (Blokdijk et al. 1995:23) refers to this theory as "the theory of rational expectations".

2.2.2 Agency theory[19] and the theory of the firm

Agency theory and the theory of the firm as we know it today, are mainly developed within the Chicago school of economics. Scholars as Frank Knight (1921), Ronald Coase (1937) and Eugene Fama (1970), have led the foundation of the current agency theory and the theory of the firm.

Positivist agency theory[20] originates from the rise of modern corporations. In the modern corporation, share ownership is widely held and managerial actions depart from those required to maximise shareholder returns (Berle and Means, 1932). "Since the relationship between the stockholders and manager of a corporation fit the definition of a pure agency relationship it should be no surprise that the issues associated with the 'separation of ownership and control' in the modern diffuse ownership corporation are intimately associated with the general problem of agency" (Jensen and Meckling, 1976:309). Jensen and Meckling (1976) integrate elements from agency theory, the theory of property rights and the theory of finance to develop a theory of the firm[21]. They define an agency relationship as *"a contract under which one or more persons (the principal(s)) engage another person (the agent) to perform some service on their behalf which involves some decision making authority to the agent."* It is assumed that both parties are utility maximizers and that principals and agents act rationally and use completed contracting to maximize their wealth. A consequence of the latter assumption may be the "moral hazard" problem, as the agents may face the dilemma of acting against the interests of their principals. Since principals do not have access to all available information at the time a decision is being made by an agent, the principals are unable to determine whether the agent's actions are in the best interest of the firm. To reduce the likelihood of this problem ("adverse

---

[19] With agency theory in this study, the agency stream is meant to which Jensen and Meckling's "Theory of the firm: managerial behaviour, agency cost and ownership structure" belongs. As within auditing literature normally to this 'stream' is referred as 'agency theory'.

[20] Agency theory has developed along two lines: positivist agency theory and 'formal' principal-agent theory (Jensen, 1983; Eisenhardt, 1989; Foss and Klein, 2006). The two streams share a common unit of analysis: the complete contract between the principal and agent and common assumptions about people, organizations and information. However, they differ in mathematical rigor, dependent variable and style. When in the field of auditing is referred to agency theory, ordinarily positivist agency theory is meant. Positivist agency theory has focused on identifying situations in which the principal and agent have conflicting goals and then describing the governance mechanisms that limit the agent's self-serving behaviour. Other than 'formal' principal-agent theory, positivist agency theory is less mathematical. The positivist agency theory, from a theoretical perspective, has been most concerned with describing the governance mechanisms that solve the agency problem whereas the focus of principal-agent researchers has been the development of a general theory that can be applied to (all possible) agency relationships (Eisenhardt, 1989).

[21] As the paper "The Nature of the Firm" by Ronald Coase (1937) commonly is regarded as the classical work in the theory of the firm, the evolution in the 1970s to theory of the firm by Jensen and Meckling and corresponding evolution in agency theory are sometimes described as "modern theory of the firm" and "modern agency theory" (Foss and Klein, 2006).

selection") and to limit the possible divergence from their interests by the agent, the principals can limit these divergences by establishing appropriate incentives for the agent and by incurring monitoring costs designed to limit the aberrant activities of the agent. In most agency relationships the principals and agent incur positive monitoring and economic bonding costs. Jensen and Meckling (1976) define agency costs as the sum of:

- monitoring costs by the principal;
- the economic bonding expenditures by the agent; and
- the residual loss.

The main objective of agency theory is to explain how contracting parties design contracts to minimize the costs associated with the problems of adverse selection and moral hazard. Following 'complete contract' theory, agency theory assumes that the existence of market and institutional mechanisms can reduce these problems. Agency theory rests upon two key concepts: asymmetric information and creation of incentives. Jensen and Meckling (1976) enlarged the sources of agency costs by giving the owner-manager (agent) the possibility to limit his 'non-pecuniary consumption' voluntarily, the bonding costs. Examples of this bonding costs, mechanisms to convince the (future) outside-shareholder that the manager will act in their best interest, are imposing budget constraints and voluntarily auditing of financial statements. Thus agency costs (monitoring and bonding costs and residual loss) are an unavoidable result of the agency relationship (Jensen and Meckling, 1976).

In general it can be concluded that "the crux of agency theory is that principals delegate authority to agents to act on their behalf. It is this delegation that allows agents to opportunistically, build their own utility at the expense of the principals' utility (wealth). Thus, agency theorist specify an intermediate condition of control, that is, first delegation and then controls to minimize the potential abuse of the delegation." (Davis et al., 1997: 120).

Why has agency theory (the theory of the firm) become a dominant theory? Is it because it is a simple theory, in which large corporations are reduced to two participants – managers and shareholders – and the interests of each are assumed to be both clear and consistent (Daily et al., 2003). Is it because economists struggled with the problem of self-interest for centuries until Jensen and Meckling (1976) provided their rationale for how the public corporation could survive and prosper despite the self-interested proclivities of managers (Daily et al., 2003). Is it because the "conventional theory of the firm is sufficiently successful, theoretically and empirically, that competitors have a hard time gaining a foothold" (Foss and Klein, 2008: 442). Or because "the fact that the dimension it focuses upon is the apparently competing interests of the most powerful players in corporate governance – the executives and major investors – in the dominant Anglo-American economies" (Clarke, 2004: 20). Despite the existence of fundamental criticism brought forward against agency theory (see chapter 2.3) agency theory (and in a broader sense: neo classical economy) is still the dominant theory (Folmer and Lindenberg, 2011). It can be concluded that in their paper 'The theory of the firm', Jensen and Meckling (1976) translate the concerns of ownership-control separation into 'fully fledged' agency problems and even more important they also identified the costs of the agency problems and trace who bears the costs and why. The 'positivist' way Jensen and Meckling formulate their theory certainly has contributed to the acceptance of the theory by mainstream management literature (including auditing) and the business textbooks, which in turn evoked the scientific interest of scholars in these fields.

Although agency theory originally has not been developed to explain the demand for audit, the theory became the paradigm for audit researchers to explain the demand for audit. From the aforementioned explanation of agency theory it can be concluded, that agency theory originates from the rise of modern corporations. As history shows, modern auditing as a profession originated in response to encountered practical complications associated with the rise of modern corporations. Therefore the existence of auditing can be related to the existence of agency-relations. Jensen and Meckling (1976) also mention auditing as a method for controlling the behaviour of the agent.

As over time audit research emerged as an individual scientific discipline, scholars adopted agency theory as the paradigm explaining the demand for audit. The presence of a spontaneous acceptance of a paradigm indicates the maturity of a scientific discipline (Kuhn, 1962). According to Kuhn, research activity within a discipline, normally is a 'puzzle-solving-activity' and problems encountered will be researched and solved within the prevailing paradigm like a puzzle piece is fitted within the puzzle. This view on science differs from, and has been criticized by, other philosophers on science, e.g. Popper (1970). According to Popper, scholars have to reject a theory which has been falsified and replace it. But, as Kuhn noticed, this is not commonly practice and "if any and every failure to fit were ground for theory rejection all theories ought to be rejected at all times" (Kuhn, 1962: 146). This study follows Kuhn in his view that research is a 'puzzle-solving-activity' within a research programme.

2.2.3 The agency theory framework explaining the demand for audit

Scholars in various fields of economics (e.g., organization, governance, strategy) have conducted a number of empirical studies to validate agency theory. Eisenhardt (1989) conducted an assessment and review of agency theory. Based on this study, she concludes that the common approach in the empirical stream of positivist agency theory is to identify a policy or behaviour in which stockholder and management interests diverge and the to demonstrate that information systems or outcome-based incentives (or monitoring controls) solves the agency problem. The reviewed studies of the positivist agency stream showed empirical results consistent with agency theory arguments. As a part of this study, I have conducted an analysis of previous empirical studies explaining the demand for audit.

2.2.3.1 Overview of empirical studies using Demand for Audit as dependent variable

The search for empirical studies revealed only a limited amount of empirical research which used the 'Demand for Audit' as a dependent variable. This can be explained by governmental regulation which requires the majority of firms to engage in mandatory audit of financial statements (Willekens, 2008). An advantage of the studies which used the demand for audit as a dependent variable is the ability to measure the explanatory power (R^2) of the, in the research model, incorporated independent variables (hypothesized relationships) on the demand for audit. The table listed below shows the identified academic studies[22] in which the Demand for Audit[23] was a dependent variable.

---

[22] This set of studies was developed through scanning journals and following up referenced articles. It is expected that all studies are identified, however due to the method it is possible that the list is not exhaustive. Working papers which are not publicized yet are not incorporated.

[23] Studies using the voluntary demand for review of interim financial statements are also not included (e.g. Ettredget et al., 1994; Haw et al., 2008).

Table 2.1 Overview of empirical studies using 'the demand for audit' as dependent variable

Authors	Date	Sample	Legal setting	Public / Private	Sample size	R^2-range
Chow	1982	USA	Non-mandatory	Public	165	.118 - .263
Buijink	1992	NL	Non-mandatory	Public	141	.040 - .253
Carey et al.	2000	AUS	Non-mandatory	Private	186	.200
Senkow et al.	2001	CAN	Non-mandatory	Private	201	.400
Seow	2001	UK	Non-mandatory	Private	32	N/A
Collis et al.	2004	UK	Mandatory	Private	332	.348
Collis	2010	UK and DK	Mandatory	Private	254	.538
					431	.594

The earliest empirical study, and also one of the earliest studies of this type using an agency theory framework, was conducted by Chow (1982). Chow uses the agency framework to analyze a firm's incentives to hire external auditing. Chow investigated if the following external agency relationships[24] affects the demand for audit:

   a.   the manager's ownership share in the firm;
   b.   the proportion of debt (leverage) in the firm's capital structure;
   c.   the number of different accounting measures in the firm's debt covenants;
   d.   the size, measured by market value of the equity of the firm plus the book value of debt.

Whereas at first glance it is clear that the first three relationships are derived from the agency theory framework, this is not the case with the expected relationship between the size of the firm and the demand for audit. In relating size to the agency theory framework Chow uses 'economy of scale'-theory, a possible explanation for the rise of the modern corporation and the emergence of the ownership-control separation, when he argues that the demand for audit is positively related to firm size. More specifically, with this relationship Chow adds a cost-benefit consideration into his model, which seems logical given the utility maximizing assumption[25] underlying agency theory.

---

[24] A crucial difference of the theory of the firm by Jensen and Meckling (1976) compared to for example Alchain and Demsetz is that the Jensen and Meckling do not think of 'team-production', and the related agency cost, to be essential in explaining the corporation. Instead, based on their definition of agency costs, they focus on the agency cost of outside equity and debt (Foss and Klein, 2006). For structuring purposes a distinction is made, based on this original focus of Jensen and Meckling, in the remainder of this study between external agency relationships and internal agency relationships.
[25] The assumptions underlying agency theory are discussed in more detail in chapter 2.3.2.

The univariate tests of Chow supports, with the exception of the manager's ownership share in the firm[26], the hypothesised relationships and the multivariate tests revealed that the proportion of debt and the number of different accounting measures in debt covenants have positive and statistically significant coefficients. However, in explaining the demand for audit the multivariate test for size showed mixed results.

Buijink (1992) replicated, as a part of his thesis, the study of Chow in a Dutch setting and extended it by:
a. making a distinction between public and private debt;
b. taking into account the presence of outside directors as an alternative control mechanism.
Buijink only concludes that the contracting cost of debt, and especially the proportion of private debt affects the demand for audit. The presence of outside directors show a significant positive association with the demand for audit. Therefore, Buijink suggests that instead of an alternative control mechanism auditing and outside directors may be complimentary as monitoring devices.

Where Chow and Buijink used public firms in a non-mandatory environment in their studies, the studies of Carey et al (2000), Senkow et al. (2001) and Seow (2001) researched the demand for audit in private firms in Australia, Canada and the United Kingdom. Carey et al. (2000) used as a proxy variable, the proportion of nonfamily participation in management and board of directors for the agency conflict arising from the ownership-control and found this variable to be positively associated with the demand for audit. Senkow et al. (2001) added, in addition to the relationships tested in the previous studies, two more relationships in their research model to explain the demand for audit. First they assumed as Abdel-khalik (1993) that the demand for external audit also could be explained by the internal agency relationship between management and employees (loss of control, discretion of delegation problem). In addition to this they added the existing relationship with the auditor, if there is any, as a possible explanatory reason for retaining an audit if this is no longer required.

Collis et al. (2004) examined the demand for audit for private firms in the UK. They add internal agency related 'management factors', such as a check on internal controls to reduce the chance of material error and the improvement of the quality of financial information. Collis (2010) extended the 2004 study comparing the drivers for the demand for voluntary audit in both the UK and Denmark. Similar to the study of 2004, data was used of companies which were

---

[26] Chow used a proxy for the management share. However, due to potential measurement errors an adequate test on management share was not possible and therefore excluded from the test.

mandatorily obliged to have their financial statements audited, which made Collis to remark: "A final point of note is that since this analysis is based on the directors' predicted audit decision, there is scope for future research to investigate actual practices" (Collis, 2010: 227).

2.2.3.2 *Overview of empirical studies using Demand for Audit as independent variable*

As mandatory requirements for auditing in many countries made it hard for scholars to conduct empirical 'demand for audit'-studies, most scholars have taken an indirect approach. By using the 'demand for audit' as an independent variable or using substitutes like audit fees and auditor choice[27] (e.g. Eichenseher and Shields, 1985; Jensen and Payne, 2003; Fortin and Pittman, 2007; Haw et al., 2008; Knechel et al., 2008), scholars have tested if the demand for audit as a monitoring mechanism holds within the agency theory framework. Relationships that have been tested, using the 'demand for audit' as an independent variable are:

1. Loss of control and/or complexity within an organization may affect the demand for audit or the auditor choice (Abdel-khalik, 1993; Hay and Davis, 2004);
2. Auditing improves the quality of financial information, reduces earnings management (Willekens, 2008);
3. Auditing reduces the cost of debt and increases the ability to attract debt financing (Blackwell et al., 1998; Hay and Davis, 2004; Willekens, 2008); and
4. External auditing as a substitute for internal auditing and improves operational efficiency (Ettredge et al, 2000; Jensen and Payne, 2003).

However, the few identified empirical studies (see table 2.2), using the demand for audit as independent variable, show mixed results for some of the expected relationships.

---

[27] Studies using a proxy for the demand for audit, such as auditor choice or audit fee, are not presented in this chapter, only those studies using the demand for audit as independent variable.

Table 2.2 Overview of empirical studies using the demand for audit as an independent variable

Dependent relationship	Authors	Expected sign	Support
Lender requirement	Abdel-khalik	Positive	++
Reduces cost of debt	Blackwell et al., Willekens	Positive	+/0
Loss of control and complexity	Abdel-khalik, Hay and Davis	Positive	++
Quality of financial information	Willekens	Positive	++
Financial health	Willekens	Positive	++
Strategic reasons	Hay and Davis	Positive	NS

Support is calculated as the mean of the found significance divided by the number of studies, whereby ++ counts for a strong positive relationship ($p \leq 0.01$); + counts for positive ($p < 0.10$); +/0 counts for mixed results and NS counts for Not Significant

2.2.3.3 Concluding remarks

From the conducted analysis of previous empirical studies using the 'demand for audit' both as dependent variable (chapter 2.2.3.1) and independent variable (chapter 2.2.3.2) it can be concluded:

1. All studies refer to the agency theory framework for their empirical research, which is consistent with the assumption of agency theory being the existing paradigm in explaining the demand for audit;

2. Over time, the paradigm shows some 'plasticity' (Kuhn, 1962). Although originally the focus was on external agency conflicts (Jensen and Meckling, 1976), other encountered relationships with the demand for audit could be fit within the agency theory framework;

3. The relatively low R^2, the explanatory value of the hypothesized and tested relationships, of the empirical studies using the 'demand for audit' as dependent variable suggests that other relationships may exist explaining the demand for audit;

4. Mostly proxy variables and 'substitutes' for the 'demand for audit' have been used in empirical studies in the absence of direct variables to explain the causal relationship with the demand for audit;

5. Comparative studies showed sometimes mixed results for hypothesized relationships. This may be a possible indicator that the demand for audit is also affected by country, size and cultural characteristics.

2.3 Criticism brought forward against the paradigm: agency theory

Recently[28], agency theory (and the theory of the firm)[29] is coming more and more 'under attack' (Davis et al., 1997; Clarke, 2004; Fukuyama, 2005; Padilla, 2007; Foss and Klein, 2008). Criticasters blame agency theory for underestimating the complexity of the phenomena (Clarke, 2004), to have an overly optimistic (Chicago school) view that various governance mechanisms have solved the agency problem (Mahoney, 2005), its evolution never taken place far away from the economic mainstream (Foss and Klein, 2008) and that it relies upon a comparative analysis between a perfect (unrealistic) and imperfect (realistic) world rather than comparing realistic worlds (Padilla, 2007).

Although agency theory appears to be the dominant paradigm underlying most auditing research, exclusive reliance on agency theory is undesirable because, particularly caused by the assumptions made in agency theory, the complexities of organizational life are ignored and therefore additional theory is needed to explain relationships based upon other noneconomic assumptions (Davis et al., 1997).

However, scientific development is not possible without taking into account the concepts of a critical open mind and progress (Kant, 1781; Feyerabend, 1975). The remainder of this chapter will therefore focus on the arguments against a number of the main assumptions underlying agency theory. Although these criticisms are brought forward against agency theory in general and are not specifically pointed towards the demand for audit deriving from agency theory, audit research should not disregard them. In adopting agency theory as the paradigm for the demand for audit, the audit research discipline has to reflect on scientific progress regarding the development of agency theory[30] and not to consider agency theory as static. Therefore, this study provides an analysis of the main criticism brought forward against a number of assumptions underlying

---

[28] Although agency theory, the theory of the firm and their originated theories (e.g. 'The nature of the firm" by Coase, 1937) have been criticized also long before by other scholars (e.g. Simon 1947; March and Simon, 1958) it is only recently that critics on agency theory derive more mainstream attention. Michel-Kerjan and Slovic (2010) remark that evidence against, for example, the rationality of individual behaviour has been downplayed by economists using these assumptions, but with a growing sense of unease among the general public, other social scientists and policy makers these critics no longer can be neglected.

[29] These critics mostly are part of a broader criticism brought forward by scholars against neo classical economy theories.

[30] Over time it seems that most scientific progress of agency theory and introducing rival theories have taken place in neighbouring economic disciplines (e.g. organizational economics, financial market economics and corporate governance) of the audit research discipline.

agency theory, so that we can then consider the potential consequences for the demand for audit research. The criticism are summarized into the following categories:

- the view of the firm as a nexus of contracts;
- the assumption of rational expectations;
- the assumption of a self-interested and utility-maximizing individual actor, and
- the dominant shareholder view.

The potential consequences of this criticism for the theory development regarding the demand for audit are discussed in section 2.4.

2.3.1   The view of the firm as a nexus of contracts

Jensen and Meckling (1976) view the firm as "one form of legal fiction which serves as a nexus for contracting relationships and which is also characterized by the existence of divisible residual claims on the assets and cash flows of the organization which can generally be sold without permission of the other contracting individuals" (Jensen and Meckling, 1976: 311). With this definition Jensen and Meckling emphasize the essential contractual nature of firms and showing that a firm in itself has little substantive content. *"The firm is not an individual"*. Therefore, according to Jensen and Meckling, questioning if a firm has a social responsibility is seriously misleading. Clarke (2004) criticized this view of the firm, by reducing economic relations to series of contracts, it fails to comprehend the complexity of corporate relationships and the need for corporations to continually adapt to changing market environments. Also Simon (1982: 5) notes that the "firm of classical economic theory is little more than an entrepreneur to whom is attached a cost curve or a production function. Since profit maximization and internal efficiency are assumed, there is little room or no room in the theory for the familiar institutional characteristics of real firms." Agency theory is an organizational theory without organizations (Kiser, 1999).

The view of the firm by 'economists' is also criticized by Fukuyama (2005) but he noticed a change in thinking from the period when economists saw firms as 'black boxes', because economics as a science likes to generate theories that produce optimizing solutions, and where the 'black box' may resemble more of a black hole from the viewpoint of theory. This change in thinking by economists represents a regression in the social sciences as "some economists recognizing the limitations of their approach are now turning to earlier theories an trying to restate them in terms of their own methodological assumptions. They are in effect reinventing a forty- to fifty-year-old wheel, which they were responsible for forgetting how to use" (Fukuyama, 2005: 61). And did not Berle and Means (1932) already envision an enterprise being transformed into an institution which resembles the state in character?

A different view of the firm, or an organization, is held by sociologists and organizational theorists. According to Simon (1997) the term 'organization' refers to a complex pattern of human communications and relationships. March and Simon (1958:23) defined organization as "assemblages of interacting human beings [that are] the largest [groups] in our society that have anything resembling a central coordinative system ... [This] marks off the individual organization as a sociological unit comparable in significance to the individual organism in biology". Also legitimacy theory views the firm to be a part of a larger social system. Legitimacy theory relies on the notion that there is a 'social contract' between a company and society that requires the company to be responsive to the environment in which it operates (Deegan 2002).

These conceptions of an organization resemble a broader view than the nexus of contracts. An organization is seen as an 'actor' in society, which is bounded by, but also exists of[31], implicit contracts, norms and values. It is expected that organizations will try to manage their legitimacy because it "helps to ensure the continued inflow of capital, labour and customers necessary for viability. It also forestalls regulatory activities by the state that might occur in the absence of legitimacy and pre-empts boycotts or other disruptive actions by external parties. By mitigating these potential problems, organizational legitimacy provides managers with a degree of autonomy to decide *how* and *where* business will be conducted" (Neu et al. 1998: 265). Also these organizations will conform their behaviour to social norms to avoid the risk that (parts) of society (stakeholders) who can affect the achievements of a corporation's purpose.

2.3.2   Rational Expectations

Rational expectations are an important assumption underpinning the agency theory framework. The presented analysis of Jensen and Meckling (1976) builds on these rational expectations: "If the equity market is characterized by rational expectations the buyers will be aware that the owner will increase his non-pecuniary consumption when his ownership is reduced" (Jensen and Meckling, 1976: 318).

---

[31] Viewing the organization as an 'actor' recognizes the existence of an 'organization culture'. As a result of the existence of an organization culture 'human beings' within the organization are bounded to implicit contracts, norms and values of the organization.

Not only in agency theory, but in almost all neoclassical economic theories (e.g. financial market equilibrium theory) rational expectations play an important role. This assumption of rational expectations is heavily criticized by scholars from other streams and other disciplines. Simon (1982) notes that the neoclassical economic theory of markets with perfect competition and rational agents is a deductive theory that requires almost no contact with empirical data once the assumptions are accepted. Neoclassical "economists attribute to 'economic man' an omniscient rationality. Economic man has a complete and consistent system of preferences that allows him always to choose among the alternatives open to him" (Simon, 1997: 87). The problem with rational expectation theory is that it assumes that participants act on basis of their best interest. This sounds reasonable, but it isn't, because participants act not on their best interests but on their perception of their best interests, and the two are not identical (Soros, 2009), which has been empirically tested by various scholars, such as Kahneman, Slovic and Tversky (1982), Michel-Kerjan and Slovic (2010) and Kahneman (2011).

In their search for development of a theory March and Simon (1958) focus on the history of formal organizations, taking the perspective of social psychologists in answering the question: How does the rationality of 'administrative man' compare with that of classical 'economic man' or with the rational man of modern statistical decision theory? The rational decision makers of economics and statistical decision theory make optimal choices in a highly specified and clearly defined environment (March and Simon, 1958: 158):

1. When we first encounter him in a decision-making situation, he already has laid out before him the whole set of alternatives from which he will choose his action. This set of alternatives is simply 'given'; the theory does not tell how this is obtained.
2. To each alternative is attached a set of consequences – the events that will ensue if that particular alternative is chosen. Here, the existing theories fall into three categories:
   a. *Certainty*: theories that assume the decision maker has complete and accurate knowledge of the consequences that will follow on each alternative
   b. *Risk*: theories that assume accurate knowledge of a probability distribution of the consequences of each alternative
   c. *Uncertainty*: theories that assume that the consequence of each alternative belong to some subset of all possible consequences, but that the decision maker cannot assign definite probabilities to the occurrence of particular consequences

3. At the outset, the decision maker has a 'utility function' or a 'preference ordering' that ranks all sets of consequences from the most preferred to the least preferred.
4. The decision maker selects the alternative leading to the preferred set of consequences.

In the case of certainty, the choice is unambiguous. In the case of risk, rationality is usually defined as the choice of the alternative for which the expected utility is greatest. Expected utility is defined here as the average, weighted by the probabilities of occurrence, of the utilities attached to all possible consequences. In the case of uncertainty, the definition of rationality becomes problematic.

Therefore March and Simon (1958: 159) argue that there are difficulties with this neoclassical model of rational man. "In the first place, only in the case of certainty does the neoclassical model agree well with common-sense notions of rationality. In the case of uncertainty, especially, there is little agreement as to the correct definition of rationality or whether, indeed, the term correct has any meaning here. A second difficulty with existing models of rational man is that these models make three exceedingly high demands on the choice-making mechanism. These models assume that (1) all the alternatives of choice are given, (2) all of the consequences attached to each alternative are known, and (3) the rational man has complete utility ordering for all possible sets of consequences."

However in practice, decision makers lack the ability and resources to arrive at optimal solutions. Bounded rationality deals with this phenomenon, it views the decision-maker as a 'satisficer', one seeking a satisfactory solution rather than the optimal one. Simon (1982: 290) argues that "(b)roadening the definition of rationality to encompass goal conflicts and uncertainty made it hard to ignore the distinction between the objective environment in which the economic actor 'really' lives and the subjective environment that he perceives and to which he responds. When this distinction is made, we can no longer predict his behaviour – even if he behaves rationally – from the characteristics of the objective environment. We also need to know something about his perceptual and cognitive processes". But when perception and cognition intervene between the decision maker and an objective environment, neoclassical economics no longer proves adequate (Mahoney, 2005: 45).

The organizational theory of 'bounded rationality' has found resonance with economists, where adapting these other views leads to a resulting theory of the firm which differ significantly from the neoclassical theory of the firm (Williamson, 2002).

2.3.3   Self-interested utility-maximizing motivation of individual actors

The assumption of self-interested behaviour is the driving force behind the agency problem (Noreen, 1988) and is the element that the theory says is ideally resolved through careful and considered contracting[32]. But as with most of the assumptions underlying agency theory the assumption of self-interested utility-maximizing motivation of individual actors also has it critics. Notably Jensen and Meckling (1994) criticized this model of man as being a simplification for mathematical modelling and an unrealistic description of human behaviour. The assumption of individual self-interest is too limited (Perrow, 1986; Fukuyama, 2005). Frank (1994) suggested that this model of man does not suit the demands of a social existence. The motivation of self-interest is assumed to be wholly extrinsic (Foss and Klein, 2006) and therefore incentives could control for the discrepancy. "If agency theory is useful in highlightening the self-interested economic inclination of agents, it misses the essential basis of trust upon which all human relations are based" (Clarke, 2004:19).

Organizational theorists view organizations as collections of individuals who manifest both cooperative and competitive or self-interested behaviour. Although agency theory provides a useful way of explaining a part of the principal-agent relationship, additional theory is needed to explain other types of human behaviour (Davis et al., 1997). Stewardship theory has been introduced as a means of defining relationships based upon other behavioural premises than self-interest. In stewardship theory "the model of man is based on a steward whose behaviour is ordered such that pro-organizational, collectivistic behaviours have higher utility than individualistic, self-serving behaviours" (Davis et al., 1997: 120). The major distinction between agency theory and stewardship theory is the focus on extrinsic versus intrinsic motivations. Where agency theory assumes that the behaviour is wholly extrinsic the focus in stewardship theory is on intrinsic rewards that are not easily quantified.

---

[32] Completed contracting is an assumption in the agency theory. Based on this assumption the self-interested utility-maximizing behaviour of individual actors can be controlled by ex ante incentive alignment or ex post monitoring. As incentives are considered to be a mechanism to align the interest of the agent with the principal, many (large) corporations introduced financial incentive schemes (bonuses, stock-based compensation), which provide rewards and punishments that are aimed at aligning principal-agent interests, as a major tool in the employment contracts. Corporate scandals (e.g. Enron, Ahold) and the financial banking crisis of 2008 revealed two important issues, namely:
- Incentives as a mechanism to align divergence between agent and principals may be imperfect;
- Individuals certainly demonstrate self-interested utility maximizing behaviour.

As the models of man, regarding their behaviour, agency theory and stewardship theory are not mutually exclusive and should be considered as complementary[33] (Donaldson and Davis, 1994). By adding stewardship (theory) to agency theory the assumption of self-interested utility maximizing individuals is relaxed.

It should be noticed that stewardship theory as described above inherently differs from the 'stewardship' hypothesis in auditing literature, which is grounded in agency literature. This stewardship hypothesis argues that the demand for auditing is generated by managers' (agents') desire to add credibility to their performance reports. These performance reports are issued to the owners (principals) to show that the agent has acted in the principals' best interest. Wallace (1980) introduced the 'Stewardship (monitoring) hypotheses' in her paper *The economic Role of the Audit in Free and Regulated Markets* as the relationship wherein one party (the agent) has delegated decision making power, the agent has an incentive to be checked if the benefits from such monitoring activities exceed the related costs. However this view of stewardship is built on a cost-benefit analysis and is still based on rational expectations and the self-interested and utility maximizing agent.

2.3.4 Dominant shareholder view

A more diffuse stream of critics points to the pre-dominant view on shareholder value by agency-theory, that has created the conditions for the disconnection of corporations from their essential moral underpinnings, encouraging them to concentrate exclusively on financial performance, and to neglect not just the wider stakeholder interests of customers and employees, but the essential interests of the economies and communities in which they operate (Clarke, 2004). Corporations should be regarded not as bundles of assets that belong to shareholders, but rather as institutional arrangements for governing the relationship between all of the parties that contribute firm-specific assets (Blair, 1995). In the theory of the firm the assets of the firm are the property of the shareholders and managers are seen as agents of shareholders with no legal obligation to any other stakeholders. Under this view "the rights of creditors, employees, and others are strictly limited to statutory, contractual, and common law rights" (Allen, 1992:10, cited in Blair 1995).

---

[33] Donaldson and Davis (1994) analyzed previous empirical studies and concluded that the results of empirical studies to validate either agency or stewardship as a 'one best way' showed mixed findings; thus there is the need for both agency theory and stewardship theory explanations of management.

The conception that business holds obligations to various groups in society and must uphold these obligations to survive has gained importance in response to the emergence of stakeholder activism in the 1970s. Freeman (1984: 25) defines stakeholders as "any group or individual who can affect, or is affected by, the achievement of the firm's objectives". Stakeholders include employees, customers, suppliers, stockholders, banks, environmentalists, government and other groups who can help or hurt the firm.

This view contrasted strongly with the view of the Chicago School, which found any broadening of the social obligations dangerous. Why is this so dangerous? Or as Friedman (1986: 133) stated: "Few trends could so thoroughly undermine the foundations of our free society as the acceptance by corporate officials of a social responsibility other than to make as much money for their stockholder as possible". "So long as the management has the one overriding duty of administering the resources under its control as trustees for the shareholders and for their benefit, its hands are largely tied; and it will have no arbitrary power to benefit from this or that particular interest. But once the management of a big enterprise is regarded as not only entitled but even obliged to consider in its decisions whatever is regarded as the public or social interest, or to support good causes and generally to act for the public benefit, it gains indeed an uncontrollable power – a power which would not be left in the hands of private managers but would inevitably be made the subject of increasing public control" (Hayek, 1979: 82). But over time also the Chicago School could no longer ignore the increasing importance of stakeholder theory, although they remain indebted to the value maximization as the organizational objective, as Jensen (2001: 6) states: "A firm cannot maximize value if it ignores the interest of its stakeholders."

In Europe, in contrast with the USA, large corporations have traditionally adhered to a stakeholder model, whereby stakeholders who have a long-term relationship with the firm continuous monitor the firm and engage in important aspects of decision-making. Also the concept of stakeholder theory is much closer to Asian business values. In the UK the possibility of considering other stakeholders interests beyond shareholder value was debated in the Review of Modern Company Law. "The conclusion was that boards should pursue 'enlightened shareholder value' in which it is by balancing the interests of different stakeholder groups to enhance cooperation between them, that the long term interests of shareholders are best protected" (Clarke, 2004:13).

2.4 Implications for theory-developing regarding the demand for audit

2.4.1 Introduction

The previous section presents a number of criticism brought forward against the assumptions underlying agency theory. Within the 'normal' scientific evolution some of these critics have been incorporated[34] (mainly by relaxing assumptions) within the current paradigm. "Still, it is surely debatable how deep the impact ... of insights from fields such as psychology, sociology ... has really been" (Foss and Klein, 2006: 3) and calls are made for more logical duels between rivalling theories (Folmer and Lindenberg, 2011). Opening itself for criticism leads to new insights, as Simon (1982) already shows how fruitful social science research can be for those who are not intimidated by disciplinary boundaries.

Where do we stand with the demand-for-audit-theory development today? Is it justified to argue in line with Karl Popper, that the existing theory, as such has been so falsified that it should be rejected? Or, to argue in line with Thomas Kuhn, have we arrived at the phase in scientific development where it becomes clear that the general accepted paradigm beginning to show signs of disruption and the academic search for rivalling theories should be strengthened? Is now the time to leave the agency theory framework? The old childhood saying 'to not throw away your old shoes before you have new ones' is a simple argument to stick to the existing paradigm. A more substantive argument is that, based on the conducted analysis of previous empirical studies, it is concluded in chapter 2.2.3.3 that the current paradigm has shown 'plasticity' over time. Using a Kuhnian view, there is no reason to leave the agency theory framework yet.

We should not ignore the criticisms and challenges brought forward against the assumptions underlying agency theory. Instead, we should investigate to which extent these criticisms and challenges help us to enlarge our knowledge regarding the drivers for the demand for audit and to see whether the current known variables driving the demand for audit should be amended or supplemented. The previous section presented criticisms brought forward against:
- The view of the firm as a nexus of contracts (chapter 2.3.1);
- Rational Expectations (chapter 2.3.2);

---

[34] An example of interaction with a neighbouring discipline can be found in Williamson's interaction at Carnegie-Mellon University and the following impact on the theory of the firm as governance structure (Williamson, 2002). Another example is the statement of Jensen (2001:6) that a firm cannot ignore the interest of its stakeholders.

-    Self-interested utility-maximizing motivation of individual actors (chapter 2.3.3); and
-    Dominant shareholder view (chapter 2.3.4).

Based on the arguments brought forward it can be concluded that cited criticasters view the firm more than a nexus of contracts. The firm is presented as an institution in society, a sociological unit. Following this line of reasoning the 'moral' or social obligations of the firm logically is a following point of criticism. Whereas agency theory focuses on the shareholder as the ultimate owner of the company, this dominant shareholder view (given the view on the firm) is challenged by other theories, such as stakeholder theory and legitimacy theory. Therefore, for the remainder of this section, the view of the firm as a nexus of contracts and the dominant shareholder will be combined. The social existence, and more specifically human behaviour, is also the line of reasoning followed by criticasters of the assumption of self-interested utility-maximizing motivation of individual actors (in this case management as 'agent') to argue that this model of man is to limited and its behaviour (or decisions) is not always based on extrinsic motivations but sometimes also driven by intrinsic motivations (stewardship theory). With regard to the model of man, agency theory assumes that the agent is 'rational' in his decision making. This view is strongly criticized by sociologists and psychologists as discussed in chapter 2.3.2, and it is argued that people, at best, are bounded rational. The 'way' people make their decision (wholly self-interested?; rational expectations?) is regarded the binding theme in the analysis of the criticism brought forward against the self-interested utility-maximizing motivation of individual actors (chapter 2.3.3) and rational expectations (chapter 2.3.2). From the analysis of the criticisms, two themes come forward that have potential consequences for theory-developing regarding the demand for audit, namely:
-    View of the firm as an institution in society
-    Decision making process of the agent

In the remainder of this section these two themes will be further discussed in light of the potential consequences for the drivers for the demand for audit.

2.4.2   View of the firm as an institution in society

When we consider the 'firm' as an institution and as an autonomous actor within society, we broaden the narrow concept of the 'firm' in agency theory. Viewing the 'firm' as an actor in society means accepting that the legitimacy of the 'firm' can be questioned by other actors. In order to convince other actors that the 'firm' acts legitimately, the company should make a statement that the company acts legitimately. The emergence of the phenomenon 'corporate social responsibility'

(CSR) can be seen as an example of the accountability of the 'firm' as an actor to other actors within society. The identification of the social responsibility of the company drives a demand for specific accounting information to be disclosed by companies[35] and subsequently drives a demand for (another type of) audit (e.g. sustainability audit).

The influence of the question of legitimacy of the company on the demand for audit becomes more visible when it is linked to a stakeholder view instead of a shareholder view. An increase in the demand for accounting information by various parties (often with different needs of information also) and an existing uncertainty by those parties about the credibility of the disclosed accounting information by the company creates a multiple demand for audit. However, honouring this question for audited accounting information by management depends on 'factors' (as shown above) taken into account in the decision process of management and the interdependence between these factors. Holding a stakeholder view (see figure 2.2) in the demand for audit theory is acknowledging the increasing complexity of the environment of the company and the need to disclose information to various parties often with different and sometimes conflicting goals, which in turn creates an uncertainty by (management of) the company if they 'operate' within the boundaries of the standards of 'powerful' stakeholders.

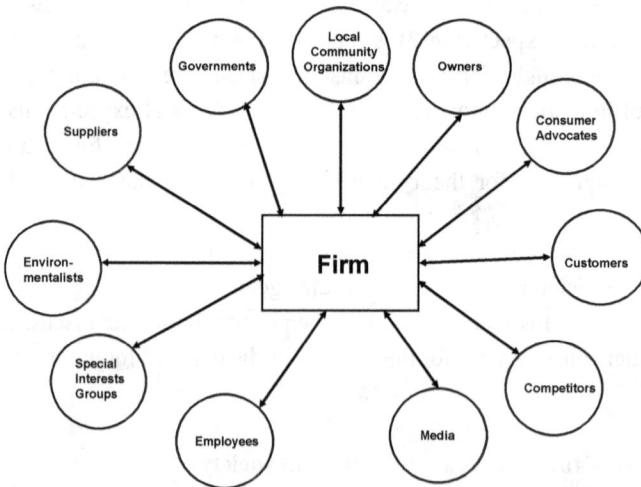

Figure 2.2: Stakeholder view of the firm (source: Freeman, 1984)

---

[35] Accounting research revealed that as a response to the development of 'CSR', companies voluntarily disclose accounting information about their 'corporate social responsibility'. Empirical studies shows that, in absence of a mandatory obligation, the decision for voluntary disclosure is based on a desire/necessity to manage companies' relations with society, proactive enlightened self interest and 'moral' obligations and duties (Neu et al., 1998; O'Dwyer, 2003).

Viewing the 'firm' as an institution, a social arrangement which pursues collective goals, controls its own performance, and has a boundary separating it from its environment reveals the existence of various agency-relations and agency-problems within the 'firm'.

Whereas the original focus of the theory of the firm (Jensen and Meckling, 1976) is on 'external' agency relationships ('the classical agency relationship') also 'internal' agency relationships exists. Scholars have recognized the existence of these 'internal' agency relationships already from the beginning as the theory roots in the organization theory (Coase, 1937; Alchain and Demsetz, 1972) and subsequently conducted a number of empirical studies to test the relationships of a number of these internal agency relationships (e.g. the loss of control) with the demand for (independent external) audit (e.g. Abdel-khalik, 1993; Jensen and Payne, 2003; Knechel et al., 2008). However, holding the view of the firm as an institution, opens the possibility to reveal additional relationships with the demand for audit not fully taken into account yet (e.g. relating the number of stakeholders involved with a company to the demand for audit; the dependence of the company on creditor and/or supply chain on the demand for audit). The number of identified stakeholders of the company will be included as a variable in this study.

2.4.3   Decision making process of the agent

An important question is: who hires the auditor? As over time the number of relations of the company have increased and became more complex, the view of who holds the decision making power has shifted from the shareholders (principal) to management (agent) (Perrow, 1986; Shapiro, 2005). The assumption that principals are in the driver's seat has become problematic when principals seek out agents for their expert knowledge and when principals are one-shotters and agents repeat players. When multiple stakeholders act as principals of the firm, how do agents understand and reconcile the duties delegated to them when they are receiving mixed messages and conflicting instructions and incentives from multiple principals? (Shapiro, 2005). In general it is assumed that in a Small and Medium Sized Enterprises (SME company) setting, it is management is responsible in the decision making process 'who hires the auditor'[36].

---

[36] This also used to be the case with public companies. However, due to further proposed regulation it is expected that within the European Union the decision power shifts to mandatory installed audit committees (although the meeting of shareholders formal appoints the auditor, based on the recommendation of the audit committee) (European Commission, 2010) .

In absence of a mandatory audit, what considerations will management take into account and how will the 'actual' choice to audit or not to audit be made? The criticisms brought forward against the assumptions underlying agency theory (see chapter 2.3) argued that the following factors may also affect the decision making process:

1. Besides extrinsic motivations also intrinsic motivations held by the decision maker have to be taken into account (see chapter 2.3.3);
2. The existence of the 'power' element in relationships (see chapter 2.3.4);
3. The bounded rationality of the decision maker (see chapter 2.3.2).

With regard to motivation, agency theory assumes that only extrinsic motivations play a role in the decision making process. In chapter 2.3.3 it is brought forward against agency theory that besides extrinsic motivations also intrinsic motivations may play a role in the decision making process. Stewardship theory argues that "the 'model of man' is based on a steward, whose behaviour is ordered such that pro-organizational, collectivistic behaviour is ordered such that pro-organizational, collectivistic behaviours have higher utility than individualistic, self-serving behaviours" (Davis et al., 1997:120). The behaviour of a steward is cooperative, collective and organizationally centred. There is anecdotic evidence that management of SME companies (in particular owner-manager and family business) in the Netherlands showed signs of this behaviour during the 2010 economic crisis followed on the 2008 financial crisis, by accepting lower net profits or lower salaries instead of reducing the number of employees. Following this line of reasoning opens the possibility that other motivators may also affect the demand for audit. For example, confronted with competing stakeholders and shareholders objectives regarding the demand for audit, management may be motivated to make a decision which is perceived to be in the best interest of the company.

Power is another element which may possibly more profoundly impact the decision making process whether or not to engage an auditor. In this case the element of 'power' is described by Luhmann as it "influence(s) the selection of actions in the face of other possibilities" (Luhmann, 1979:112, cited in Bachman, 2001: 350). Therefore 'power' can be considered also to be a mechanism to co-ordinate and control the dynamics of a relationship (Bachman, 2001) and it is considered to be an important aspect in the agency relationship (Davis et al., 1997). Whereas in a mandatory audit environment it was clear that government held the balance of power and companies were required to have their financial statements audited if they met the criteria, this no longer is certain in a voluntary environment. In the absence of a mandatory requirement for audit the 'actual' decision 'to audit or not to audit', will be the subject of negotiation, in which it is likely that the 'power-element' plays a role. The relationship between the providers of debt capital and the company is expected to be a relationship whereby the providers of debt capital are in the possession of the 'power-element' to co-ordinate the behaviour of the other party (in this case the company) and that therefore this element probably will play a more profound role in the decision making process to engage an auditor.

Following the theory of bounded rationality (March and Simon, 1958; Simon, 1982; Simon, 1997) it is assumed that the decision maker uses a limited, approximate, simplified model of the real situation and the elements of the situation are not given but are the outcome of a psychological and sociological process, including the choosers' own activities and the activities of others in the choosers' environment. Whereas agency theory, based on rational expectations, implies that management will make a rational choice based on a complete and consistent set of preferences that allows management to choose correctly among the entire set of solutions available it follows that the question to audit or not to audit in an agency relation is considered as (one of the) solutions (March and Simon, 1958). Whether or not an audit eventually will be chosen depends also on the consequences of the various solutions and the utility function or preference ordering of the decision maker. Other than is assumed in agency theory (and neoclassical economic theory in general) bounded rationality recognizes that the alternatives in the choice process are not given but must be sought. From psychological research it is known that decision makers' (this study: management who decides whether or not to opt for an audit) information about their environment is actually less than an approximation of the real environment. This difference is mainly caused by perception[37] in the decision makers' mental model and is actually an active process to focus the attention to a very small part of the whole and to exclude almost all that is not within the scope of attention. In the view of behavioural theorists, like Simon and Kahneman, it is already questionable if management will consider auditing as an alternative/solution to the arisen agency problem not even to mention the assessment of the consequences. Using another view of decision making, like bounded rationality, is accepting that the decision also will be influenced by perceptions and 'general' thinking. A perception of 'auditors exist by the grace of the legislator' therefore has the potential to negatively affect the decision making process, as having this perception limits the decision-maker to look beyond the mandatory obligation and to exclude other potential benefits of an audit in his decision making process.

---

[37] Perception is defined in this study as the interpretation of 'reality' after information/stimuli is filtered out, selected, organized using existing knowledge, needs, beliefs, values, assumptions and attitudes.

Whereas a positive perception of the added value of auditing and a deliberately widened view has the potential to positively affect the decision making process. Scholars should not underestimate the notion of perception[38]. Last decennia much importance has been given to the notion of rationality in economics and evidence against the rationality of individual behaviour tended to be dismissed or downplayed (Michel-Kerjan and Slovic, 2010; Folmer and Lindenberg, 2011). Using an agency theory framework for the demand for auditing assumes that the choice to audit or not to audit will be made on (economic) facts. But as 'bounded rationality' theory argues, a real-life decision exist of more than (economic) facts (knowledge), it also involves perceptions and some inferences drawn from the perceptions and facts (Simon, 1982). Perceptions of the decision maker will be included as explanatory variables in this study.

2.4.4 Towards a post-modern[39] agency theory, explaining the demand for audit?

It seems that the criticism brought forward in this chapter (see chapter 2.3) against agency theory, the existence of other (rivalling) theories and the discussion of possible implications for theory-development not have led to 'logical duels' between scholars yet (Folmer and Lindenberg, 2011). With regard to the demand for audit, the urgency for a continuing 'Kuhnian puzzle-solving activity' regarding the drivers for the demand for audit may not have been high in the last decennia, mainly due to the existing mandatory audit regimes[40] in many countries. It is only recently that research regarding the demand for audit has (re-)gained some importance[41]. This serves, to some extent, as a justification why scholars have used the agency theory framework based on the theory of the firm of Jensen and Meckling (1976) in explaining the demand for audit. Although it is

---

[38] Due to the power of perception on decision making it is possible that whole programs/products can disappear. An anecdotic example is the introduction of Buckler (an alcohol free beer) by Heineken in the Netherlands. Whereas due to a negative perception/association of this beer by consumers Heineken ultimately removed this beer off the market.

[39] As 'agency theory' and the 'theory of the firm' as we know it today originally roots in the work of Knight (1921) and Coase (1937), The current agency theory and theory of the firm is also defined as 'modern' (Foss and Klein, 2006), therefore the term 'post modern' is introduced in this study.

[40] As a result of the mandatory audit regimes the demand for audit has become 'inelastic' to some extent (Maijoor, 1991). Whereas, according to Willekens (2008) the existing mandatory audit regimes are (partly) responsible for the lack of empirical studies regarding the demand for audit.

[41] Debates regarding the role and position of the auditor in a response on the various accounting scandals and financial crises in the beginning of the 21th century and governmental actions to lessen the administrative burden for (private) companies (e.g. MARC, 2010, Greenbook – Audit Policy of the European Commission, 2010; ACCA, 2011) resulted in a gained interest of scholars regarding the 'audit market' and the 'added value of auditing' (e.g. Willekens, 2008; Niemi et al., 2009; Pfeijffer, 2011).

also concluded that the agency theory framework ('the paradigm') shows 'plasticity', as other relationships until now have been incorporated

The 'renewed' interest in the drivers for the demand for audit and knowing that the paradigm does not fit the entire explanation for the existence of auditing[42] justifies both on-going theoretical and empirical research regarding "why is there a demand for audit'. Also knowing that society has been, and still is, changing considerably over time and relevant scientific progress achieved in other disciplines (e.g sociology, organizational theory and governance theory) the question should be asked: what is at risk if auditing academics remain committed solely to the agency theory framework to explain the demand for audit?

The answer: A lack of insight why contemporary society, in absence of mandatory regulation, demands an (independent) audit accommodates the risk of not meeting the needs and expectations of society and as a result risking auditing being perceived as having no added value and becoming redundant or will be marginalized (Limperg, 1932; Power, 1997; Strikwerda, 2007).

Given the purpose of this study to 'enrich' our understanding in the drivers for the demand for audit in a non-mandatory environment, the analysis of the main criticism brought forward against agency theory (chapter 2.3) and the possible implications for theory development regarding the demand for audit (chapter 2.4.2 and chapter 2.4.3) opens the possibility to broaden our 'playing field' within the current generally accepted scientific research programme[43] of the search for relationships affecting the demand for audit as the following, not exhaustive, identified relationships in chapter 2.4.2 and 2.4.3[44] could also be a driver for the demand for audit:

- Agents are not only demanding an audit ex-ante from a 'bonding' point of view, but can also, not mutually exclusive, demand an audit because

---

[42] As Buijink (1992) already concluded: "given the weak complete models results, to some extent the question remains: why do companies engage external auditors in an unregulated environment?" Or more recently, Knechel et al. (2008): "The value of an audit is multi-dimensional and the optimum mix of different benefits may vary across stakeholders and organizations and next to the classical agency theory argument for auditing, auditing may be valuable for other reasons".

[43] The research programme is, according to Kuhn (1962), part of the scientific community. Whereas the scientific community consists of practitioners who have undergone similar education and share a paradigm.

[44] With this overview I do not claim that scholars researching the demand for audit have not paid attention to this relationships yet. Indeed some scholars already refer to some of these relationships. For example Knechel et al. (2008) refer in a footnote to likeliness that the rationality of a decision in a small firm may be 'bounded' although this is directly related to an efficient cost-benefit analysis. However, in my opinion, a more explicit attention to these potential drivers in the research for the demand for audit is desirable.

of other reasons, such as intrinsic motivation (stewardship) and corporate social responsibility;

- Holding a broader stakeholder view[45] implies that there are other possible 'principals' with potential 'principal-agent' conflicts;
- In absence of a mandatory requirement for auditing, the element of 'power' in the decision making process needs to made more 'visible' in the identified relationships, such as the relationship with providers of debt capital and creditors/supply chain, explaining the demand for audit;
- It is questioned (e.g. bounded rationality theory) if actors are able to make rational choices and it is argued that the decision making process of management whether or not to audit is also influenced by perceptions held.

2.5 Concluding remarks

Empirical research to confirm the paradigm of the agency theory has increased our insight in variables affecting the demand for auditing. The results suggest that besides agency variables also other reasons (may) exist which drive the demand for audit, although, to date, the paradigm is able to assimilate these new insights.

Using a Kuhnian view on science development, a 'puzzle solving' approach is followed, whereby with an open 'critical view' attention is paid to recent developments in other disciplines. The literature review revealed, taken into account critics brought forward against a number of assumptions underlying agency theory, that existing predicted relationships in 'real life' may also be influenced by other factors (e.g. the influence of perception on decision making) and other possible relationships exist which also may be a driver for the demand for audit.

History tells us that societies are constantly changing and therefore the factors driving the demand for audit may be subject to change. Living in a time of globalization, technical progress, an exponential increase in information (information overload) and the risk of possible 'devastating' impact of unknown

---

[45] This in itself contains the classical agency theory conflict. Next to this, recognizing the existence of a 'broader group' of principals increases the risk of the company being confronted with goal conflicts and different accounting information needs; which leads in turn to increasing uncertainty by both stakeholders (principals) and management (agent) to which extent the needs of the stakeholders has/have to be fulfilled. Auditing can serve as a possible mechanism to reduce this uncertainty.

and unintended consequences on the possessed wealth[46] of actors, creates what Ulrich Beck calls a 'risk society' (1992). Due to the fact that the environment of individuals and organizations has become more risky (Power, 2004), the need to reduce uncertainty also increases. Social theory (Beck, 1992; Giddens, 1990; Möllering, 2006) shows that two mechanism exist to reduce the uncertainty resulting from the (perceived) risk, namely trust and/or control. The extent to which a choice is made between trust and/or control depends largely on the uncertainty (risk aversion) of actors regarding the behaviour of other actors and the nature of the relationship between those actors. Auditing[47], as both a 'trust and control-concept', is a mechanism to reduce uncertainty regarding information asymmetry risk and non-conforming behaviour between actors in economic society. Therefore, auditing can serve as a (social) control mechanism to provide actors with reliable information at (given) 'reference points' to reduce their uncertainty only if auditing is able to fulfil the needs of society. This in itself justifies a critical scientific examination of known relationships regarding the demand for audit still holds.

This study offers an empirical research into the drivers for the demand of auditing, using data of Dutch private SME companies which due to a deregulation no longer fulfil the criteria for a mandatory audit. Besides the empirical examination of known relationships (chapter three presents an overview of the known relationships) this study also:
- adds some variables as possible drivers for the demand for audit, derived from the literature review of this chapter;
- use direct variables (as the actual decision is observed) besides proxy variables measuring the relationship with the demand of audit.

---

[46] Examples of these possible 'devastating' impact are: the nuclear crisis in the aftermath of the earthquake in Japan in 2011, the banking crisis of 2008-2010, the euro crisis and the impact of sovereign debts of national 'euro-countries'.
[47] Möllering (2005) noticed that the concepts of trust and control should not be perceived as a dualism (which suggests that they mutually exclude each other) but as a duality (trust and control each assume the existence of each other, refer to and create each other). Perceiving trust and control as a duality, it can be noted that the concept of auditing united both the trust as control concepts. As the practical enactment of auditing is aimed at control, trust in the performer of these tasks is a prerequisite.

Chapter 3.   Study into variables explaining the demand for audit, hypotheses development and research model

3.1   Introduction

To answer the research question: *what are drivers for the demand for audit in a non-mandatory environment?*, this chapter provides an overview of variables used to explain the demand for audit and the development of the research model. It is concluded in the previous chapter that the agency theory framework still is to be considered the most important paradigm to explain the demand for audit. But also developments in other disciplines were signalled which could have an influence on our current knowledge regarding the drivers for the demand for audit. Whereas chapter 2.2.3 presented an overview of empirical demand for audit research related to the agency theory framework, this chapter provides a more detailed overview of previous empirical research on a 'relationships-level' with the demand for audit (section 3.2), which subsequently will serve as the basis for the hypotheses development and research model of this study (section 3.3).

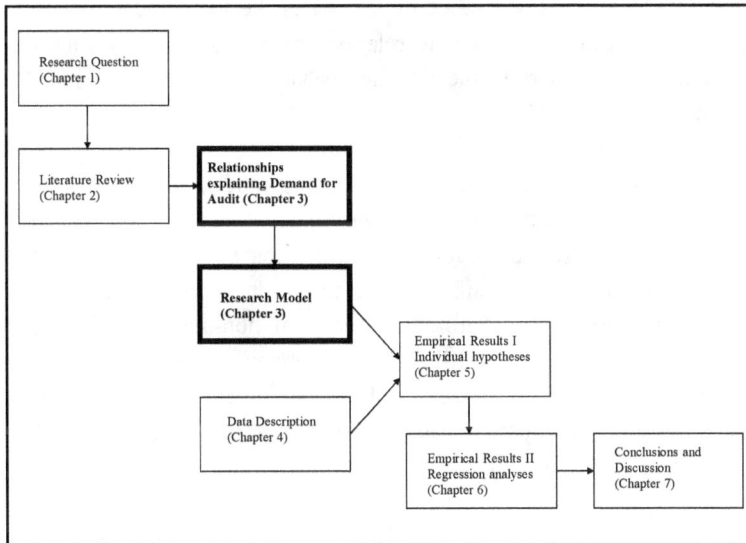

Figure 3.1 Overview of the structure of the study

3.2 Overview of previous empirical research into variables explaining the demand for audit

As originally the focus of explaining the demand for audit within the agency theory framework was on external agency conflicts, the so-called 'classical agency relationships'[48] (see also chapter 2.3.1.3), the structure of this section is divided in three categories, namely: external agency relationships, internal agency relationships and other considerations. The external agency relationships are divided in the two potential agency conflicts described in Jensen and Meckling (1976) seminal paper "Theory of the Firm":

- the agency costs of outside equity (the (shareholder) owner – manager relationship);
- the agency costs of debt (the existence of debt in the capital structure of the company).

3.2.1 External agency relationships

3.2.1.1 Shareholder (owner) – manager relationship

Empirical research has viewed the relationship between the shareholder (owner) and manager from two different angles, namely: from the manager point of view (the classical view) and from the point of view of the shareholder. The classical example of the principal – agent relationship is the relationship between shareholders and managers of the firm and is viewed as a bonding mechanism (Jensen and Meckling, 1976).

Based on aforementioned theory, Chow (1982) hypothesized that the smaller the manager's ownership share in the firm, the higher the probability that the firm voluntarily engages external auditing because when the manager only owns a small portion of his firm's equity shares, he has incentives to allocate firm's resources in ways that may harm the interest of non-managing shareholders. Chow examined a sample of NYSE and OTC companies in the USA for the year 1926. However, due to measurement problems an adequate test on management ownership share was not possible. Buijink (1992) replicated the study of Chow in a Dutch setting and found no significant differences between audited and non-

---

[48] As already noticed in footnote 24, the distinction between external agency relationships, internal agency relationships and other considerations is deliberately chosen. Following Foss and Klein (2006) in their historical analysis of the theory of the firm literature the choice between external agency relationship and the other relationships (including internal agency) is made as the external agency relationships ('the classical agency relationships') represents the originally focus of Jensen and Meckling (1976) in their development of the theory of the firm.

audited firms to support the hypothesized relationship between manager's ownership share[49] in the firm and the demand for audit. Whereas the studies of Chow and Buijink used data of public companies, Senkow et al. (2001) used data of private companies but they also found no direct evidence that the level of management ownership was significantly related to the likelihood of retaining an audit. Seow (2001) conducted an exploratory study and found that in private companies a positive relationship exists between the presence of non-management-shareholders and the demand for audit. Also auditor choice studies show mixed results between audit (choice) and the percentage of management ownership. Simunic and Stein (1987) and Niskanen et al. (2009) found a (marginally) positive relationship. However, Francis and Wilson (1988) and Lennox (2005) found no significant- nor nonlinear relationship (negative within the low and high regions of managerial ownership).

The use of a 'non-family management' variable can be considered as a further specification of the management ownership variable. Carey et al. (2000) used data of private companies and in particular of 'family businesses'. They argue that when family owners delegate responsibility to non-family members, this can be seen as a loss of control and therefore they will exhibit greater demand for monitoring to reduce management shirking due to information asymmetry[50]. The results showed that the demand for audit is positively correlated with the proportion of non-family management. Others also found a positive relationship between the level of family-ownership and the demand for audit (Collis et al, 2004; Niemi et al., 2009; Collis, 2010).

Seow (2001) noticed that with the agency costs arising from the ownership – manager relation it is commonly argued that:
- agency costs increase in relation to size and complexity, or the situation where an audit may be demanded by shareholders (Simunic and Stein, 1987); or
- an audit is perceived to improve the quality and credibility of the financial statements (Wallace, 1981).

It can be questioned if this is also the case in an SME setting. Agency costs in a SME company may arise in the situation where the company has shareholders who are no company directors as these shareholders are unable to directly observe or control the activities of management. The results of the exploratory study of Seow show some support for the hypothesis that shareholders who were remote

---

[49] To measure management ownership share Buijink used a proxy, namely: the proportion of common and preferred (cumulative) shares issued that is listed.

[50] It can be argued to which extent other (intrinsic) motivations and factors (e.g. culture, belonging to the same 'blood' line) drives this demand besides information asymmetry.

from the day-to-day operations of the company were more willing to demand an audit. Collis (2010) also tested the relationship whether the existence of shareholders without access to internal financial information has a positive relationship on the demand for audit. Collis only found some support for this relation in the UK sample but not in the comparative Danish sample[51].

Collis (2010) also studied the relation between shareholders' need for audited financial statements and the decision for a voluntary audit if the company would classify for an audit exemption. These results show that this variable was highly significant in the Danish sample but not significant in the UK sample, Collis did not provide an explanation for this difference. From audit fee studies it is known that the existence of majority shareholders reveals mixed results and the conducted meta-analyse showed an insignificant result (Hay et al., 2006).

3.2.1.2 Existence of debt in the capital structure of the firm

Introduction
Besides the relationship between shareholders and management according to agency theory the relationship between shareholders and bondholders may give rise to conflicts of interest. Chow (1982) argues that when a firm has debt outstanding, shareholders or managers, acting in the interest of shareholders, have incentives to undertake financing, investment or production activities that benefit themselves at the expense of bondholders. Changing the firm's variance of return and diluting the coverage on existing debt by issuing new debt with a higher priority, are activities which are examples of wealth-transfer mechanisms. However, bondholders will include the expected losses while pricing the bonds in an efficient capital market according to Jensen and Meckling (1976). As a result, the shareholders will ultimately bear the costs of their expected wealth transfers from bondholders. The wealth transferring activities, caused by the shareholder-bondholder conflict of interest, is ultimately a negative-sum game. According to Chow (1982) these transfers of wealth by shareholders from bondholders can result in a decline of firm value, because they involve suboptimal investment policies. Jensen and Meckling (1976) state that when shareholders would contract to limit their own ability to transfer wealth from bondholders, they would benefit from an increase in firm value. Namely, such contracts have the ability to reduce the probability of suboptimal investment activities. In addition, they would also receive a higher price for the bonds. In order to prevent the transfer of wealth

---

[51] As possible explanations for the difference found between the UK sample and the UK sample, Collis refers to a lower level of trust with unrelated shareholders in the UK and to the existence of company law in the UK that protects the needs of minority shareholders for audited financial statements.

activities, debt covenants or lending requirements can be used to limit the shareholder-bondholder conflict of interests. A common negotiated requirement is the firm's ability to pay dividends only when minimum solvency ratios are met. The following variables are used in previous empirical studies to test the company – 'debt capital provider' relationship:
- audit enhanced the credibility of the company towards external users;
- leverage;
- the existence of debt covenants/lender requirements;
- cost of debt capital;
- improvement of credit rating.

Enhancing credibility

The main function of auditing is adding credibility to the financial information of companies and as a result (external) users of the financial information 'can put more trust' in this information. Also in an economic setting trust plays an important role for companies. Because of the trust others have in the company they can get 'credit lines', long-standing relations with customers, etc. Therefore management has an incentive to enhance credibility to third parties by showing voluntary cooperative behaviour even if this is not formally requested by these third parties and even if management does not know explicitly that the benefits will outweigh the costs. Qualitative research by Humphrey and Stuart (1986) regarding the nature of the audit in small companies revealed that management believed that bank and inland revenues would use audited financial statements but management also add that they did not know exactly what they would rely on the audit, although a number of interviewees refer to reputation as something these external users would rely on. Collis et al. (2004) also found that perception of management that audit plays a supportive role in the agency relationships of the company with the bank and inland revenue are factors management considers in their decision to opt for a voluntary audit.

Leverage

Chow (1982) focuses on the proportion of debt in the capital structure when stating, along the line of Jensen and Meckling (1976), that shareholders have a greater incentive[52] to transfer wealth from the bondholders as the proportion of debt in a firm's capital structure increases and therefore shareholders tend to be

---

[52] Jensen and Meckling (1976: 334) reason that agency costs arise form the capital structure of the firm as they noticed that if firms are financed almost entirely with debt type claims (i.e., non-residual claims) this would have a negative effect on the owner-manager's behaviour. Potential creditors will not loan $ 100,000,000 to a firm in which the entrepreneur has invested of $ 10,000. With such at financial structure the owner-manager will have a strong incentive to engage in activities (investments) which promise very high payoffs if successful even if they have a very low probability of success. If they turn out well, he captures most of the gains, if they turn out badly, the creditors bear most of the costs.

more willing to bonding contracts to raise additional debt. Chow further argues that whether the shareholders of a given firm would offer monitoring/bonding contracts to its bondholders depends on the severity of their conflict of interest and it is expected that the higher the proportion of debt in a firm's capital structure is the severity of their conflict increases. Therefore Chow hypothesized that the higher the proportion of debt in a firm's capital structure, the higher the probability that the firm voluntarily engages external auditing.

Chow (1982) researched the relation between leverage and voluntary audits for a sample of public firms. Chow's positive and significant results imply that the higher the proportion of debt in a firm's capital structure, the higher the probability that the firm will voluntarily purchase audit services. The results from Chow's study confirm the idea that leverage may act as an explanatory variable in relation to voluntary audits. Buijink's (1992) results also indicated that the proportion of total debt, the leverage ratio, is higher for audited public firms.

Leverage as an explanation for the demand for (voluntary audit) is also tested in a number of other studies. Ettredge et al. (1994) used leverage to explain the demand for quarterly reviews, Carey et al. (2000) if there is a relationship between leverage and voluntary auditing by family businesses and Hay and Davis (2004) in their study of the demand for voluntary audit by incorporated societies. The findings of these studies confirm a positive relation between leverage and the demand for audit. However, Seow's (2001) study of the demand for audit in small companies in the UK and the Senkow et al. (2001) study of the effects of deregulation in Canada, did not show a significant association between the debt-to-asset ration and the likelihood of retaining an audit.

Debt covenants / Lending requirements
To mitigate the agency problems arising from the existence of debt in the capital structure of the firm shareholders and/or management have an incentive to limit their behaviour through the inclusion of requirement in lending agreements. As accounting numbers are of importance in these lending requirements and accounting numbers are derived from the financial statements the shareholders (and management) will provide these accounting numbers to the debt providers, which are audited by independent auditors (Chow, 1982). Therefore Chow hypothesized that the more different accounting numbers are used in debt covenants the higher the probability would be that the firm voluntarily engages external auditing. Using data of public listed debt of NYSE and OTC companies Chow found a positive significant relationship. Abdel-khalik (1993) looks at the existence of a lender requirement as an explanatory variable for the demand for audit in private companies. He proposes that the owners would voluntarily

demand external audits in order to comply with constraints placed on the organization by lenders. An empirical model is used to test the relationship between lenders' requirement of audited financial statements and audit fees. He found that the lender's requirement is a significant determinant for the demand for audit and that this lender's requirement might be related to the concern of lenders about the existence of loss of control.

A number of studies, focussing on the decision made by the loan officer (Johnson et al., 1983; Berry et al., 1993; Bandyopadhyay and Francis, 1995; Bollen, 1996; Bamber and Stratton, 1997; Wright and Davidson, 2000), have investigated to which extent the loan decision is influenced by the level of attestation of the financial statements. The results of the studies showed mixed results. Whereas the studies of Berry et al. (1993), Bandyopadhyay and Francis (1995), Bollen (1996) and Bamber and Stratton (1997) found that the level of attestation is important in the lending decision, the studies of Johnson et al. (1983) and Wright and Davidson (2000) found no significant relation between the level of attestation and the lending decision. Collis et al. (2004) and Niemi et al. (2009) investigated the relationship between the demand for audit and the existence of an agency relationship with the bank. Both the studies found that the existence of an agency relationship with the bank has a significant influence on the demand for audit. This implies that firms who are seeking for additional debt finance have a higher chance that they will voluntarily engage in audits. Seow (2001) found some evidence that management chose to purchase external audits when lenders had specific requirements or the request to have the financial statements audited. Senkow et al. (2001) found a strong positive relationship between the existence of a lender requirement for audited financial statements and the likelihood of retaining an audit.

Cost of debt capital
Blackwell et al. (1998) analyzed if the economic value of auditing leads to reduced cost of debt. They argue that auditing reduces lenders' monitoring costs interest rates. Competition will force banks to pass along these cost reductions to borrowers in the form of lower interest rates. The empirical results of their study of small private firms in the US showed that voluntary audited companies pay lower interest rates. Kim et al. (2007) complements and extends the study of Blackwell et al. (1998) using Korean data of privately held companies and also concluded that private companies with voluntary audits pay significantly lower interest rates. However, Willekens (2008) found no evidence to support the relationship between the cost of debt capital and the demand for auditing, using a Belgian sample of private companies.

Other studies (Johnson et al., 1983; Bandyopadhyay and Francis, 1995; Bamber and Stratton, 1997; Wright and Davidson, 2000) searching for the relation between the cost of debt capital and auditing (additionally) focused on:
- the decision making process of loan officers; and
- the perceptions of loan officers and/or companies management of the effect of auditing on the cost of debt capital.

Reasoning that audited financial statements would reduce risk and uncertainty of loan officers and as a result influence interest rates charged, Bamber and Stratton (1997) found that loan officers in an experimental setting associate uncertainty-modified audit reports with a greater likelihood of loan rejection, higher risk assessments and higher interest rates. Bandyopadhyay and Francis (1995) found also evidence that interest rates are related to the level of attestation. However, Johnson et al. (1983) in their experiment found no significant relation between interest rates and auditing. Wright and Davidson (2000) also conducted an experiment with loan officers to test if auditing influences the interest rates charges and also concluded that no significant relationship was found between interest and auditing.

Improvement of credit rating

Similar to the reasoning behind the 'cost of debt capital'-assumption, it is argued that agency problems related to obtain supplier credits and debt financing persuade private firms to improve the precision and credibility of their financial information and subsequently their credit rating. Fortin and Pittman (2007) studied in a private firm setting if auditor choice positively affects the obtained credit rating from qualified credit agencies, but they failed to find a significant relationship. Collis (2010) found that if management of companies perceive that there is a beneficial effect of the audit on the company's credit rating score, this perception subsequently significantly influences the choice to audit or not to audit. Lennox and Pittman (2011) studied for private firms, in a non-mandatory audit setting, if auditing affects the obtained credit rating. They found support that voluntarily audit companies receive significantly higher credit ratings.

3.2.1.3 *Size*

To explain the relationship between the size of the firm and the demand for auditing 'economy of scale'-theory can be used. Chow (1982) argues that as the total amount of potential wealth transfers increases, the related benefits of undertaking monitoring increase and furthermore the marginal costs of monitoring systems are believed to decrease with firm size. When a firm is twice the size of another company that is audited, it does not take double the costs to audit. The amount of wealth transferred and the marginal costs in relation to size, leads to the hypothesis that the larger a firm, the higher the probability that it will have its financial statements audited. Although this hypothesis sounds plausible, research on the factor size led to contrasting results. On one hand, Chow (1982), Ettredge et al. (1994), Collis et al. (2004) and Collis (2010) found support for the importance of firm size. However, research by Carey et al. (2000), and Senkow et al. (2001) found that size is no significant factor in explaining voluntary demand of audits.

3.2.2   Internal agency relationships

Introduction
Besides the relationships labelled as 'external agency relationships' in the previous section a number of other relationships, using the agency framework, have been identified in previous empirical literature. The following relationships are in this study labelled as 'internal agency relationships':
- loss of control;
- the existence of outside directors;
- auditing as a substitute for internal control;
- improvement of quality of financial information / earnings management.

Loss of control (complexity)
Although fully private firms do not have the risk of moral hazard emanating from separation of ownership and control, they are subject to problems of moral hazard "internal" to the operation of the firm (Abdel-khalik, 1993). Using agency theory the employees of a company can be considered as agents, whereas management can be considered as principals. In this case, management seeks to exercise control to ensure that employees take actions that are in the interest of the company as a whole. However, the larger the company in number of employees the more hierarchical levels will evolve as there is a limit to the 'span of control' a manager is able to exert over employees. The latter limits management in capability and capacity to control all agents, therefore this situation leads to loss of control, which holds the risk of potential losses for the company. The larger the company grows the more complex and difficult the company becomes as an increase in locations and activities may reduce overall efficiency and increasing risk of moral hazard problems of employees as management may not be able to control the operations by direct supervision (Knechel et al., 2008).

Abdel-khalik (1993) was the first to study the relationship between organizational loss of control and the demand for auditing by management as a compensatory control system. Using an audit fee model, the results of his empirical study showed that the hypothesized relationship appears to be significant. Senkow et al. (2001) researched the existence of a positive relationship between the demand for audit and the potential loss of control in a company but their study did not find a significant relationship. From auditor choice and audit fee research it is known that a positive relationship with the complexity of the organization exists (Hay and Davis, 2004; Knechel et al., 2008). Also the audit fee – meta analysis and the results of Hay et al. (2006), showed a significant positive relationship between complexity and audit fee.

Existence outside directors

To mitigate agency problems next to external auditing there are other monitoring mechanisms available that have the potential to constrain management's wealth transfer possibilities, such as internal auditing, management control systems and outside directors (Jensen and Meckling, 1976; Anderson et al., 1993). As accounting literature has viewed the monitoring role of the external auditors as endogenous to a contracting equilibrium in a firm (Watts and Zimmerman, 1990: 152), it follows that in an efficient contracting equilibrium a set of monitoring mechanisms will be used to achieve corporate governance (Anderson et al., 1993). It is therefore expected that the existence of outside directors as a monitoring mechanism would have a substitute effect on the demand for external auditing. Buijink (1992) conducted an empirical study to derive to which extent the presence of outside directors affects the demand for audit. Buijink found a positive relationship between the number of outside directors and the demand for audit, suggesting that both mechanisms are complementary. Anderson et al. (1993) also examined the relationship between the existence of both outside directors and auditing as monitor mechanism. They found that the greater (measured by assets in place and size) the firm the smaller the relative expenditure on monitoring from directors compared to auditing, also suggesting that both mechanism are complementary. However, Ettredge et al. (1994) did not find a significant relationship between the percentage of outside directors and the demand for a timely review of financial statements.

From the overview of empirical studies, it is obvious that no conclusive support is found for the substitute hypothesis. Instead, some evidence suggests that the two monitoring mechanisms -outside directors and external auditing- are complementary. Why are the monitoring mechanism of external auditing and outside directors complementary? Eichenseher and Shields (1985) suggest that this is probably because of the increased effects of regulation and liability. As outside directors are generally high-reputation members who have the role of supervising the actions of management and voting on behalf of shareholders, directors have to deal also with the increased effects of regulation and liability.

This may have contributed to the tendency of board of directors to hire (high quality) auditors. Buijink (1992) suggests that this is probably because outside directors are not always a monitoring mechanism, but measures antagonism among shareholder factions.

Auditing as a substitute for internal control[53]

Managers, but also all other users, value the integrity of financial information because that allows them to make better decisions. To provide assurance regarding the integrity of financial information, control systems are established and maintained comprised of both internal and external mechanisms (Eilifsen et al., 2001). Control systems reduce the costs of poor decisions as well with information risk in general and although there are many types of control mechanisms (e.g. internal auditors, external auditors, boards, audit committees) their purpose is often similar. Therefore, it seems reasonable that some internal and external control mechanisms may be viewed as substitutes (Jensen and Payne, 2003). The chosen monitoring arrangements are determined by their agency costs and by the relative costs and effectiveness of the various forms of control mechanism available to them (Ettredge et al, 2000). To choose a best option, managers have to decide on an cost-benefit analysis how to design a control system. With regard to the substitution of internal for external auditing, Ettredge et al. (2000) did not found a significant relationship, but the results of the study of Carey et al. (2000) showed the existence for external auditing to be a potential substitute for internal auditing in private family businesses.

For some companies the financial benefits of an internal control system will not outweigh the costs of such a system. Chow (1982) argues that due to economics of scale an external auditor may be in the position to perform a task more efficiently than internal auditors. If a internal control system is not beneficiary, other options have to be taken in mind. Also management may demand external audit services caused by management's need for an independent review or audit on internal controls to decrease the chance of material error and to improve operational efficiency (Wallace, 1981; Collis et al., 2004; Knechel et al., 2008). Collis et al. (2004) state that in a small context setting the likelihood of material misstatements (inherent risk) and the chance of the accounting control detecting any material misstatements (control risk) may be high. Furthermore external auditors may be chosen for internal control purposes if there is a smaller chance that the auditors will conspire with manager's subordinates. Collis et al (2004) and Niemi et al. (2009) found a significant relationship between the demand for audit and the belief of management that the audit acts as a check on internal

---

[53] The treatment of external auditing as a substitute for internal control, includes in this study also external auditing as a substitute for internal auditing.

controls. However, Collis (2010) found mixed results for this relationship. From audit fee studies it is known that empirical results also showed mixed results of the relationship between audit fees and internal control (Hay et al., 2006).

The existence of a lack of accounting expertise within the company, based on agency theory combined with the cost-benefit argument, may be a potential driver for management to demand an audit. Jensen and Payne (2003) found empirical evidence for managers viewing external audit (in this case audit quality) as a substitute for at least some elements of the internal control system such as a compensation for the lack of accounting expertise within the company. Seow (2001) tried to test a hypothesized relationship between the demand for audit and the accounting expertise within the company, but due to measurement problems he was not able to test this hypothesis.

Improvement of quality financial information / earnings management
Research on the relationship between the quality of the prepared financial information and auditor choice (quality differences) has revealed that auditor choice has a positive effect on the quality of the prepared financial information. Also a number of auditor choice studies have tested the relationship between earnings management and auditor quality, by reasoning the more earning management the lower the quality of the reported earnings (Willekens, 2008). Auditing is a control mechanism (monitoring) to reduce uncertainty of users of financial information about the quality of the presented financial information by management. Willekens (2008) therefore hypothesized that the quality of the prepared financial information will be higher and earnings management will be lower of audited financial statements than not audited financial statements. Willekens empirically tested this hypotheses in a Belgian setting, using the mandatory disclosure of differences between last year's calculated payable taxes on profit and actual paid taxes in the financial statements and a proxy for earnings management based on a model of abnormal working capital accruals. She found a positive relationship between both the quality of the prepared financial information and earnings management and the demand for auditing. Haw et al. (2008) examined whether a relationship between earnings management and the demand for voluntary interim audits exists. Using data of Chinese public firms, they found also support for the existence of the relationship.

Ettredge et al. (2000) studied whether a voluntarily timely review is associated with the quality of prepared financial information, by looking at the number of adjustments recorded in the fourth quarter. Their empirical results provide evidence that the number of adjustments is positively related to the purchase of a timely review. The relationship between the quality of the financial information and the demand for audit has also been tested by Collis et al. (2004), Niemi et al. (2009) and Collis (2010), using data from the UK, Finland and Denmark. All these studies showed that, based on the perception of management, an audit provides the benefit of improving the quality of financial information.

3.2.3   Other considerations for the demand for audit

Introduction
The aim of this chapter is to present an overview of relationships used in previous empirical studies explaining the demand for audit with the purpose, as set out in chapter 2.5, to conduct a critical examination of known relationships regarding the demand for audit still holds. Besides the relationships which have been labelled as external or internal agency relationships, previous empirical research have tested also a number of other relationships expected to be drivers for the demand for audit. The following relationships have been tested, which are labelled as 'other considerations':
-    audit fee / cost of audit;
-    dependence on auditor relationship;
-    type of audit report issued in previous year(s);
-    financial health;
-    strategic reasons.

Audit fee / Cost of audit
Using economic price theory, it is argued that management will be willing to incur the cost of auditing as long as the marginal benefits exceed the marginal costs. Various studies have described the relationship between audit fee and the benefit of the audit to the client, using an audit quantity or audit quality view (Simunic, 1984; Palmrose, 1986; Hay et al., 2006). Also researchers hold different views on the direction of the relationship of the audit fee and the demand for audit. Senkow et al. (2001) hypothesized a positive relationship between audit fee and the likelihood of retaining an audit, holding the view that when management is willing to pay higher audit fees the higher management perceives the benefits of the audit. The results of their study showed a significant positive relationship. A contrary view of the relationship of audit fee and the demand for audit is held by Collis (2010) and a negative relationship between audit fee and the demand for audit is hypothesized. Also Collis, although opposite of Senkow et al., found a significant negative relationship.

Dependence on auditor relationship

In the literature it has been suggested that potential efficiencies exist through the joint production of auditing and other services, due to 'knowledge spillovers'. Simunic (1984) gathered evidence supporting efficiencies when clients obtain both management advisory services and auditing services. Senkow et al. (2001) investigated whether a company is more likely to retain an audit if other services are provided to the company. It was predicted that the provision of other services may have an impact on the company's decision as to whether to retain an audit but the results of their study did not support this proposition. Seow (2001) also tested if the company is highly dependent on its auditor for the provision of other non-audit services, the company is more likely to continue the audit? Besides this, Seow tested whether the company is likely to continue the audit if there is a long-standing relationship with the auditor. Based on his exploratory research no significant relationship for both hypotheses was found.

Type of audit report issued in previous year(s)

Niemi et al. (2009) argue that the demand for voluntary auditing will also be based upon prior experiences of management from mandatory auditing and the auditor. Holding the view that issuing of a modified audit report the result is of an agency conflict between management and the auditor under a mandatory regime, it is hypothesized that the likelihood of management choosing a voluntary audit decreases with prior conflicts arisen from modified audit reports. However, they found no support for this relationship.

Financial Health

Using economic theory it can be reasoned that 'risky' companies will gain most from a decrease in information asymmetry between management and users of financial information (Simunic, 1980; Willekens, 2008). As auditing contributes to reducing uncertainty of users of financial information, it can be argued that there is a higher chance that a company engages in voluntary audits when it is financial 'risky' due to a bad financial health in order to increase the likelihood of receiving new loans because being audited reduces (partly) the financial risk. In other words the more financial risk the higher the probability users will demand an audit. Willekens (2008) tested the relationship between financial health and auditing and hypothesized that audited companies have better financial performance than not audited companies and found to some extent support for this relationship. Niemi et al. (2009) hypothesised that the likelihood of choosing a non-mandatory audit increases with financial distress but found no support for their hypothesis.

On the other hand, from a cost saving perspective it can be expected that when a company is in bad financial health there is less chance that a company demands an audit. Following this line of reasoning, Seow (2001) examined whether companies with financial distress are less likely to demand an audit. The results of his study showed no support for this relationship.

Strategic reasons
In the decision process whether or not to have the financial statements audited, management may also have 'strategic' reasons to opt for a non-mandatory audit, as it has been suggested that companies might engage an auditor to signal good performance. Hay and Davis (2004) tested for a New Zealand sample of incorporated societies whether the strategic reasons may play a role in the demand for audit and found some support.

3.3   Hypotheses development and research model

Before the research model used in this study will be described, we start this section with a general hypotheses development of predicted relationships by presenting, based on section 3.2, a chronological overview of relationships tested in previous empirical demand for audit studies. Although, it is argued in chapter 2.5, that only the incorporation of known relationships derived from previous empirical studies in the research model already is justified to see if these relationships still holds, it is the purpose of this study to contribute to the enrichment of our existing knowledge regarding the drivers for the demand for audit (see chapter 1.3). To fill in the calls for a greater integration of literature, chapter two analyzed some of the main criticism against agency theory. In chapter 2.3, using a broader view, some other relationships are presented which may influence the demand for audit also. The general hypotheses development based on the chronological overview will be complemented with some hypotheses derived from the literature review of chapter two.

3.3.1   Chronological overview of variables used in empirical demand for audit studies and hypotheses development

As there is a limited amount of empirical research regarding the demand for audit (Willekens, 2008) a chronological overview has been prepared of the relationships tested in previous empirical studies[54] (see table 3.2). This chronological overview only presents studies which have used the demand for audit as dependent or independent variable. Besides the studies identified in table

---

[54] Footnote 22 describes the 'search' method used in identifying previous empirical studies.

2.1 and 2.2. of chapter 2.2.3, this overview also includes three identified working papers using the demand for audit as variable and two published papers using the demand for voluntary interim review as variable. It is decided not to include identified working papers using the demand for voluntary interim review as variable. Also empirical studies using a substitute for the demand for audit, such as audit choice or audit fee, are not included in this overview. For classification purposes it is decided to group more or less identical variables into 'variable themes'. A total of sixteen previous empirical studies has been identified using the demand for audit as (dependent or independent) variable. Consistent with the evolution of the current 'paradigm' explaining the demand for audit, as discussed in chapter two, an initially strong focus on the variables related to external agency relationships in the first empirical studies is noticeable. Also, the number of variables used in studies increased over time, whereby the external agency variables 'management-ownership share', 'leverage' and 'size' are extended with other variables. Whereas the first studies used data of public companies, in recent years a shift to SME companies is noticeable. Overall nineteen variables are identified, being used in previous empirical studies to proxy for predicted relationships with the demand for audit. Based on this overview of previous empirical research the following general hypotheses can be formulated (see also chapter five for a more detailed hypotheses development):

**Table 3.1 General hypotheses development
based on previous empirical studies**

		Expected sign
	External agency variables	
1	The higher the manager's ownership share (or family ownership share) in the company, the lower the probability that the company demands an audit.	-
2	The demand for audit increases with the existence of shareholders with no (direct) access to internal financial information of the company.	+
3	The demand for audit increases with the perception held by management that the audit improves the credibility of financial information.	+
4	The higher the proportion of debt in the company's capital structure, the higher the probability that the company demands an audit.	+
5	The demand for audit increases with the existence of debt covenants / lender requirements.	+
6	The cost of debt is lower when the company will have the financial statements audited	+
7	The credit rating score of the company is higher when the company will have the financial statements audited.	+
8	The larger the size of the company, the higher the probability that the company demands an audit.	+
	Internal agency variables	
9	The larger the number of employees (loss of control), the higher the probability that the company demands an audit.	+
10	The existence of outside directors increases the demand for audit	+
11	The demand for audit increases when the company considers audit also to be a substitute for internal audit/internal control.	+
12	The demand for audit increases when the company does not have a financial department or hires employees with low levels of accounting expertise	+
13	The quality of financial information is higher and earnings management lower when the company will have the financial statements audited.	+

Other considerations

14	The demand for audit increases when the company considers the benefits of the audit to be greater than the costs.	+
15	The demand for an audit increases if the auditor has been serving the company for a longer period of time.	+
16	The demand for an audit increases with the number of other services provided by the auditor.	+
17	The demand for an audit increases if an unqualified audit report has been issued in previous year(s).	+
18	The demand for an audit increases if the company is faced with financial distress or making a loss.	+
19	The demand for an audit increases if management believes an audit is desirable for strategic reasons.	+

Besides these general hypotheses derived from previous empirical studies, based on the conducted literature review of chapter two, this study will add three additional hypotheses. The following hypotheses will be added:

20.   The larger the number of shareholders in the firm, the higher the probability that the company demands an audit (additional shareholder-manager variable);

21.   The larger the number of relevant stakeholders depending on the financial information of the company, the higher the probability that the company demands an audit (based on chapter 2.4.2);

22.   The demand for an audit increases with the perception held by management that the audit of financial statement is desired by existing shareholders (direct variable, based on chapter 2.3.2).

Table 3.2 Chronological overview of variables[55] used in empirical demand for audit studies

	Chow (1982)	Buijink (1992)	Abdel-khalik (1993)	Ettredge et al. (1994)*	Blackwell et al. (1998)	Carey et al. (2000)	Senkow et al. (2001)	Seow (2001)	Hay and Davis (2004)	Collis et al. (2004)	Kim et al. (2007, wp)	Haw et al. (2008)*	Willekens (2008)	Niemi et al. (2009, wp)	Collis (2010)	Lennox and Pittman (2011, wp)	Total
External agency variables																	
Managementownership share	✓	✓				✓	✓	✓	✓	✓				✓	✓		9
Shareholders without access to internal financial information		✓						✓									2
Perception audit adds credibility to external users				✓										✓			
Leverage	✓	✓		✓	✓	✓	✓	✓	✓	✓	✓	✓	✓	✓			13
Debt covenant / Lender requirement	✓						✓	✓					✓		✓	✓	6
Cost of debt			✓		✓						✓						3
Improves credit rating (incl perception)															✓	✓	2
Size	✓	✓	✓	✓	✓	✓	✓	✓	✓	✓	✓	✓	✓	✓	✓	✓	16
Internal agency variables																	
Loss of control/complexity			✓	✓			✓		✓								4
Existence outside director		✓	✓	✓													3
Substitute for internal control (incl. perception)				✓		✓		✓		✓			✓				5
Quality of employees financial department														✓			1
Quality financial information / earningsmanagment (incl. perception)								✓		✓			✓	✓	✓		5
Other considerations																	
Cost of audit							✓								✓		2
Audit tenure							✓										1
Other services rendered from auditor							✓	✓						✓			3
Type of audit report issued in previous year														✓			1
Financial health								✓			✓	✓	✓				4
Strategic reasons												✓					1

* = study has voluntary demand of **review** of interim financial statements as a dependent variable

[55] For presentation purposes not all control variables used in the regression models of the previous studies are presented in this overview.

3.3.2 Research model of this study

The aim of this study is to contribute to the existing literature by enlarging the existing body of knowledge regarding the drivers for the demand for audit. The following empirical study consists of comprehensive testing whether previously used variables for explaining the demand for audit also will hold in a Dutch private SME setting as drivers for the demand for audit. Previous empirical research regarding the demand for auditing learns us that, due to difficulties in data selection, limited research has been carried out and often shows mixed results in different settings. This in itself justifies additional empirical research, to test if already identified relationships show similar results in a Dutch setting. Furthermore, this study uses data of companies which are exempt from the mandatory audit regime. This creates a rare opportunity (Senkow et al., 2001; Willekens, 2008; Lennox an Pittman, 2011) and creates the possibility to use direct variables related to the demand for audit, where other studies have used proxy variables to test the hypothesized relationships.

As the research question of this study has been formulated in chapter 1.3 as: *what are drivers for the demand for audit in a non-mandatory environment?*, we are interested in both the individual relationships of identified variables with the demand for audit as well as the answer to the question which of the variables are driving the demand for audit. To test the latter, multivariate regression has to be conducted to identify the most important drivers for the demand. Following the presented classification of variables in this chapter, the general regression model for the demand for audit (DVA) of this study can be formulated as follows:

DVA = f(external agency variables, internal agency variables, other variables)

In chapter four the context for auditing in the Netherlands, the data selection, data description and descriptive statistics are presented. Subsequently the empirical results are presented in chapter five (individual hypotheses) and chapter six (regression analyses).

Chapter 4. Data description

4.1 Introduction

The research question of this study is: *what are drivers for the demand for audit in a non-mandatory environment?* To empirically answer this question, this chapter deals with the description of the data used in this study (see figure 4.1). As data of private Dutch SME companies is used, this chapter also provides the context of auditing in the Netherlands. Therefore this chapter, consists of two parts. Section 4.2 starts with an overview of auditing in the Netherlands and section 4.3 describes the data selection and the descriptive data of the sample used in this study.

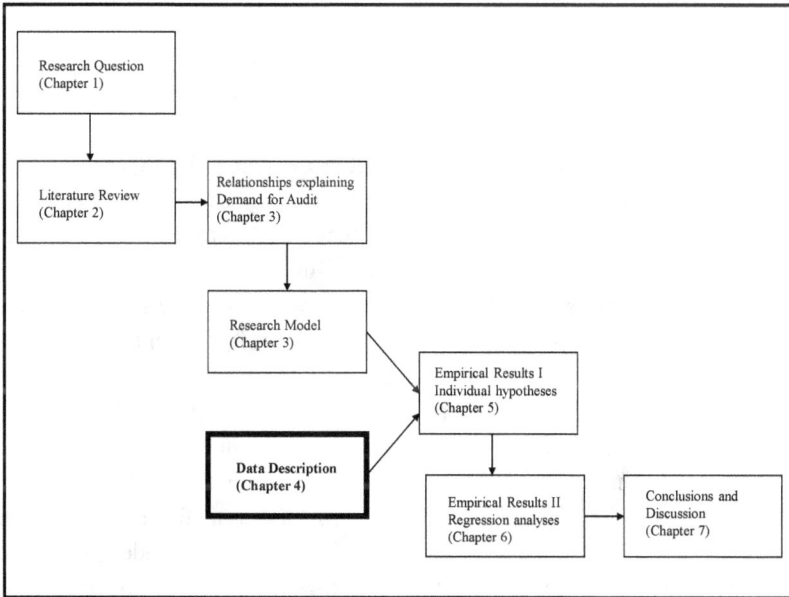

Figure 4.1 Overview of the structure of the study

4.2 Auditing in the Netherlands

In chapter 1.1 it is postulated that auditing is a social control mechanism. And although the mechanisms (e.g. risk, uncertainty, trust and control) underlying the concept of auditing are universal, it is also important, due to the fact that country specific data is used, to take into account country specific legal, social and cultural elements (the context) which potentially could have an influence on the drivers for the demand and supports interpreting the results of this empirical study compared to previous studies. Based on the sociological notion of 'path dependence' it is argued that developments in the past will have an impact on the current and future situation[56]. We therefore start this chapter with a brief historical overview of auditing (and audit regulation) in the Netherlands. Special attention is given to the differences in development of auditing in the Netherlands compared to the Anglo-Saxon countries because of the dominant influence of their concept of auditing (both in research as in practice) since the 1980s. We will especially focus on the cultural differences between the Netherlands, the United Kingdom (as a representative of the Anglo-Saxon countries) and Finland. The rationale behind the comparison of the cultural differences with these countries is the attempt to explain the results of this study with the results of conducted studies in both the United Kingdom and Finland (chapter 6.5).

4.2.1   Historical development of the audit profession

Like in most Anglo-Saxon countries, the audit profession in the Netherlands arose in the aftermath of the first 'broad' fraudulent reporting scandals at the end of the 19th century. They were seen as the 'negative outcrops' of the rapid industrialization process and the separation of ownership and management in, ever becoming larger, companies. In general, the 'Pincoffs affair' in 1871 is considered the marking point of the rise of the audit profession in the Netherlands (De Vries, 1985). According to Blokdijk, Drieënhuizen and Wallage (1995) the primary reason for the existence of the independent audit in the Netherlands, was the creation of a separation between management and ownership. The assumption that a potential conflict of interest may arise between the management of a company and its owners (the shareholders), forms the basis for the theory of the independent audit. It is thus concluded by the authors that the independent audit in the Netherlands originated from the need to examine the accounting of the amount of money entrusted to the management of a company, on behalf of those who had a direct financial interest in a company's results. "As such, the origin of the audit profession can be seen as consistent with the ideas of agency theory" (Meuwissen and Wallage, 2008: 168).

---

[56] 'Path dependence' can be described as the dependence of (economic) outcomes on the path of previous outcomes, rather than simply based on current conditions. History matters in 'path dependence', as history has an enduring influence. Choices made on basis of changing conditions and persist long after those conditions have changed. Thus, explanations of the outcome of processes requires also looking at history, rather than simply at current conditions.

However, Blokdijk et al. (1995) point out that in comparing the development of auditing in the Netherlands with the development in the Anglo-Saxon countries, there are some important differences. These differences have led to a historical development of some concepts in Dutch audit theory that differ from those in other countries and to some extent still have an impact on auditing in the Netherlands nowadays, namely:

- the early focus on the development of a theory of auditing and auditing education;
- cultural differences and legal system.

4.2.1.1   *The early focus on the development of a theory of auditing and audit education*

Already in the infant stage of the audit profession, auditors were involved in the development of a consistent audit theory. The first body of accountants was founded in 1895, the 'Netherlands Institute of Accountants' (Nederlandsch Instituut van Accountants, N.I.V.A). However, in absence of legislation, anyone could set up an association of auditors, which resulted that during the following years other bodies of accountants were founded besides the N.I.V.A (De Vries, 1985). With the number of bodies growing, discussion about the quality of the audit arose. Under leadership of professor Th. Limperg, during the early 1920s a consistent theory of auditing was developed resulting in the 'theory of inspired confidence'. This normative and dynamic theory has heavily influenced auditing and audit education in the Netherlands. "It connects the community's need for reliable financial information to the technical possibilities of auditing to meet these needs; it also takes into account the evolution of the needs of the community and of auditing techniques over the course of time. According to this theory, changes in the needs of the community and changes in auditing techniques result in changes in the auditor's function" (Blokdijk et al., 1995: 23). The theory of inspired confidence states that the auditor's report derives its added value (confidence) form expert work, on which the audit opinion is formed, therefore the auditor should act in such a way that he does not disappoint the (rational) expectations of those who may use the audit report (general audit norm). "Limperg argued that there was no need for specific technical auditing standards; the general auditing norm, directly linked to users' rational expectations, would suffice to perform any audit" (Blokdijk et al., 1995: 24). Although there was an extensive discussion about the application of the general auditing norm and these discussion evolved into comprehensive theories, the development in the USA of auditing standards was not followed in the Netherlands until the 1970s.

With regard to the auditing education in the Netherlands, "Dutch auditors felt that business economics should form the basis of accountancy education in the Netherlands. The auditor should grasp the underlying concepts of business economics in order to understand the role of financial statements in decision making processes and to be able to form an independent opinion on such statements" (Blokdijk et al., 1995: 30). Given the historical development to finance the growth of companies by retained earnings and/or borrowing from banking institutions instead of raising new capital (the common situation in Anglo-Saxon countries), the Dutch focus of auditing was on meeting the requirements of owners and others who were entitled to the profits of the company. The focus on 'understatement of net profits' (the attention for the profit and loss account) led to the development of a specifically Dutch discipline, 'Administrative and Accounting Organization' (AAO)[57], strongly based on the concepts of business economics. With this perspective Dutch auditors and management held a mutual interest in the 'AAO system' of the company. The findings and recommendations of the auditor to management regarding the improvement of the existing 'AAO system' generally are viewed as an added value of audit by management for own purposes. Until the late 1980s audit education has been heavily influenced by the general Limpergian norm of inspired confidence. However, due to internationalization and the creation of big audit firms, audit education in the Netherlands makes an increasing use of Anglo-American audit literature. But AAO and internal controls together with a broad business economics approach are still corner stones in the education of auditors in the Netherlands nowadays.

4.2.1.2 *Cultural differences and legal system*

As Blokdijk et al. (1995) noticed, another explanation for the differences in the way auditing and the audit profession have developed between the Netherlands and the Anglo-Saxon countries, are existing cultural differences. These differences may also cause the existence and/or serve as an explanation of possible differences between the factors driving the demand for audit in the decision making process of managers between different countries.

---

[57] "AAO deals with the organization of the collection and processing of data by an entity, in order to make relevant and reliable information available on a timely basis for operational, managerial and financial accounting purposes. It has three basic concepts:
- the economic substance of the business: 'what is really happening in the company?';
- the circular flow of values within a company, which may appear as a 'flow of goods and cash values' through the entity; and,
- -the classification model of business entities, which serves as an analytical tool for the design of an 'AAO system' in a given entity.

Emphasized are the internal controls on the completeness of revenue recognition." (Blokdijk et al., 1995:14-15).

Hofstede (2001) found that cultural differences between countries exist and that these differences in 'national culture' can be ordered along five dimensions:
- power distance;
- uncertainty avoidance;
- individualism versus collectivism;
- masculinity versus femininity;
- long-term versus short-term orientation.

Table 4.1 presents an overview of Hofstede's classification along these dimensions of the Netherlands compared to the United Kingdom and Finland. In chapter 6.5 differences between the results of this study and similar studies in both countries are explained.

Table 4.1 Classification of cultural differences			
	The Netherlands	United Kingdom	Finland
Power distance	Low	Low	Low
Uncertainty avoidance	Weak	Weak	Strong
Individualism/collectivism	Individualism	Individualism	Individualism
Masculinity/femininity	Feminine	Masculine	Feminine
Long-term/short-term orientation	Long-term[58]	Short-term	Long-term
Source: Hofstede (2001)			

What implications do these cultural differences have on the development of auditing and the audit profession in the different countries? Blokdijk et al. (1995) relate the development of a principle based approach to auditing and the large degree of uniformity within the Dutch audit profession, even in absence of standards and regulation to the following Dutch cultural factors:
- the existing consensus and compromise culture;
- the substance over form attitude; and
- aversion to detailed laws and regulations to ensure compliance.

According to Hofstede, accountants (and also auditors, HBD) and accounting systems "can also be considered uncertainty-reducing rituals, fulfilling a cultural need for certainty, simplicity and truth in a confusing world" (Hofstede, 2001: 382) and as accounting is a field in which technical imperatives are weak, it is, according to Hofstede, logical for the rules of accounting and the way they are

---

[58] With the long-term/short-term orientation Hofstede (2001:359) remarks: "Among western societies, the Netherlands scored relatively highest on LTO; the Dutch have been teased by other Europeans for their stinginess and have been called "the Chinese of Europe".

used to vary along national cultural lines. Using the five dimensions Hofstede points towards a number of differences in the role of accounting systems and the people involved:

- in large power distance countries, accounting systems serve to justify the decisions of the top power holders;
- in strong uncertainty avoidance countries, accounting systems will contain more detailed rules and will be more theoretically based, whereas in low uncertainty avoidance countries more will be left to the professional judgement of the accountant;
- in collectivist countries the accounting profession is likely to carry lower status than in individualistic countries;
- in more masculine countries, accounting results are more likely to be presented in such a way that a responsible manager is pictured as a hero of a bum;
- in more masculine countries, accounting systems stress the achievement of purely financial targets more;
- in more masculine countries, accounting professionals tends to be less conservative and more optimistic in evaluating accounts;
- in short-term oriented countries, accounting systems stress the importance of short-term results more.

Acknowledgement of these differences supports our understanding why auditing (and auditors) in the Netherlands originally focused on the broad business environment of the company and 'precautionary principle' in preparing and auditing the annual accounts was prevalent for long.

With regard to the differences in legal system, the Netherlands is to be considered part of the Rhineland governance model, which differ in various ways from the Anglo-Saxon governance model. The legal system in the Rhineland governance model is based on 'civil code' and in the Anglo-Saxon governance model on 'common law'. With regard to ownership structure and litigation risks the difference between civil code law and common law is prominent. Auditors in a civil code law governance model generally face lower risks than in the common law governance model. Blokdijk et al. (1995) noticed that compared to the United States there have only been a few cases against auditors. And of those, most are settled out of court. However, it can be questioned to which extent these differences in ownership structure and litigation risks between civil code and common law also hold in the case of SME companies (Niemi et al., 2009).

4.2.2 Audit regulation

The history of independent auditors in the Netherlands goes back to 1879 and the first accountancy body, N.I.V.A, was already founded in 1895. Nevertheless, it took a while before auditing was regulated by company law in the Netherlands. Although a revision of the Dutch company law in 1929 did mention the possibility of an external audit, it should be emphasized that this was optional (Buijink, 1992). However, as the revision tightened disclosure requirements for larger Dutch companies, this may have influenced the demand for accounting expertise of external auditors at that time. The development of larger companies voluntarily choosing to have their financial statements audited may also be attributed to a further internationalization and the need for larger Dutch companies to join common practice in the Anglo-Saxon countries (were auditing at that time already was mandatory). As such, the 1958 mandatory requirement of the Amsterdam Stock Exchange can be seen, as of that time an external independent audit of financial statements information in security issue prospectuses is required.

First in 1970 companies in the Netherlands were obliged to have their financial statement audited. As a result of the major revision of Dutch company law, leading to the passing of the Law on the Financial Statements of Companies (Wet op de Jaarrekening van Ondernemingen) all public companies, large private companies and large co-operative societies had to disclose audited annual accounts (Maijoor, 1991). But it took until 1983, when a second major legislation change took place (the passing of Title 8, book 2 of the Dutch Civil Code) that besides aforementioned companies also middle-sized companies were required to audit their financial statements. Under Title 8 all public companies, private companies, and co-operative societies are obliged to disclose annual accounts. However, small and middle-sized firms are allowed to submit abridged annual accounts. All large and middle-sized firms subjected to Title 8 were required to audit their annual accounts. The legislation change also concerned the requirements for the auditing and content of annual accounts. The legislation change was effective in 1984 and with this change Dutch law was adapted to the Fourth EC Directive on Company Law. Within Title 8, there was a temporary provision for middle-sized private companies with respect to the mandated audit. Until 1990 only large private companies (size criterion based on "old' legislation) were required to have their financial statements audited (Maijoor, 1991).

Figure 4.2 shows that the number of auditors in public practice grew steadily until 1970 and then rapidly expanded. This increase in the number of auditors from 1970 till 1990 is mainly the result of the demand-side regulation (Maijoor, 1991;

Meuwissen and Wallage, 2008). However, the increase in the number of auditors during the 1990's is mainly caused by the effects of the implementation of the Eighth EU Directive, whereby members of the Dutch Association of Certified Accountants are also allowed to conduct statutory audits. However, most of these certified accountants in public practice do not conduct statutory audits, but are mainly involved in rendering compilation and tax services to small companies.

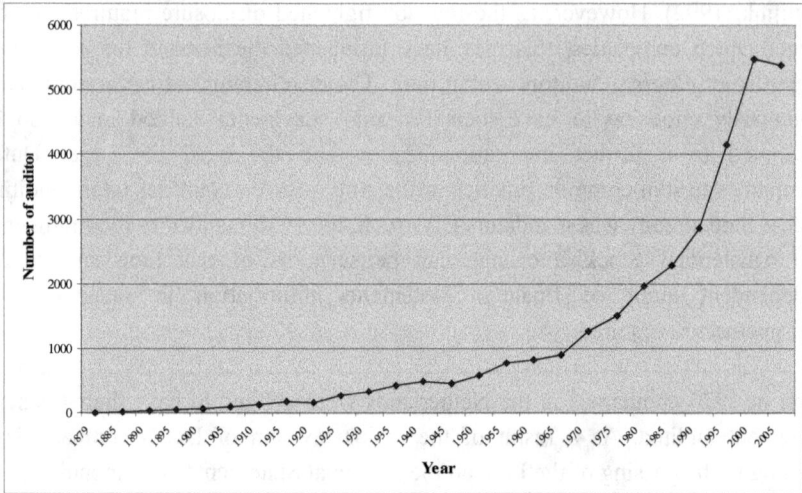

Figure 4.2: The Dutch market for audit services, 1879-2005 (source: Meuwissen and Wallage, 2008)

In 2006, as a response to US and European accounting scandals, the Supervision of Auditors' Organizations Act (Wet Toezicht Accountants) was implemented together with a independent oversight board for statutory auditors. "All other auditors and audit firms – i.e. those conducting non-statutory audits – are subject to inspections by the professional bodies" (Meuwissen and Wallage, 2008). As from 2006 audit firms which conduct mandatory statutory audits should obtain a license from the Netherlands Authority for Financial Markets (AFM), the oversight board. Only licensed audit firms and the by these firms AFM-licensed auditors are allowed to conduct mandatory statutory audits after being approved by the AFM, whereby a difference is made in licenses for the mandatory statutory audit of Public Interest Entities (Organisaties van Openbaar Belang) and other mandatory statutory audits. Due to this additional layer of control the number of audit firms and auditors with a licence decreased significantly. Only 475 (of which 16 audit firms with a OOB-license and 459 with a general license) audit firms of the 1.939 audit firms in the Netherlands applied for a license from the AFM. Also the number of auditors which are registered to perform mandatory statutory auditors decreased to 2.266 (of the number of 8.691 auditors working in public practice)[59].

From the history of audit regulation it can be concluded that the mandatory audit for middle sized companies in the Netherlands only exists for about three decades and that Dutch small companies in the Netherlands have never been faced with a mandatory audit regime. Unlike some other European countries, only a small percentage (2%) of the number of companies are mandatorily required to have their financial statement audited. The table listed below (table 4.2) shows the number of companies in the Netherlands under the mandatory audit regime compared to several other (European) countries.

Table 4.2. shows that the number of companies falling under a mandatory statutory audit regime related to the total number of enterprises for the Netherlands is relatively low. Comparing the Gross Domestic Product (GDP) of these countries, it shows that the Netherlands has one of the highest GDP. On a global scale the Netherlands is the 16th largest economy of the world[60]. It appears that audit regulation in the Netherlands is less stringent compared to e.g. the Scandinavian countries. Furthermore, the majority of enterprises in the Netherlands can be classified as 'small' and therefore are exempted from the mandatory audit regime.

---

[59] Source: Accountant Adviseur, September 2009. The numbers presented are as of January 2009 and contains both the number of Registered Auditors (Registeraccountants) and Certified Accountants (Accountants-Administratieconsulenten).
[60] International Monetary Fund, World Economic Outlook Database, April 2011: Nominal GDP list of countries. Data for the year 2010.

Table 4.2 Number of companies falling under a national mandatory audit regime and GDP

	number of companies mandatory audit[61]	number of enterprises[62]	GDP (million €)[63]
Belgium	18,300	424,600	339,000
Denmark	75,000	212,100	223,000
Finland	370,000	213,800	171,000
France	200,000	2,569,100	1,907,000
Ireland	140,000	92,700	160,000
The Netherlands	9,000	540,300	572,000
Norway	207,000	253,900	273,000
Spain	29,000	2,712,400	1,054,000
United Kingdom	179,000	1,670,600	1,563,000
Sweden	280,000	560,800	293,000
Switzerland	170,000	312,900	354,000

4.2.3 Summary

In interpreting the empirical results of this study, the context of the environment should be taken into account as to some extent factors driving the demand for voluntary audit for SME companies in the Netherlands probably are caused by sociological influences as 'path dependence' and 'national culture'. These influences, in turn may also impact the decision making process whether or not to opt for a non-mandatory audit. This section has described a number of historical and sociological developments which potentially influence (both positively as negatively) the demand for audit in the Netherlands, such as:

- the broad knowledge of Dutch auditors of business economics;
- the 'shared focus' with management on the quality of the 'AAO-system' of the company;

---

[61] Source: De Accountant, June 2007. The numbers are an estimate of the numbers of companies falling under a mandatory audit regime as of July 1, 2006. Due to the estimate of these numbers no clear explanation can be given why the number of companies falling under a mandatory audit regime for Finland and Ireland exceeds the total number of enterprises. However numbers implicate that as a result of a more stringent audit regulation in both Ireland and Finland the majority of companies are mandatory required to have their financial statements audited.

[62] Source Eurostat 2009 presenting the 2007 figures (Ireland, 2006), whereby an enterprise is defined as: the enterprise is the smallest combination of legal units that is an organisational unit producing goods or services, which benefits from a certain degree of autonomy in decision-making, especially for the allocation of its current resources. An enterprise carries out one or more activities at one or more locations. An enterprise may be a sole legal unit.

[63] Source Eurostat: Keyfigures on Europe – 2011 edition, presenting 2009 figures

- the relatively low number of private companies which are subject to a mandatory audit and the relatively short period of the existing mandatory regime for middle-sized companies in the Netherlands;
- the traditional aversion of (detailed) laws and regulations to ensure compliance coupled with the recent installed additional layers of controls on auditing (and audit profession);
- the existence of a large number of audit firms and auditors in public practice which are not conducting mandatory statutory audits but providing other services (e.g. compilation services).

4.3   Data selection

4.3.1   Introduction

As we know from the preceding section, in the Netherlands all incorporated companies with limited liability, whether their shares are publicly traded or privately held, are required to disclose financial statements following the requirements stated in the Dutch Civic Code. But only large and medium sized companies are required to have their annual financial statements audited by an independent certified public accountant. The classification in company law is made by size criteria as mentioned in article 2:396 section one and article 2:397 section one of the Dutch Civil Code[64].

Due to a number of developments, Dutch government was faced with an increasing call of the Dutch business environment to lessen the administrative burden[65]. Already in 2003 the first governmental studies were undertaken to explore opportunities to lessen this burden. One of the suggested possibilities was raising the current size criteria by 25%. A study commissioned by the department

---

[64] The full text of these articles (in Dutch) is as follows. Artikel 2:396 BW lid 1: "De leden 3 tot en met 8 gelden voor een rechtspersoon die op 2 opeenvolgende balansdata, zonder onderbreking nadien op 2 opeenvolgende balansdata, heeft voldaan aan 2 of 3 van de volgende vereisten: (a) de waarde van de activa volgens de balans met toelichting bedraagt, op de grondslag van verkrijgings- en vervaardigingsprijs, niet meer dan € 4.400.000; (b) de netto-omzet over het boekjaar bedraagt niet meer dan € 8.800.000; (c) het gemiddeld aantal werknemers over het boekjaar bedraagt minder dan 50.". Artikel 2:397 BW lid 1: "Behoudens art. 396 gelden de leden 3 tot en met 7 voor een rechtspersoon die op 2 opeenvolgende balansdata, zonder onderbreking nadien op 2 opeenvolgende balansdata, heeft voldaan aan 2 of 3 van de volgende vereisten: (a) de waarde van de activa volgens de balans met toelichting, bedraagt, op de grondslag van verkrijgings- en vervaardigingsprijs, niet meer dan € 17.500.000; (b) de netto-omzet over het boekjaar bedraagt niet meer dan € 35.000.000; (c) het gemiddeld aantal werknemers over het boekjaar bedraagt minder dan 250."
[65] This was not only a Dutch phenomenon, but also occurs in other countries. The members of the European Union therefore agreed to simplify and reduce the administrative burden in the EU in the Lisboa-agreement.

of Justice showed that the number of companies, which due to this deregulation no longer classify as medium sized, would decrease with almost 1,000 companies (from 7,690 to 6,706)[66]. At that time the European Union was also in the process of revising the criteria for classification of companies as set out in the 4th Directive. This made the Dutch government decide to follow the revised criteria as proposed by the EU. In October 2006 the criteria for classification were revised as of January 1, 2006. Table 4.2 shows an overview of the revised and old criteria for classification as a 'small' company.

Table 4.2 Revised criteria and criteria before October 2006 for classification 'small' sized companies

	Revised criteria	Criteria before October 2006
Total amount of assets (in €)	≤ 4,400,000	≤ 3,650,000
Total amount of revenue (in €)	≤ 8,800,000	≤ 7,300,000
Total number of employees	< 50	< 50

The revision of the law led to an increase of the size criteria. Thus, a group of companies that, due to the revision, did not fall within the "middle" sized company range anymore was faced with the decision whether they continue with the practice of having their financial statements audited voluntarily by external auditors. It is this deregulation which created the opportunity for an empirical study regarding the drivers for the demand for voluntary audit choice.

4.3.2 Sample selection

As all Dutch companies resorting under company law are mandatorily required to file their annual accounts at the Chamber of Commerce, the total population of companies could be extracted from the files of the Chamber of Commerce. The population consists of companies that, according to the Chamber of Commerce, fell in the specified range for at least two out of three size criteria. The companies of interest fall in the range between the old size criteria and the new size criteria of article 2:396 section one of the Dutch Civil Code. A request was made to the Chamber of Commerce to produce a list of companies which based on the size criteria classified as medium sized in 2005 and, according to the revised criteria, classified as small in 2006. This process resulted in a number of 759 companies

---

[66] Source: letters of the minister of Justice to Parliament – March 1, 2006 and April 15, 2004 (brief 29515, nr. 130 van de minister van justitie aan de tweede kamer der Staten-Generaal, d.d. 1 maart 2006 en brief 29515, nr. 8 van de minister van justitie aan de tweede kamer der Staten-Generaal, d.d. 15 april 2004).

(the total population)[67]. Based on article 2:396 section one of the Dutch Civil Code companies are only allowed to apply the exemptions for small companies if they fulfil to the size criteria for two concessive years. This implicates that of the population only companies who fulfil the size criteria for small companies for two concessive years are allowed to apply the other sections of article 2:396 of the Dutch Civil Code, including the exemption for a mandatory audit[68]. However, due to the deregulation, a provisional clause exists whereby companies were allowed to apply the other sections of article 2:396 of the Dutch Civil Code already in 2006 if, according to the new size criteria the company would have been classified as small in 2005 (it showed that 52% of the respondents meet this provisional clause in 2006)[69].

4.3.3   Data collection

4.3.3.1 Methodology

To gather the necessary data to answer the research question of this study, besides publicly available data, the survey as research method will be used. With the use of survey studies a number of common difficulties are identified such as low target populations, the difficulty of achieving adequate levels of response and non-response bias. Nonetheless, survey research can be used to obtain multi-faceted data regarding the behaviour and perceptions of the respondent (Henn et

---

[67] This number is lower than the originally estimated number by the Minister of Justice, although for that estimation also the figures of the Chamber of Commerce has been used. A possible explanation for the difference is that the estimation of the Minister of Justice is based on 2002-figures.

[68] The existence of this 'step-on'/'step-off' period in Dutch Civil Code may have consequences for the population of this study. As a result of this 'step-on'/'step-off' period it could occur that over time not all companies of the population are allowed to apply for the exemptions for small companies under Dutch Civil Code. Companies which are facing the exemptions for small companies, due to their size, in 2006 but finally do not meet these criteria for two concessive years (in this case the adapted 2005 figures or the 2007 figures) may not apply for the small-company-exemptions. Althouh the focus of this study is on the (renewed) audit decision in a non-mandatory setting it was recognized, in the construction of the questionnaire, that the possibility exists that not all companies of the population finally could apply for this exemption.

[69] Besides the 52% of the respondent companies which already in 2006 meet the legal requirements of a small company according to article 2:396 section 1 of the Dutch Civil Code, 37 % classified as small company in subsequent years. It showed, that of the respondents, although facing the possibility of a non-mandatory audit decision in 2006, finally 11% (17 of the 154) could not apply for the small company exemptions. Chapter 6.2.2 discusses the need of a minimum number of cases related to the number of independent variables incorporated in the regression model to produce statistical reliable outcomes. Given the research question of this study (chapter 1.3), an aim of this study is to include as many as possible expected drivers for the demand for audit in the regression model (see chapter 6.3). Therefore it is decided to include in the final sample also the responses of companies which finally could not apply for the small company exemptions. An additional performed non-parametric Mann-Whitney (see Appendix VI) showed that no significant differences exists between characteristics of the companies which ultimately did and companies which did not classify as small company.

al, 2006). As this study is focused on enrichment of our understanding of the factors driving the demand for audit in the decision making process of management, both publicly available data and private data is needed. The publicly available data (e.g. total assets, number of employees, leverage and audit report) are collected using databases of Chamber of Commerce, REACH and Company.info. To collect the private data, consisting of factual private data (e.g. management-ownership share and existence of outside directors) and psychological (perceptions) data (e.g. perceptions regarding audit improves credibility of financial statements), it was decided to use a survey method. To mitigate the mentioned difficulties, as they are in essence 'technical' in nature, proposed solutions in designing (e.g. covering letter, specific targeting to respondents, follow-up procedures, easy to understood and quick to answer questions) and pilot testing of the survey (Smith, 2003; Henn et al., 2006) are executed to overcome these difficulties

Survey research can be divided into three main types of data collection methods: the face-to-face interview, postal questionnaires (including e-mail and internet) and telephone interviews. For this study, the postal questionnaire has been chosen as survey method, mainly due to the size of the population. The main advantage of using postal or electronic questionnaires is that they can be used for large-scale survey and this method of data collection ensures a degree of privacy for the respondent and produces less distortion than face-to-face and telephone interviews (Henn et al., 2006). In addition, the costs are relatively low compared to interviews. It was decided to use a traditional postal questionnaire accompanied with a cover letter as, based on anecdotic evidence, it is expected that the response rate of management (the targeted respondents) would be higher than using an electronic survey.

In designing the questionnaire (see appendix I) and the construction of the detailed questions for gathering data for the identified variables driving the demand for audit the following steps were executed. First, several interviews were conducted to explore the issues and test whether the questions are clear and to test the sequence of the questions[70]. Subsequently in November 2009 a pilot survey[71] was sent out to the management of a number of companies outside the population to test the designed questionnaire. The lay-out of the questionnaire

---

[70] As "one of the most serious criticism of survey research is that the questions asked are often complex" (Smith, 2003: 121). To mitigate the risk of to complex questions and to test if reasonably can be expected that the asked questions can be answered without having to search or look up for details (which would increase the risk of a low response rate) pilot testing of the questionnaire was conducted.

was constructed in a way that all questions, including intentionally created blank space to give respondents the opportunity to add some qualitative remarks[72], fit within a four page survey which were double side folded on a one A3-paper.

4.3.3.2 Collection of the survey data and response rate

The postal questionnaire was accompanied by a cover letter explaining the purpose of the survey that also highlighted the importance for (SME) companies to gather insights in the demand for voluntary audit decision. The cover letter, the questionnaire and a prepaid envelope were addressed to the management of the companies of the population[73]. The questionnaire was sent on January 18, 2010. From the original total population of 759 companies a total of 36 companies were removed due to parent-subsidiary-relation, resulting in a total of 723 sent questionnaires. As the data used in this study combines public available data with private data and the perception of management regarding the audit decision, each questionnaire was given an unique reference code so that the returned questionnaires could be connected to the individual company and public data and also the non-respondents could be identified. A reminder was sent on March 2, 2010. In order to maximise the response rate, the reminder consisted of a new cover letter together with a copy of the original cover letter and the questionnaire. Also the effective number of companies surveyed was reduced to 695 due to the elimination of 28 companies that were subsequently found to be out of scope and were excluded for the reasons shown in table 4.3.

Table 4.3 Breakdown of companies excluded from survey

Reason	No. of companies
Not trading/(in) liquidation/ bankrupt	6
Owner overseas/unavailable	5
Questionnaire returned 'moved to another address'	17
Total	**28**

A total of 154 filled-in questionnaires were returned, resulting in a response rate to the questionnaire survey of 22% (22.2%). This is higher than the 17% achieved

---

[71] The pilot survey was conducted under 189 middle sized companies. As these companies still felt under the mandatory audit regime it was asked if they would forgo with a voluntary audit if the existing mandatory audit regime would no longer exist.

[72] It showed that 16 of the 154 respondents have taken the opportunity to add some qualitative responses. Of the respondents who have added qualitative responses 75% opt not to continue with the audit.

[73] It should be noticed that, although the questionnaires have been addressed to management of the companies, the possibility exists that the questionnaire not have been filled-in by management but by other employees of the company on behalf of management.

by the postal survey of Collis et al. (2004) and the realized response rate of 12% of the electronic survey of Niemi et al. (2009), but lower than the 32% achieved by the postal survey of Senkow et al. (2001).

As non-response is a concern in almost all survey research, a check was carried out to test for evidence of non-response bias. In previous research it is suggested that non-respondents behave like late respondents. Therefore an additional test was conducted to see whether the characteristics of late-respondents (received at least 6 days after sending the reminder) significantly deviated form early respondents. A non-parametric Mann-Whitney test on a number of key characteristics was conducted. The results (see appendix II) showed that the null hypothesis (there is no difference between the two groups of respondents) for all these characteristics, was confirmed and no indication of non-response bias existed in this study. Another concern (although occurring in most forms of research) is the existence of missing data. This study has also to deal with the existence of missing values and has initially treated missing values based on a list wise deletion. A more in detail explanation the way this study has dealt with missing values is provided in chapter 6.3.2 and appendix IV.

Furthermore, the research focuses on a population of companies which due to deregulation no longer meets the 2006 size criteria for medium sized companies. The companies were selected from the data of the Chamber of Commerce. However the population may be biased to some extent for two reasons. First, although all companies are mandatorily required to file their financial statements at the Chamber of Commerce, not all companies fulfil this requirement and therefore companies which fulfil the requirements for selection could be missing[74]. Second, although with a number of questions the views of management were asked at the time of decision making, due to the existing 'time-gap', the perceptions held at time of responding on the questionnaire may be 'coloured' by later events.

---

[74] As described in chapter 4.3.1, all incorporated companies with limited liability in the Netherlands are required to disclose their annual financial statements at the Chamber of Commerce. Supervision of this obligation is executed by the Tax Authorities and companies which do not fulfil their filing obligation risk a penalty. Research has revealed that about 13% of the companies in the Netherlands do not file their financial statements yearly at the Chamber of Commerce. Due to the large absolute and relative number of small companies in the Netherlands, it is tentative to expect that the majority of

4.3.4   Description of the variables in this study

The objective of this study is to test empirically the possible variables that could explain the demand for audit and to enlarge our understanding of the drivers for the demand for audit in a non-mandatory environment. Chapter 3.3 provided an overview of general hypotheses (table 3.1) already tested in previous 'demand for audit' studies. Of the total of nineteen identified general hypotheses, eighteen will be included in this study. The general hypothesis related to 'the cost of an audit' (no. 14 of table 3.1) was not included. Also it was decided not to include the hypothesis related to 'earnings management' (the second part of hypothesis no. 13 of table 3.1). The reason is the expected impossibility to gather the necessary data from publicly available information due to existing disclosure exemptions[75]. Besides these eighteen hypotheses an additional three hypotheses are included in this study of which one hypothesis will use a 'direct' variable measuring the influence of the need of shareholders for audited financial statements in the decision making process. The other two hypotheses are related to the shareholders-company relationship and stakeholder-company relationship. Whereby the number of shareholders is included as an additional proxy variable to measure the potential external ('classical') agency relationship between the owner and the manager. The number of relevant stakeholders as identified by management is added as a new variable to measure the stakeholder-company relationship, following the critics brought forward against agency theory (e.g. stakeholder theory) and also the acknowledgement of Dutch historical and cultural factors.

The following variables will be included in the analysis, showing the label used in this study, the description, the source of the data (public data or data obtained through questionnaire), the expected sign and the reference to the corresponding hypothesis tested in chapter five:

---

the companies which do not fulfil their filing duties are 'small companies' and the potential impact on the population of this study is negligible.

[75] The test for earnings management commonly uses the abnormal working capitals accruals method, or a similar model. For these methods is data needed which, due to disclosure exemptions for SME companies, are not publicly available. With regard to the audit fee SME companies are also exempted to disclose the audit fee. Initially, in the pilot survey, a question was introduced regarding the audit fee. However, based on the responses and the decision that the survey should be easily to answer prevails, it was decided not to incorporate an audit fee question in the final questionnaire.

Table 4.4 Description of variables in this study

Label	Description	Source of data	Expected sign	Hypothesis tested
DVA	Whether the company opts for a non-mandatory audit of its financial statements	Dependent variable		
	EXTERNAL AGENCY VARIABLES			
SHRH#	The number of shareholders of the company	Questionnaire	Positive	H1a
SHRHAC	If **all** shareholders have direct access to internal financial information of the company. This is treated as a categorical variable coded as "1" if the company has shareholders with **no** access to internal financial information and "0" otherwise	Questionnaire	Positive	H1b
STAKE#	The number of relevant stakeholders identified by management of the company next to shareholders.	Questionnaire	Positive	H1c
MOWN50	The percentage of shares held by the company's management. This is treated as a categorical variable coded as "1" if management owned 50% or more of the shares and "0" otherwise	Questionnaire	Negative	H1d
SHRHND	Perception of management that the decision is related to the need of existing shareholders of the company for audited financial statements (1 = disagree, 5 = agree).	Questionnaire	Positive	H1e
CREDIBLY	Perception of management that the audit improves the credibility of the financial information to external users (1 = disagree, 5 = agree).	Questionnaire	Positive	H2a
LVRG	The proportion of debt as measured by debt-to-asset ratio	Public	Positive	H2b
LRQM	The existence of a lender requirement for an audit at the time of change in legislation. This is treated as a categorical variable coded "1" if a lender requirement exists at the time and "0" otherwise	Questionnaire	Positive	H2c

88

LENDPLUS	Perception of management that audit has a positive effect on lending conditions (1 = disagree, 5 = agree).	Questionnaire	Positive	H2d
COMPCRED	Perception of management that audit improves the company's credit rating (1 = disagree, 5 = agree).	Questionnaire	Positive	H2e
ASSETS	Size of company as measured by the natural log of balance sheet total in €		Positive	H3
CATOMZ	Size of the company as measured by turnover. This is treated as a categorical variable coded "1" if the turnover does not fit in the small category and "0" otherwise	Questionnaire	Positive	H3
CATEMPLS	Number of employees represents both size of the company and hierarchical levels within company and therefore serves as a proxy for complexity. This is treated as a categorical variable coded "1" if the number of employees does not fit in the small category and "0" otherwise		Positive	H3 + H4

INTERNAL AGENCY VARIABLES

OUTDIR	The existence of outside directors. This is treated as a categorical variable coded as "1" if the company has outside directors and "0" otherwise.	Questionnaire	Positive	H5
CHECK	Perception of management that audit provides a check on accounting records and systems (1 = disagree, 5 = agree).	Questionnaire	Positive	H6a
FINAFD	Whether the company has a financial department. This is treated as a categorical variable coded as "1" if the company has a financial department and "0" otherwise	Questionnaire	Negative	H6b
EDUFIN	Whether the company has a qualified head of financial department. This is treated as a categorical variable coded as "1" if the company has a qualified head of the financial department and "0" if the company has a	Questionnaire	Negative	H6c

	qualified head of financial department			
QUALITY	Perception of management that audit improves the quality of the financial information (1 = disagree, 5 = agree).	Questionnaire	Positive	H7
	OTHER VARIABLES			
AUDTERM	The number of years the current auditor has been engaged with the company.	Questionnaire	Positive	H8a
AUDSERV	The number of other services, such as MAS and taxation services, provided by the audit firm besides the audit.	Questionnaire	Positive	H8b
AUDREP	Whether an unqualified audit report has been issued in previous year(s). This is treated as a categorical variable coded as "1" if an unqualified audit report has been issued and "0" otherwise.	Public	Negative	H8c
HEALTH	Whether the company makes profit or not. This is treated as a categorical variable coded "1" when the company makes profit the previous year and "0" otherwise	Public	Positive	H9
STRAT	Perception of management that the expected future growth of the company has been part of the decision making process (1 = disagree, 5 = agree).	Questionnaire	Positive	H10

4.3.5 Descriptive data

Table 4.5 provides the descriptive statistics of this study. The variables presented are described in the number of cases (N), the mean, the median and the standard deviation from the mean. The descriptive statistics of the independent dichotomous variables are not presented in this table, as the calculation of the mean, median and the standard deviation from the mean is not meaningful. However, in the individual hypotheses testing of chapter five the mean and standard deviation of the dichotomous independent variables are presented.

Table 4.5 Descriptive statistics

		Total Sample	DVA = 'Yes'	DVA = 'No'
SHRH#	N	154	95	59
	Mean (Median)	3.05 (2.00)	3.61 (2.00)	2.15 (1.00)
	Std.Dev.	6.127	7.478	2.658
STAKE#	N	154	95	59
	Mean (Median)	2.94 (3.00)	3.01 (3.00)	2.81 (3.00)
	Std.Dev.	1.089	1.162	0.955
SHRHND	N	141	88	53
	Mean (Median)	3.08 (3.00)	3.70 (4.00)	2.04 (1.00)
	Std.Dev.	1.536	1.288	1.344
CREDIBLY	N	154	95	59
	Mean (Median)	3.77 (4.00)	4.05 (4.00)	3.31 (3.00)
	Std.Dev.	1.053	0.880	1.149
LVRG	N	154	95	59
	Mean (Median)	0.70 (0.56)	0.81 (0.56)	0.53 (0.55)
	Std.Dev.	1.443	1.816	0.319
LENDPLUS	N	154	95	59
	Mean (Median)	3.29 (3.00)	3.42 (3.00)	3.07 (3.00)
	Std.Dev.	1.282	1.234	1.337
COMPCRED	N	152	94	58
	Mean (Median)	2.88 (3.00)	3.03 (3.00)	2.64 (3.00)
	Std.Dev.	1.239	1.248	1.195
ASSETS	N	154	95	59
	Mean (Median)	15.71 (15.51)	15.67 (15.46)	15.76 (15.62)
	Std.Dev.	0.978	1.081	0.791
CHECK	N	154	95	59
	Mean (Median)	3.36 (4.00)	3.72 (4.00)	2.80 (3.00)
	Std.Dev.	1.119	0.986	1.095
QUALITY	N	153	94	59
	Mean (Median)	2.93 (3.00)	3.29 (3.00)	2.37 (2.00)
	Std.Dev.	1.134	0.957	1.173
AUDTERM	N	136	86	50
	Mean (Median)	9.71 (7.50)	11.31 (10.00)	6.96 (4.00)
	Std.Dev.	9.105	9.298	8.136
AUDSERV	N	154	95	59
	Mean (Median)	2.47 (2.00)	2.39 (2.00)	2.60 (2.00)
	Std.Dev.	1.661	1.586	1.782
STRAT	N	126	74	52
	Mean (Median)	2.13 (2.00)	2.34 (2.00)	1.83 (1.50)
	Std.Dev.	1.088	1.126	0.964

The results of the descriptive data showed that 62% of the companies choose for a non- mandatory audit. Compared to the study of Senkow et al. (2001), the only other study using data of companies which are facing a non-mandatory audit decision, this percentage is 12% lower. However, it should be noticed that the study of Senkow et al. consists of private large Canadian companies, whereas this study consists of private SME Dutch companies. Compared to the study of Collis et al. (2004) the percentage of companies choosing an audit is almost identical (62% vs. 63%).

In general the respondents agree that the auditing has a positive effect on the credibility of the financial information (CREDIBLY) and provides a check on accounting records and systems (CHECK). This is also the case for the responses of management with regard to their perception that the decision is related to the need of existing shareholders for audited financial statements The mean of these variables for the sample as a whole is above three (out of five) and the relative low standard deviations imply that with regard to these variables considerable consensus exist between the population as a whole. The differences in the mean for these variables between the respondents which opt for a non-mandatory audit and those who did not suggest that these could be a driver for the demand for audit. Also the differences in a number of other variables (e.g. SHRH#, LVRG, QUALITY, AUDTERM) suggest that these may be statistically significant. To which extent this indeed will be the case, will be presented in the next chapter. Chapter five deals with the hypotheses testing of the identified individual relationships with the demand for auditing.

Chapter 5. Empirical Results I – Individual hypotheses

5.1 Introduction

Following the structure of this study, chapter five presents the empirical results of the individual hypotheses.

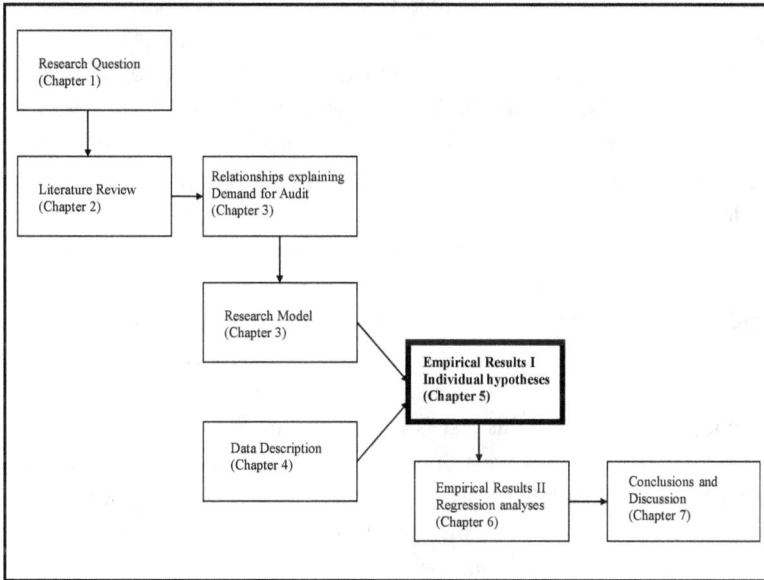

Figure 5.1: Overview of the structure of this study

What are drivers for the demand for audit in a non-mandatory environment? To empirically answer the research question, based on literature review, chapter 3.3.2 presented the regression model of this study.

DVA = f(external agency variables, internal agency variables, other variables)

In this regression model, the demand for audit (DVA) is the dependent variable. And as we observe the decision of management whether or not opt for a non-mandatory audit, the outcome of this dependent variable can only be a 'yes' or 'no'. As DVA is characterized as a dichotomous variable, logistic regression will be used. Like linear regression, logistic regression allows us to study the association of various independent variables on a dichotomous dependent variable. Using a dichotomous dependent variable in a linear regression model is problematic because this would lead to a violation of one of more of the assumptions underlying linear regression models[76]. An advantage of using logistic regression in this study is that besides analyzing the association of independent variables on the dichotomous dependent variable the mutual influence of the different types (continuous and categorical) independent variables can be analyzed.

Before conducting the regression analyses this chapter presents the bivariate analyses of the independent variables (see chapter 4.3.4) related to the DVA. Based on hypothesized relationships with the demand for audit it will be tested if significant relationship between the individual independent variables and the dependent DVA exist. Due to the different types of variables (ratio, ordinal and dichotomous), various statistical tests are conducted to test whether statistical significant relationships exist with DVA. The tables provided show the statistical results taking into account the two groups of dependent variable DVA, 'Yes' or 'No'. Independent t-tests are used to test the independent ratio variables in this study. Where appropriate, one-tailed tests are conducted and presented next to the standard two-tailed test[77]. Fisher's exact tests are used to test the ordinal (dichotomous) independent variables. The use of Fisher's exact test in this study is twofold, as the standard statistic output of this test provides the one-tailed significance test[78] also and this test is more accurate than the conventional Chi-square test for 2x2 tables. To test the significance of the association between the independent ordinal variables and DVA, Kendall's tau-b[79] is used. The non-parametric Mann-Whitney tests are conducted to test the other ordinal variables as univariate analysis shows that these independent variables are not normally distributed.

---

[76] The use of regression models is bounded by four basic assumptions:
  a. the relationship between the independent(s) and dependent variables is linear in nature;
  b. the errorterms are normally distributed
  c. the errorterms are not correlated
  d. the errorterms are homoskedastic
By using logistic regression the assumptions of correlation and homoskedastic of the errorterms disappear.
[77] As on forehand the direction of the predicted relationships between the independent and dependent variable can be predicted it is allowed to conduct one-tailed tests instead of a two-tailed test (De Vocht, 2010: 126).
[78] Normally the one-tailed significance of the two-tailed Chi-square test can be calculated by dividing the outcome of the two-tailed Chi-square significance by 2. However, this is only allowed in the case of 'normal distribution' of the frequencies and the requirement of at least 50 observations and no cells with less than 5 observations.
[79] Another commonly used association test is the Spearman's rank correlation. However, statistical literature seems to prefer the use of Kendall's tau-b above the use of Spearman's rank correlation

The structure of this chapter follows the structure of relationships as presented in chapter three. First we start with the individual hypotheses related to the external agency relationships in section 5.2. Section 5.3 presents the individual hypotheses related to other relationships, divided in internal agency relationships and other considerations. A table summarizing the empirical results of this chapter is presented in section 5.4 and section 5.5 deals with the conclusion of the outcome of these empirical results. Although to some extent an overlap with chapter three exists, it is decided from a readers point of view to reiterate briefly the motives for the formulation of the hypotheses before elucidating the hypotheses and the statistical results.

5.2 External agency relationships

5.2.1 Shareholder(owner) – manager relationship

The relationship between shareholder and manager as principal and agent is to be considered as the foundation of agency theory. Following the structure of chapter three, this study will test the following relationships with respect to the shareholder (owner) – manager relation and the decision of management whether or not to have the financial statements audited:
- the number of shareholders and stakeholders to which management of the company has to provide financial information (general hypotheses 20 and 21 of chapter 3.3.1);
- the impact of the existence of shareholders, who have no direct access to internal financial information (general hypothesis 2 of table 3.1);
- the proportion of management's share in the equity of the firm (general hypothesis 1 of table 3.1);
- perceptions held by management with respect to existing shareholders' need for audited financial statements and the enhancement of credibility of the financial information (general hypothesis 22 of chapter 3.3.1).

5.2.1.1 *The position of shareholders to the company*

Agency theory considers auditing of financial statements as agency costs and therefore, following the line of reasoning of agency theory, from an profit maximizing point of view it is likely to expect that management will not continue the audit in case a mandatory audit becomes voluntary. The relation between

---

because of the fact that the use of Kendall's tau-b can be extended to more variables (Mortelmans and Dehertogh, 2007: 182).

shareholder and manager and more specific the extent to which shareholders place trust in management and the risk shareholders are willing to take, will have an effect on this decision. However, the greater the number of shareholders involved in the equity of the company, the more likely it is that these shareholders have different levels of trust and risk bearing, which leaves management with greater uncertainty whether to discontinue the audit of financial statement is in his best interest. This leads to the following hypothesis.

Hypothesis 1a: The larger the number of shareholders in the firm, the higher the probability the company will have the financial statements audited.

Variable SHRH# is used to test this relationship between the identified groups (DVA 'no' and 'yes'), whereas SHRH# counts for the number of shareholders of the company. As SHRH# is treated as a nominal value, independent t-test (see table 5.1a) are executed to test for the difference between the two groups. Results of this test show a statistical significance difference ($p < 0.05$) between the mean number of shareholders, where the companies opting for an audit indeed have a higher mean of shareholders (3.61 compared to 2.15). The results of the test are consistent with hypothesis 1a.

Table 5.1a - Independent t-tests on number of shareholders (hypothesis 1a)						
Label	DVA	N	Mean	Median	Std. Dev.	Sig.
SHRH#	No	59	2.15	1.00	2.658	0.043**
	Yes	95	3.61	2.00	7.478	
	Total	154	3.05	2.00	6.127	

Table 5.1a present descriptive statistics for the variables used in the examination of individual 'external agency' relationship of hypothesis 1a. The table presents the means, medians and standard deviations of the ratio variable and t-statistics measuring the difference between the companies that opt for an audit or not. ***$p<0.01$, **$p<0.05$ and *$p<0.10$; one-tailed

As the existence of information asymmetry between shareholder and manager is also to be considered to play an important role in the demand for auditing, it can be further hypothesized that shareholders who are solely depending on the financial information provided by management and have no other direct access to internal financial information of the company will be more uncertain about the presented financial information of management and therefore, to reduce this uncertainty/risk, more likely to demand an audit than shareholders who have also direct access to internal financial information (see also chapter 3.2.1.1).

96

Hypothesis 1b: The existence of shareholders with no access to internal financial information is associated with a higher probability the company will have the financial statements audited.

Variable SHRHAC is used to test for this relationship. SHRHAC is a dichotomous independent variable which counts '0' if **all** shareholders of the company also have access to internal financial information and '1' if the company has shareholders with no access to internal financial information. The 2x2-table presented in table 5.1b shows that from the companies having shareholders with no access to internal financial information, 70% choose for an audit compared to 57% of the companies where all shareholders have also access to internal financial information. This counts for a mean of 0.39 for companies with opting for an audit compared to a mean of 0.27 for the companies which did not. The Fisher's exact test shows some significance at the one-tail level. Although, it is not a strong association as Kendall's tau-b shows only a weak non-significant relation between the existence of shareholders with no access to internal financial information and the demand for audit. The results of the Fisher's exact test are consistent with hypothesis 1b, showing some statistically significant difference with regard to the access of shareholders to internal financial information and the demand for audit.

Table 5.1b - Fisher's exact tests on shareholders access to internal financial information (hypothesis 1b)							
Label		DVA		N	Sig. 2-tailed	Sig. 1-tailed	Kendall's tau-b	Sig.
		No (%)	Yes (%)					
SHRHAC	Access	43	58	101				
	No access	16	37	53				
	Total	59	95	154	0.164	0.091*	0.121	0.135
	Mean	0.27	0.39					

Table 5.1b presents descriptive statistics for the variable used in the examination of individual 'external agency' relationship of hypothesis 1b. The table presents the boxplot, the means, Fisher's exact test for both two-tailed as one-tailed p-statistics measuring the existence of a relationship between the variable and demand for audit, whereby Kendall's tau-b and significance are measuring the strength of the relationship. ***p<0.01, **p<0.05 and *p<0.10.

Agency theory originally focused on the shareholders as the ultimate bearers of potential residual loss of the company based on the conception that the assets of the company are the property of the shareholders and management is viewed as agents of shareholders the "rights of creditors, employees, and others are strictly limited to statutory, contractual and common law rights"[80]. But it is mainly due to stakeholder activism of the 1980s that the conception that companies hold obligations (stakeholder theory) to various groups in society has (re)gained importance (Freeman, 1984). When companies are confronted with an increase in the demand for accounting information by various parties, which often have different interests, a multiple demand for audit is created. The situation where multiple stakeholders act as principals of the firm and management as agents have difficulties to understand and reconcile the duties delegated to them together with the possibility of receiving mixed messages and conflicting instructions of these multiple stakeholders management may be more likely to demand an audit as a information risk reducing mechanism for the presented information to different stakeholders. This situation is expected to be more prevalent in the Netherlands as the Dutch environment can be characterized as part of the 'Rhineland-governance model' (see chapter 4.2.1.3). The business-environment of the 'Rhineland-system' differs from the 'Anglo-Saxon-system' with regard to the (historical) importance of the role and power of stakeholders within the economic system. Therefore the following relationship is postulated:

> Hypothesis 1c: The larger the number of relevant stakeholders depending on the financial information of the company, the higher the probability that the company will have the financial statements audited.

Stakeholders of companies are considered to play a more important role in Dutch society and it is expected that management of the companies take also in to account the 'company-obligations' to those stakeholders this relationship is tested. Hereby STAKE# is the independent variable used to count for the number of relevant stakeholders, identified by management, of the company that receive, besides the shareholders, a copy of the financial statements of the company. As STAKE# is treated as a nominal value, independent t-test (see table 5.1c) are executed to test for the difference between the two groups, showing a slightly higher mean (3.01 compared to 2.81) of the number of different stakeholders for the companies which opt for an audit. However, the difference is not statistical significant and therefore individual hypothesis 1c is not consistent with the presented results.

---

[80] Allen, 1992:15, cited in Blair M.M., 1995.

Table 5.1c- Independent t-tests on number of stakeholders (hypothesis 1c)

Label	DVA	N	Mean	Median	Std. Dev.	Sig.
STAKEH#	No	59	2.81	3.00	0.955	0.138
	Yes	95	3.01	3.00	1.162	
	Total	154	2.94	3.00	1.089	

Table 5.1c present descriptive statistics for the variable used in the examination of individual 'external agency' relationship of hypothesis 1c. The table presents the means, medians and standard deviations of the ratio variable and t-statistics measuring the difference between the companies that opt for an audit or not. ***p<0.01, **p<0.05 and *p<0.10; one-tailed.

5.2.1.2   *The proportion of management's share in the equity of the firm*

Based on the literature study of chapter three and following Chow (1982) with regard to the shareholder (owner) – manager relationship, it is expected that when a manager holds no or only a small portion of the equity shares of the company, he has the incentive to allocate the companies resources in a way that may harm the interest of non-managing shareholders. To limit this risk, shareholders will implement monitoring / bonding contracts in order to minimize the negative effects of the manager – shareholder conflict of interest. Management compensation, which is based on financial measures of performance, is a common example of a bonding contract. Jensen and Meckling (1976) argue that managers have the incentive to produce the necessary information, such as financial statements, in order to prove their compliance with the contracts. Shareholders want to verify this information and management can do this by voluntarily engaging in audits. As we know from the literature review of chapter 3.2.1.1, the same argument was used in the studies by Buijink (1992), Carey et al. (2000), Senkow et al. (2001), Seow (2001), Collis et al. (2004), Niemi et al. (2009) and Collis (2010) and based on their results, it is expected that management ownership share and voluntary audits negatively relate to each other. In order to research this relation the following hypothesis has therefore been formulated:

Hypothesis 1d: The higher the manager's ownership share in the company, the lower the probability the company will have the financial statements audited.

To test this hypothesis in the Dutch sample variable MOWN50[81] was used. MOWN50 is a dichotomous variable which is '1' if management owns 50% or more of the shares and '0' otherwise to test hypothesis 1d. The 2x2 cross table presented in table 5.1d shows that when management owns 50% or more of the shares of the company still 59% choose for an audit compared to 64% of the companies where management holds no or less than 50% of the shares. This counts for a mean of 0.39 for companies which opt for an audit compared to a mean of 0.44. Fisher's exact test showed no significant relationship, which is not consistent with hypothesis 1d. However, it should be noticed that, although it is a non-significant weak association, Kendall's tau-b shows the expected negative correlation between management ownership and DVA, showing that higher manager's ownership has a negative association with the demand for audit.

Table 5.1d - Fisher's exact tests on
management ownership share (hypothesis 1d) variable

Label		DVA		N	Sig. 2-tailed	Sig. 1-tailed	Kendall's tau-b	Sig.
		No (%)	Yes (%)					
MOWN50	< 50%	33	58	91	0.614	0.322	-0.051	0.531
	> 50%	26	37	63				
	Total	59	95	154				
	Mean	0.44	0.39					

Table 5.1d presents descriptive statistics for the variable used in the examination of individual 'external agency' relationship of hypothesis 1d. The table presents the boxplot, the means, Fisher's exact test for both two-tailed as one-tailed p-statistics measuring the existence of a relationship between the variable and demand for audit, whereby Kendall's tau-b and significance are measuring the strength of the relationship. ***p<0.01, **p<0.05 and *p<0.10.

5.2.1.3   *Perception of management of shareholder's need*

In chapter two the assumptions of rational expectations and self-interested utility-maximizing motivation of individual actors underpinning the current mainstream auditing theory have been discussed. Using bounded rationality theory (Simon, 1982), we expect managers not to take all (economic) facts in consideration in their decision whether or not to have the financial statements of the company audited. Instead we expect that managers use a limited, simplified model of the real situation. The manager as decision maker is a 'satisficer' (Simon, 1982),

---

[81] Publicly available information shows only data if management or another shareholder has a 100% ownership of the shares of the company. Therefore a question about management ownership was included in the questionnaire. Following the study by Senkow et al. (2001) it is questioned whether management holds shares in the company and if so, this percentage in the shares of the company exceeds 50%.

focussing only the attention to a very small part of the whole and to exclude almost all that is not within the scope of attention (see also chapter 2.4.3). As shareholders are logically[82] to be considered to be of the most importance for the manager it is expected that the perception of the view of existing shareholders with respect to auditing decision with regard to DVA is in the scope of attention of management and will have an association with management's decision making process. Therefore hypothesis 1e has been formulated.

> Hypothesis 1e: The perception held by management that an audit of financial statements is desired by existing shareholders is associated with a higher probability that the company will have the financial statements audited.

Variable SHRHND is used to test hypothesis 1e. Other than the variables used for the hypotheses 1a, 1b and 1c, this variable is considered to be an independent variable directly measuring the relationship with the demand for audit. Respondents were asked to which extent the need for audited financial statements by existing shareholders was taken into account. The data used for the variable SHRHND are obtained through a 5-point likert-scale question and are treated in this research as an ordinal variable[83]. Table 5.1c show the results of the Mann-Whitney test[84] with regard to the statistical significant relationship between SHRHND and DVA. The mean rank for management's perception of shareholders' need for audited financial statements is almost double for DVA 'Yes' compared to DVA 'No' (87.01 vs. 44.42). This difference indicates that a significant relationship between SHRHND and DVA may exist. The p-value showed to be strong significant, which is consistent with hypothesis 1e.

---

[82] Based on article 2:132 and article 2:242 of the Dutch Civil Code.

[83] Within the statistical literature there is some discussion whether data obtained by a likert scale question can also be treated as an interval variable. In the case of 'locked' questions and a regular distance between the responses (1,2,3 etc.) social science treats likert scale questions as interval variable (a metric value), based on continuity. This is commonly accepted if a question has at least 6 or 7 intervals (Mortelmans and Dehertogh, 2007). In this study the likert-scale questions consist of 5 intervals and therefore is treated as an ordinal variable.

[84] To test for significant relationships between two variables in a cross-tabulation also Chi-square tests can be used. To use the Chi-square test three conditions have to be fulfilled (De Vocht, 2010, p. 157):
- the number of cases in the sample must be $\geq$ 50;
- all expected cell frequencies (E) have to be $\geq$1;
- less than 20% of the expected cell frequencies (E) are lower than 5.
Although for all individual independent variables in this chapter using data from likert-scale questions these conditions have been met, only the non-parametric Mann-Whitney tests are shown as the data is considered to be ordinal and not normally distributed. As an additional test also the Chi-square tests have been performed. No differences in statistical significance with the Mann-Whitney tests were found.

Table 5.1e - Mann-Whitney tests on variable management perception of shareholder's need for audited financial statements (hypothesis 1e)

Label	DVA	N	Mean rank	Sum of ranks	Mann-Whitney U	Wilcoxon W	Z	P
SHRHND	No	53	44.42	2354.50				
	Yes	88	87.01	7656.50				
	Total	141			923.50	2354.5	-6.149	0.000***

Table 5.1e presents descriptive statistics for the variable used in the examination of hypothesis 1e of the individual 'external agency' hypotheses. The table presents the Mann-Whitney test. ***p<0.01, **p<0.05 and *p<0.10; two-tailed.

5.2.2 Existence of debt in the capital structure of the firm

Besides the relationship between shareholders(owners) and managers, the relationship between shareholders (and managers acting in the interest of shareholders) and providers of debt capital can also give rise to the existence of agency conflicts. Based on the literature review of chapter two and the analysis of previous empirical studies in chapter three, the following relationships regarding the existence of debt in the capital structure of the firm and the demand for voluntary audit will be empirically tested in this study:

- Enhancing credibility to external users (general hypothesis 3 of table 3.1);
- Leverage (general hypothesis 4 of table 3.1);
- The existence of lending requirements (general hypothesis 5 of table 3.1);
- Improves lending conditions (general hypothesis 6 of table 3.1);
- Improves credit rating (general hypothesis 7 of table 3.1).

5.2.2.1 Enhancing credibility to external users

The objective of auditing financial statements is adding credibility to the financial reporting of companies for intended users of this financial information. Certainly this argument has vehemently been used by regulators in history to impede additional layers of control around the audit profession in response of the various financial crises of the 20th century, as already noticed in chapter 1.1. It is the belief of regulators that auditing plays an important role in the trust people place in financial markets by adding credibility and therefore trust in the role of the auditor should be protected. Building on decision making theory, as set out in chapter 2.4.3, this belief will have a powerful influence on perception because it creates the context through which perception is filtered. Thus, if one believes auditing is important as it provides the trust people (users) place in financial information, this creates the construct through which the perceptions of (economic) facts are filtered (Simon, 1982). Therefore it is expected that the belief held by management that users of financial information of the company as a result of the audit put more trust on the financial information of the company will have an influence on the decision making process and will positively affect the choice for (retaining) a voluntary audit. Based on the literature study of previous research in chapter 3.2.1.2 (Collis, 2004; Niemi et al., 2009; Collis, 2010) the following hypothesis regarding enhancing credibility is formulated.

> Hypothesis 2a: The perception held by management that the audit improves the credibility of financial information to external users is associated with a higher probability that the company will have the financial statements audited.

The variable CREDIBLY is used to test for this relationship and the data is also obtained through a 5-point likert scale question. The mean rank for management's belief that an audit improves the credibility of financial statements counts 88.56 ('Yes') compared to 59.69 ('No') and also the p-value shows a strong significant relationship. Therefore hypothesis 2a is consistent with the presented results in table 5.2a.

Table 5.2a - Mann-Whitney tests on variable
enhancing credibility of financial information to external users (hypothesis 2a).

Label	DVA	N	Mean rank	Sum of ranks	Mann-Whitney U	Wilcoxon W	Z	P
CREDIBLY	No	59	59.69	3522.00				
	Yes	95	88.56	8413.00				
	Total	154			1752.00	3522.00	-4.104	0.000***

Table 5.2a presents descriptive statistics for the variable used in the examination of hypothesis 2a of the individual 'external agency' hypotheses. The table presents the Mann-Whitney test. ***p<0.01, **p<0.05 and *p<0.10; two-tailed.

5.2.2.2 Leverage

The relation between leverage and a company deciding for a voluntarily audit, depends on the severity of the conflict of interest between shareholders and bondholders. As set out in chapter 3.2.1.2 it is commonly reasoned that this severity depends on the level of debt in the firm's capital structure as it is expected that if leverage increases, shareholders have a greater incentive to undertake activities that transfer wealth from the bondholders to themselves. To limit this behavior "in an efficient capital market, bondholders would anticipate such shareholder behavior after the bonds have been issued. Potential bondholders would allow for these expected losses in pricing the bonds. The result is that the shareholders bear the cost of their expected wealth transfers from bondholders … [b]ecause shareholders bear the cost … they have incentives to do so at the least cost. Jensen and Meckling (1976) postulate that having the manager to supply externally audited financial reports is such an alternative" (Chow, 1982: 275). This relation has been tested in a number of audit studies (e.g. Chow, 1982; Abdel-khalik, 1993; Blackwell et al., 1998; Hay and Davis, 2004 and Kim et al., 2007). Although the results of these studies showed mixed results, most studies found a positive relation between leverage and the demand for audit. Therefore the following hypothesis has been formulated:

> Hypothesis 2b: The higher the proportion of debt in the company's capital structure, the higher the probability the company will have its financial statements audited.

Variable LVRG is used to test for this relationship. Independent t-tests (see table 5.2a) show that this hypothesized relationship is not significant between the two groups, which is not consistent with hypothesis 2a.

Table 5.2b Independent t-tests on leverage (hypothesis 2b)						
Label	DVA	N	Mean	Median	Std. Dev.	Sig.
LVRG	No	59	0.526	0.551	0.319	0.121
	Yes	95	0.807	0.562	1.816	
	Total	154	0.699	0.558	1.443	

Table 5.2b present descriptive statistics for the variable used in the examination of hypothesis 2b of the individual 'external agency' hypotheses. The table presents the means, medians and standard deviations of the ratio variable and t-statistics measuring the difference between the companies that opt for an audit or not. ***$p<0.01$, **$p<0.05$ and *$p<0.10$; one-tailed.

5.2.2.3 Debt covenants / Lending requirements

In addition to the leverage hypothesis and following the line of reasoning of the agency theory in previous studies as presented in chapter 3.2.1.2 (e.g. Chow, 1982; Senkow et al., 2001 and Seow, 2001)) it is expected that bondholders, as a consequence of the utility maximizing shareholder/manager and to prevent the risk of the transfer of wealth activities from the bondholder to the shareholder/manager, use debt covenants and lending requirements to limit the shareholder-bondholder conflict of interest. To monitor the fulfillment of the debt covenants and lending requirements, bondholders often demand that the financial results and measures are audited. It can be the case that at the time of the change in legislation in the Netherlands, companies had loans outstanding that were agreed upon under the condition that the company has to meet certain debt covenants and that lenders may have required companies to provide audited financial statements, which will increase the likelihood that a firm will continue to have their financial statements audited. The expected positive relation between lender requirements and the demand for audit gives rise to the following hypothesis:

> Hypothesis 2c: The existence of debt covenants / lender requirements is associated with a higher probability that the company will have the financial statements audited.

Dichotomous variable LRQM is used to test for this relationship. From the 2x2 cross table it can be derived that of 79% of the companies with a lender requirement choose for an audit. Also the mean for the companies which opt for an audit is substantially higher, namely 0.35 compared to 0.15. Fisher's exact test show to be strong significant an also Kendall's tau-b show to be strong significant, which is consistent with hypothesis 2b.

Table 5.2c Fisher's exact test on the existence of a lending requirement (hypothesis 2c)

Label		DVA		N	Sig. 2-tailed	Sig. 1-tailed	Kendall's tau-b	Sig.
		No	Yes					
LRQM	No	50	62	112	0.009***	0.006***	0.213	0.004***
	Yes	9	33	42				
	Total	59	95	154				
	Mean	0.15	0.35					

Table 5.2c present descriptive statistics for the variable used in the examination of hypothesis 2c of the individual 'external agency' hypotheses. The table presents the boxplot, Fisher's exact test for both two-tailed as one-tailed p-statistics measuring the existence of a relationship between the variable and demand for audit, Kendall's tau-b and significance measuring the strength of the relationship. ***p<0.01, **p<0.05 and *p<0.10.

5.2.2.4   *Cost of debt capital and lending conditions*

Watts and Zimmerman (1983) argued, using classical economic theories, that if auditor assurance reduces lenders' monitoring cost, competition will force banks to pass along these cost reductions to borrowers in the form of lower interest. From the literature review of chapter 3.2.1.2 we know that various studies, using different datasets from different countries, have tested if there is a relationship between the demand for audit and loan interest (Blackwell et al, 1998; Kim et al., 2007; Willekens, 2008). However the results of this studies are mixed. Some studies found significant relationships, while others did not.

In obtaining debt finance Dutch SME companies are in general not active on a securities market, the primary source of outside capital would be banks (Bollen, 1996). As through national and international banking regulation (e.g. Basel II) the bank has to classify the risk for each issued loan, which will have an impact on the corresponding interest rate and loan securities (e.g. mortgages, personal liability). Although the criteria used by the banks to classify the risk on the loan are not transparent, there is some anecdotic evidence that whether or not the financial statements are audited is not an element in this risk assessment. However, there is some empirical evidence that whether or not the financial statements are audited has a positive impact on the perception of loan officers (Bollen, 1996; Berry et al., 1993) and that the financial statements of the company are, next to the bank's knowledge of the customers, an important source of information (Bollen, 1996; Collis, 2010). Therefore, it is reasoned that as companies deal with loan officers in the pre phase of an application for a loan, that whether or not the financial statements are audited will have an impact on the decision making process of the loan officer.

Another possible positive effect on lending conditions (e.g. delay of payment of invoices granted by suppliers) is related to the credit rating the company obtained from credit institutions. Lennox and Pittman (2011) tested this relationship in a non-mandatory audit environment, expecting a positive relationship with the demand for audit. The results of their study show that companies which opt for an audit received higher credit ratings.

> Hypothesis 2d: The perception held by management that the audit has a positive effect on lending conditions is associated with a higher probability the company will have the financial statements audited.

> Hypothesis 2e: The perception held by management that the audit has a positive effect on the credit rating of the company is associated with a higher probability the company will have the financial statements audited.

Variable LENDPLUS is used to test for the relationship with the lending conditions and variable COMPCRED is used to test for the relationship with the credit rating of the company. Data for both variables are obtained through a 5-point likert-scale question in the questionnaire and are treated in this research as an ordinal variable. Table 5.2d shows the results of the Mann-Whitney test with regard to the statistical significant relationship of the variables with DVA. It appears that there is not a significant difference between the companies with a voluntary audit and the companies without regarding the perception that the audit will have a positive effect on lending conditions. However, with regard to the perception of the added value of the audit on the credit rating of the company there appears to be a significant difference between the two groups. Therefore hypothesis 2c is not consistent with and hypothesis 2d is consistent with the presented results in table 5.2d.

Table 5.2d - Mann-Whitney tests on lending conditions (hypothesis 2d) and company's credit rating (hypothesis 2e)

Label	DVA	N	Mean rank	Sum of ranks	Mann-Whitney U	Wilcoxon W	Z	P
LENDPLUS	No	59	70.64	4167.50				
	Yes	95	81.76	7767.50				
	Total	154			2397.50	4167.50	-1.542	0.123
COMPCRED	No	58	68.29	3961.00				
	Yes	94	81.56	7667.00				
	Total	152			2250.00	3961.00	-1.859	0.063*

Table 5.2d presents descriptive statistics for the variables used in the examination of hypothesis 2d and hypothesis 2e of the individual 'external agency' hypotheses. The table presents the Mann-Whitney test. ***$p<0.01$, **$p<0.05$ and *$p<0.10$; two-tailed.

5.2.3 Size

Furthermore it is commonly argued, based on agency theory, that the total amount of wealth that is transferred (for a given management ownership share and debt / equity ratio) increases with firm size. This implies that monitoring and bonding contracts provided to the agent can yield a higher benefit when firm size increases. Although size does not have a direct relationship with agency theory, size is commonly used in both audit demand literature and empirical research to explain the need for auditing. Also, European legislators used size-criteria to determine whether companies should have their financial statements audited or not. In this respect the size criteria can be considered as 'proxy variables' to count for the increased risk that wealth is transferred at the expense of one or more principals, based on the reasoning that the larger the company in size the more likely agency relationships will exist which incur agency cost to mitigate the risk and uncertainty of the principal.

Studies by Chow (1982), Ettredge et al. (1994) and Collis et al. (2004) found a relation between a firm's size and a voluntary audit, while other studies by Senkow et al. (2001) and Carey et al. (2000) were not able to confirm this relation (see chapter 3.2.1.3). Due the conflicting results found in previous studies it would be interesting whether this study will be able to find a relation between size and the demand for audit. Turnover, total assets and number of employees have been used (which are also the legal criteria in the Netherlands to determine whether a company is mandatory required to have their financial statements audited) to test the relationship with the demand for audit. The hypothesis to examine this relation is stated as follows:

> Hypothesis 3: The larger the size of the company, the higher the probability that the company will have the financial statements audited.

The variables ASSETS, CATOMZ and CATEMPLS are used to test the relationship between size and the demand for audit. ASSETS is the natural log of the total assets measured by balance sheet total. CATOMZ is a dichotomous variable measuring the size of the company by turnover and CATEMPLS is a dichotomous variable measuring the size of the company by the number of employees. CATOMZ and CATEMPLS counts '0' if the company is 'small' in size based on turnover or employees an '1' otherwise.

Table 5.3a - Independent t-tests on size variable assets						
Label	DVA	N	Mean	Median	Std. Dev.	Sig.
ASSETS	No	59	15.764	15.621	0.791	0.288
	Yes	95	15.673	15.459	1.081	
	Total	154	15.708	15.509	0.978	

Table 5.3a present descriptive statistics for the variable used in the examination of individual 'external agency' hypotheses. The table presents the means, medians and standard deviations of the ratio variable and t-statistics measuring the difference between the companies that opt for an audit or not. ***p<0.01, **p<0.05 and *p<0.10; one-tailed.

Table 5.3a shows that no significant relationship exists between the independent variable ASSETS and the dependent variable DVA. Table 5.3b shows that there also is no significant relationship between the independent variable CATOMZ and DVA.

Only variable CATEMPLS shows to be significant (see table 5.3b). However it can be questioned to which extent this variable alone counts for the size of the company and therefore for the existence of an external agency relationship. The variable employees has also been used in other studies as a proxy for 'loss of control' by managers of the company (e.g. Abel-khalik, 1993). This latter situation of 'loss of control' combined with the responsibilities of management with regard to the 'ongoing' business activities could point towards a demand for auditing based on organizational theory (see also chapter 5.3.1).

Table 5.3b - Fisher's exact tests on size variables turnover and number of employees

Label		DVA		N	Sig. 2-tailed	Sig. 1-tailed	Kendall's tau-b	Sig.
		No	Yes					
CATOMZ	Small	17	20	37				
	Nsmall	41	75	116				
	Total	58	95	153				
	Mean				0.251	0.168	0.094	0.258
CATEMPLS	Small	52	69	121				
	Nsmall	7	26	33				
	Total	59	95	154				
	Mean				0.026**	0.017**	0.184	0.013**

Table 5.3b presents descriptive statistics for the variables used in the examination of individual 'external agency' hypotheses. The table presents the boxplots, Fisher's exact test for both two-tailed as one-tailed p-statistics measuring the existence of a relationship between the variable and demand for audit, whereby Kendall's tau-b and significance measuring the strength of the relationship. ***$p<0.01$, **$p<0.05$ and *$p<0.10$.

5.3   Internal agency relationships

Next to the relationship between management and outsiders, the external agency theory argument, auditing can also apply for agency relationships within the company (e.g. between management and subordinates). Following previous literature and empirical studies on internal agency relationships (chapter 3.2.2) these internal agency relationships also will be investigated in this study. In chapter 4.3.4 an overview of the variables used and the reference to the hypotheses has been presented. In this chapter the empirical results of the derived hypotheses from the following relationships with the demand for audit are presented:

- Loss of control (general hypothesis 9 of table 3.1);
- The existence of outside directors (general hypothesis 10 of table 3.1);
- External audit as a substitute for internal control (general hypothesis 11 of table 3.1);
- Improvement of the quality of the financial information (general hypothesis 13 of table 3.1).

5.3.1   Loss of control

An increasing number of employees and locations may reduce overall efficiency in the company and give rise to the risk of loss of control as management is not able to control the operations by direct supervision anymore. Loss of control can be compensated by the work performed by auditors, as they make management aware of the existing risks within an organisation. It is thus expected that when the complexity of the company increases management is more willing to opt for an audit to reduce risk arising from complexity. Therefore the following hypothesis has been formulated:

> Hypothesis 4: The larger the number of employees (loss of control), the higher the probability the company will have the financial statements audited.

Abdel-khalik (1993) used the number of employees as a proxy for loss of control. He argued that the number of employees counts for the hierarchical levels within an organization. With the increase of the number of employees it is expected that the number of hierarchical levels increases, resulting in a longer chain of command and decreased observability of subordinates. To compensate for this loss, management can demand an audit as a compensatory device. Using the variable CATEMPLS (see chapter 5.2.3) to serve as a proxy for the loss of control the empirical results shows to be significant and consistent with hypothesis 4.

5.3.2   Existence of outside directors

The existence of outside directors is considered to be one of the monitoring mechanisms in corporate governance structure of the company and therefore it is expected to have an effect on the demand for external auditing. The results of previous empirical research (see chapter 3.2.2) showed that outside directors and auditing are complementary monitoring mechanisms (Buijink, 1992; Anderson et

110

al., 1993). As outside directors normally are regarded as generally high-reputation members of society, outside directors have to deal with the increased effects of regulation and liability (Eichenseher and Shields, 1985). This reputation risk may lead that the existence of outside directors has a positive tendency to demand for audit, in a response on reducing 'personal risk'. This leads to the following hypothesis:

> Hypothesis 5: The existence of outside directors is associated with a higher probability the company will have the financial statements audited.

Variable OUTDIR is used to test for this relationship. OUTDIR is a dichotomous variable, which counts for a yes or no if the company has outside directors. The one-tailed Fisher's exact test show that the relationship is significant. Given the direction of the hypothesis that the existence of outside directors would increase the probability of audited financial statement, the presented results in table 5.4 are consistent with hypothesis 5.

Table 5.4 - Fisher's exact tests on variable outside directors (hypothesis 5)								
Label		*DVA*		*N*	*Sig. 2-tailed*	*Sig. 1-tailed*	*Kendall's tau-b*	*Sig.*
		No	Yes					
OUTDIR	No	50	71	121	0.104	0.066*	0.137	0.072*
	Yes	8	24	32				
	Total	58	95	153				
	Mean	0.14	0.25					

Table 5.4 present descriptive statistics for the variable used in the examination of hypothesis 5 of the individual 'internal agency' hypotheses. The table presents the boxplot, Fisher's exact test for both two-tailed as one-tailed p-statistics measuring the existence of a relationship between the variable and demand for audit, whereby Kendall's tau-b and significance measuring the strength of the relationship. ***p<0.01, **p<0.05 and *p<0.10.

5.3.3   Audit as a substitute for internal control

Managers as principals in an internal agency setting (may) have a need to monitor their employees (agents). To monitor their employees to provide assurance regarding the integrity of financial information, managers establish and maintain internal control systems. Implementing and maintaining an internal control system in SME companies may not be efficient or economically justified. From the literature review of chapter 3.2.2 we know that Jensen and Payne (2003) found that managers see the external audit as a substitute for at least some elements of the internal control system. They determined that directors can use external auditors as being a part of their internal control system. The demand for external audit services may also be explained by management's need for an independent review or audit on internal controls to decrease the chance of material error (Collis et al., 2004; Niemi et al, 2009). It is therefore hypothesized that there is a positive relation between managers belief that external audit is a substitute of the internal control system and the demand for voluntary audit.

Hypothesis 6a: The perception held by management that the audit provides a check on accounting records and systems (internal audit / internal control) is associated with a higher probability the company will have the financial statements audited.

Variable CHECK counts for the perception of management that an external audit also functions as an internal control. Data for this variable has been obtained through a 5-point likert-scale question. The Mann-Whitney test (see table 5.6 on page 119) shows a strong significant relationship with the DVA, which is consistent with hypothesis 6a.

Another line of reasoning for the substitution of external auditing has been presented by Jensen and Payne (2003) and Seow (2001) and is related to the lack of accounting expertise within the company (see chapter 3.2.2). Jensen and Payne argues that managers rely on accounting personnel to capture and report relevant financial information useful for decision making, to establish and follow internal control activities When hiring accounting personnel there is a risk related to the accounting functions. Managers can reduce this risk by hiring high qualified accounting personnel. However hiring of highly qualified accounting personnel is not always possible and some managers may find it more efficient to hire accounting personnel with relatively low levels of accounting expertise or even not to hire accounting personnel at all and then to compensate by hiring external auditors. This leads to the following two hypotheses:

Hypothesis 6b: The likelihood of management opting for an audit of the financial statements is associated with a higher likelihood that the company does not have a financial department

Hypothesis 6c: The likelihood of management opting for an audit of the financial statements is associated with a higher likelihood that the company hire employees with low levels of accounting expertise.

Variable FINAFD is a dichotomous variable and counts for whether or not the company has a financial department. The 2x2 cross table presented in table 5.5 shows that there are only 12 companies which do not have a financial department. Of these companies only 33,3% choose for an audit of the financial statements. Although the Fisher's exact test show a significant relationship between FINAFD and the demand for audit, the results are not consistent with hypothesis 6b. As the results do not confirm the expected relationship.

To test hypothesis 6c variable EDUFIN is used, which counts for whether or not the head of the financial department has a qualified accounting degree. The one-tailed Fisher's exact test show that a significant relationship between the education of the head of the financial department and the demand for audit exists. However, the results of this 2x2 table do not confirm the expected direction and is not consistent with hypothesis 6c.

Table 5.5 - Fisher's exact tests on variables financial department (hypothesis 6b) and education of head of financial department (hypothesis 6c)

Label		DVA		N	Sig. 2-tailed	Sig. 1-tailed	Kendall's tau-b	Sig.
		No	Yes					
FINAFD	No	8	4	12	0.060*	0.038**	0.170	0.058*
	Yes	51	91	142				
	Total	59	95	154				
	Mean	0.86	0.96					
EDUFIN	No	18	17	35	0.119	0.083*	0.132	0.122
	Yes	40	70	110				
	Total	58	87	145				
	Mean	0.69	0.80					

Table 5.5 presents descriptive statistics for the variables used in the examination of hypotheses 6b and 6c of the individual 'internal agency' hypotheses. The table presents the boxplots, Fisher's exact test for both two-tailed as one-tailed p-statistics measuring the existence of a relationship between the variable and demand for audit, Kendall's tau-b and significance measuring the strength of the relationship. ***p<0.01, **p<0.05 and *p<0.10.

5.3.4 Improvement of quality financial information

Following Willekens (2008) it is hypothesized that the quality of the prepared financial information of audited financial statements will be higher than not audited financial statements. Also other studies indicated that the management-related factors, such as improved quality of information, play a role in explaining voluntary audits (Collis et al., 2004; Niemi et al. 2009; Collis, 2010).

Hypotheses 7: The perception held by management that the audit improves the quality of the financial information is associated with a higher probability the company will have the financial statements audited.

Variable QUALITY is used to test for this relationship and the data has been obtained through a 5-point likert scale question. From the statistical analysis as shown in table 5.6, a significant relationship between the management perception that auditing improves the quality of the financial information which is consistent with hypothesis 7.

Table 5.6 Mann-Whitney tests on variables check on internal controls (hypothesis 6a) and improving quality of financial information (hypothesis 7)

Label	DVA	N	Mean rank	Sum of ranks	Mann-Whitney U	Wilcoxon W	Z	P
CHECK	No	59	55.61	3281.00				
	Yes	95	91.09	8654.00				
	Total	154			1511.00	3281.00	-5.008	0.000***
QUALITY	No	59	56.06	3307.50				
	Yes	94	90.14	8473.50				
	Total	153			1537.50	3307.50	-4.840	0.000***

Table 5.6 presents descriptive statistics for the variables used in the examination of hypotheses 6a and 7 of the individual 'internal agency' hypotheses. The table presents the Mann-Whitney test. ***$p < 0.01$, **$p < 0.05$ and *$p < 0.10$; two-tailed.

5.4 Other considerations

Next to the agency related relationships (both external as internal) the literature review of previous empirical research in chapter 3.2.3 revealed some other possible considerations regarding the demand for voluntary audit. Based on this literature review a number of variables (see table 4.1 in chapter 4.3.4) are included in this study. This section presents the empirical results of hypotheses formulated regarding the following expected relationships with the demand for audit:

- Auditor relationship (general hypotheses 15, 16 and 17 of table 3.1);
- Financial health of the company (general hypothesis 18 of table 3.1);

114

- Strategic reasons based on expected future growth (based on general hypothesis 19 of table 3.1).

5.4.1 Auditor relationship

The relationship with the auditor is a relationship which possibly also influences management's decision whether or not to continue with the audit. Derived from the literature review of chapter 3.2.3 the following relationships with regard to the relation between the auditor and the company will be tested:
- Auditor tenure (hypothesis 8a);
- Other services provided by the auditor (hypothesis 8b);
- Type of audit report received in previous years (hypothesis 8c).

Companies often purchase both attest and non-attest services from their auditor. It is therefore possible that the existence of a continuing business relationship with the auditor that goes beyond the audit, may cause a reluctance on part of the client to harm the existing auditor-client relationship and as a result choose to retain the audit. To which extent the long-standing relationship with the auditor affects the decision of management to continue with the audit has been previously tested by Seow (2001), see also table 3.2 of chapter three. Also the existence of 'knowledge spillovers' and potential efficiencies between the audit and other services makes it more likely that the management of a company will choose to retain the audit has been previously tested by Senkow et al. (2001) and Seow (2001). This leads to the following hypotheses:

> Hypothesis 8a: The longer the auditor has been serving the company, the higher the probability the company retains the audit.

> Hypothesis 8b: The likelihood of management retaining the audit is associated with a higher likelihood that the auditor also provides a number of other services.

But when prior experiences of management from mandatory auditing has given rise to agency conflicts between management and the auditor it can be argued that management is less willing to continue with the audit. Issuing a not unqualified auditor report can be regarded as a situation where an agency problem between management and auditor occurred (Niemi et al., 2009). Therefore it is hypothesized:

Hypothesis 8c: The likelihood of management retaining the audit is associated with a lower likelihood if a not unqualified audit report has been issued in previous years.

The variables AUDTERM, AUDSERV and AUDREP are used to test the three aforementioned hypotheses. AUDTERM is the number of years the current auditor has been servicing the company. The conducted independent t-test (table 5.7) showed that a significant relationship exists between the number of years the auditor is servicing the company and the likelihood the company retains the audit of the financial statements, which is consistent with hypothesis 8a.

Table 5.7 Independent t-tests on variables audit term (hypothesis 8a) and other services provided by auditor (hypothesis 8b)

Label	DVA	N	Mean	Median	Std. Dev.	Sig.
AUDTERM	No	50	6.96	4.00	8.136	0.003***
	Yes	86	11.31	10.00	9.298	
	Total	136	9.71	7.50	9.105	
AUDSERV	No	59	2.59	2.00	1.782	0.231
	Yes	95	2.39	2.00	1.586	
	Total	154	2.47	2.00	1.661	

Table 5.7 presents descriptive statistics for the variables used in the examination of individual 'other considerations' hypotheses. The table presents the means, medians and standard deviations of the ratio variables and t-statistics measuring the difference between the companies that opt for an audit or not. ***p<0.01, **p<0.05 and *p<0.10; one-tailed.

Variable AUDSERV measured the number of other services the auditor renders to the company besides the audit of the financial statements. The empirical tests did not reveal a significant relationship between the number of other services and the demand for audit. Also the mean for AUDSERV of the subsample 'Yes' (2.39) is lower than the subsample 'No' (2.59), which do not confirm the expected direction. Therefore hypothesis 8b is not consistent with the presented results in table 5.7.

The hypothesis that the type of audit report received in previous years would have a significant influence on the retaining the audit, was tested by using the dichotomous variable AUDREP, measuring whether the company received an unqualified audit report or not. From the conducted Fisher's exact test it showed that this relationship is significant, whereas Kendall's tau-b also showed to be significant, which is consistent with hypothesis 8c.

Table 5.8 Fisher's exact tests on variable audit report (hypothesis 8c) and financial health (hypothesis 9)

Label		DVA		N	Sig. 2-tailed	Sig. 1-tailed	Kendall's tau-b	Sig.
		No	Yes					
AUDREP	Unqualified	38	80	118	0.028**	0.021**	0.189	0.033**
	Not Unq.	15	12	27				
	Total	53	92	145				
	Mean	0.72	0.87					
HEALTH	Profit	48	79	127	0.829	0.469	0.023	0.777
	Loss	11	16	27				
	Total	59	95	154				
	Mean	0.81	0.83					

Table 5.8 presents descriptive statistics for the variables used in the examination of hypotheses 8c and 9 of the individual 'other considerations' hypotheses. The table presents the boxplots, Fisher's exact test for both two-tailed as one-tailed p-statistics measuring the existence of a relationship between the variable and demand for audit, Kendall's tau-b and significance measuring the strength of the relationship. ***p<0.01, **p<0.05 and *p<0.10.

5.4.2 Financial health

It can be assumed that companies that are facing financial difficulties are less likely to engage in voluntary external auditing, due to the costs that are associated with this audit (Seow, 2001). On the contrary, it can also be assumed that when a company is in financial distress, they would like to increase their transparency to other parties and this can be done by performing an audit. Furthermore, it may be more difficult for a company to receive new loans when lenders are confronted with the fact that the company is making losses. An audit of the company may give the lenders more information and may make them more comfortable about lending money to that specific company (Willekens, 2008; Niemi et al., 2009). The different possibilities make it uncertain whether the financial health of a company will positively or negatively affect the likelihood that a company will perform a voluntary audit. A positive effect is assumed to investigate the relationship between the financial health of a company and the likelihood that a company will have its financial statements audited. This leads to the ninth hypothesis:

Hypothesis 9: The probability that a company will have its financial statements audited voluntarily is positively associated when it is making profits.

Dichotomous variable HEALTH (see table 5.8) counts for the situation that the financial statements of the company showed a profit in the previous year or not. The test showed no significant relationship between HEALTH and the demand for audit, which is not consistent with hypothesis 9.

5.4.3   Strategic reasons based on expected future growth

In absence of a mandatory audit regime, management may have various strategic reasons for having the financial statements audited. In previous empirical research it has been suggested that companies might engage an auditor to signal good performance (Hay and Davis, 2004). An expected business transfer in coming years or the expected added value of an audit of financial statements to attract a specific population of customers are examples which may serve as drivers for management to opt for an audit. A strategic reason, more focused on the population of this study, may be the expectation of management of future growth of the company. As we know from the data description of chapter 4 the population of this study consists of companies which no longer met the size criteria for medium-sized in 2006 and therefore probably are exempted from the mandatory audit (see also chapter 4.3.2), the expected future growth of the company may be a driver for management to retain the audit. Using a cost-benefit analysis, taking into account the expected initial cost of an (renewed) audit engagement, management probably will continue the audit if due to expected future growth the company will be classified under the mandatory regime again in coming years. It is therefore hypothesized that:

> Hypothesis 10: The likelihood of management retaining the audit is positively associated with expectation of management about future growth of the company.

Variable STRAT was used to test for this relationship. As the Mann-Whitney tests, see table 5.9 showed a significant relationship between STRAT and the demand for audit, the results are consistent with hypothesis 10.

Table 5.9 Mann-Whitney tests on variable strategic decision (hypothesis 10)								
Label	DVA	N	Mean rank	Sum of ranks	Mann-Whitney U	Wilcoxon W	Z	P
STRAT	No	52	54.07	2811.50				
	Yes	74	70.13	5189.50				
	Total	126			1433.50	2811.50	-2.547	0.011**

Table 5.9 present descriptive statistics for the variable used in the examination of hypothesis 10 of the individual 'other relation' hypotheses. The table presents the Mann-Whitney test. ***p<0.01, **p<0.05 and *p<0.10; two-tailed.

5.5   Summary of the individual hypotheses

The following table summarizes the empirical results of the independent variables with the DVA, used in this chapter to test individual hypothesized relationships with the demand for audit. The table shows the means of both subsamples (Non-Mandatory Audit (DVA) 'No' and Non-Mandatory Audit (DVA) 'Yes') and whether the results shows a statistical significance (+++ = p < 0.01; ++ = p <0.05; + = p <0.10 and NS = not significant).

Table 5.10 Summary of Individual Hypotheses

Label	Description	Hypo-thesis	Expected sign	No Mean	Yes Mean	Statistical Significance
				Dependent variable		
DVA	Whether the company opts for a non-mandatory audit of its financial statements					
EXTERNAL AGENCY VARIABLES						
SHRH#	The number of shareholders of the company.	H1a	Positive	2.15	3.61	++
SHRHAC	The existence of shareholders of the company who have no direct access to internal financial information. Treated as a categorical variable coded as "1" if the company has shareholders with no direct access to internal financial information and "0" otherwise.	H1b	Positive	0.27	0.39	+
STAKEH#	The number of stakeholders identified by management of the company next to shareholders.	H1c	Positive	2.81	3.01	NS
MOWN50	The percentage of shares held by the company's management. Treated as a categorical variable coded as "1" if management owned 50% or more of the shares and "0" otherwise.	H1d	Negative	0.44	0.39	NS
SHRHND	Extent of agreement that existing shareholders' need for audited financial statements plays a role in the audit decision (1 = strongly disagree, 5 = strongly agree).	H1e	Positive	44.42	87.01	+++
CREDIBLY	Extent of agreement that the audit improves the credibility of the financial information (1 = strongly disagree, 5 = strongly agree).	H2a	Positive	59.69	88.56	+++
LVRG	The proportion of debt as measured by debt-to-asset ratio	H2b	Positive	0.53	0.81	NS
LRQM	The existence of a lender requirement for an audit at the time of change in legislation. This is treated as a categorical variable coded "1" if a lender requirement was existence at the time and "0" otherwise	H2c	Positive	0.15	0.35	++
LENDPLUS	Extent of agreement that the audit reduces the cost of lending (1 = strongly disagree, 5 = strongly agree).	H2d	Positive	70.64	81.76	NS
COMPCRED	Extent of agreement that the audit improves the company's credibility towards external parties (1 = strongly disagree, 5 = strongly agree).	H2e	Positive	68.29	81.56	+
ASSETS	Size of company as measured by natural log of balance sheet total in €	H3	Positive	15.76	15.67	NS
CATOMZ	Size of the company as measured by turnover. This is treated as a categorical variable coded "1" if the company measured by turnover only classify as medium or large and "0" otherwise	H3	Positive	0.71	0.79	NS
CATEMPLS	No. of employees represents both size of the company and hierarchical levels within the company and therefore serves as a proxy for complexity. This is treated as a categorical variable coded "1" if the company measured by number of employees only classify as medium or large and "0" otherwise	H3 + H4	Positive	0.12	0.27	++

INTERNAL AGENCY VARIABLES

OUTDIR	The existence of outside directors. This is treated as a categorical variable code as "1" if the company has outside directors and "0" otherwise.	H5	Positive	0.14	0.25	+
CHECK	Extent of agreement that the audit provides a check on accounting records and systems (1 = strongly disagree, 5 = strongly agree).	H6a	Positive	55.61	91.09	+++
FINAFD	Whether the company has a financial department. This is treated as a categorical variable coded as "1" if the company has a financial department and "0" otherwise	H6b	Negative	0.86	0.96	+ (opposite direction)
EDUFIN	Whether the company has a qualified head of financial department. This is treated as a categorical variable coded as "1" if the company has a qualified head of the financial department and "0" otherwise	H6c	Negative	0.69	0.80	+ (opposite direction)
QUALITY	Extent of agreement that the audit improves the quality of the financial information (1 = strongly disagree, 5 = strongly agree).	H7	Positive	56.06	90.14	+++

OTHER VARIABLES

AUDTERM	The number of years the current auditor has been engaged with the company.	H8a	Positive	6.96	11.31	+++
AUDSERV	The number of other services such as MAS and taxation services provided by the audit firm.	H8b	Positive	2.59	2.39	NS (opposite direction)
AUDREP	Whether an unqualified audit report has been issued in previous year(s). This is treated as a categorical variable coded as "1" if an unqualified audit report has been issued and "0" otherwise.	H8c	Positive	0.72	0.87	+++
HEALTH	Whether the company makes profit or not. This is treated as a categorical variable coded as "1" when the company makes profit the previous year and "0" otherwise	H9	Positive	0.81	0.83	NS
STRAT	Extent of agreement that expected future growth of the company has been part of the decision making process (1 = strongly disagree, 5 = strongly agree).	H10	Positive	54.07	70.13	++

5.6   Concluding remarks

This study is, besides the study of Senkow et al. (2001), as known the only one using data of companies which due to a deregulation face the decision whether or not to continue with the audit. By that means, it provides further insight if predicted relationships with the demand of audit show to be significant or not.

Based on the literature review of previous empirical research using the demand for audit as a dependent or independent variable, chapter three provides an overview of support for identified relationships from earlier studies (see chapter 3.2.4). We start with comparing the results of this study with the (mean) results of previous empirical studies (table 5.11). To show the relation between the results of the individual hypotheses as presented in table 5.10, references to individual hypotheses are included in the table 5.11.

As we can conclude from table 5.11, the results of this study confirm for a number of already identified relationships the association with the decision for the demand for auditing. Whereas the results of the external agency relationships showed mixed results in this study, the internal agency relationship show to be all statistical significant. Also for some of the other relationships this study found positive associations with the demand for audit. This supports the claim of Knechel et al. (2008) that an audit or providing assurance for smaller non-public companies may have added value for other reasons than the 'classical' (the external) agency relationship between management and outsiders. Comparing this study with previous studies the differences in support found for the following relationships with the demand for audit are noticeable, which will be discussed more in detail in this section:
-    Shareholder (owner) – manager relationship;
-    Leverage;
-    Cost of debt capital;
-    Substitute for internal control;
-    Dependency on auditor relationship.
Although the support found for the relationship 'Size' in this study comparing to the other studies initially do not give rise for a more in detail discussion, the results of this relationship will also be discussed.

Table 5.11 Comparing results of this study with previous empirical demand for audit studies			
Relationship	Support found in previous	Support found in this study	Reference Individual Hypotheses
External agency relationships			
Shareholder (owner) – manager relationship	0	+/++	1a, 1b, 1d, 1e
Stakeholder – company relationship	N/A	-	1c
Enhancing credibility	+	++	2a
Leverage	+	-	2b
Existence debt covenants /lender requirements	++	++	2c
Cost of debt capital	0	-	2d
Improvement of credit rating of the company	+	+	2e
Size	0	0	3
Internal agency relationships			
Loss of control (complexity)	+	+	4
Existence outside directors	+	+	5
Substitute for internal control	+	++	6a, 6b, 6c
Improvement of quality of financial information	++	++	7
Other relationships			
Dependency on auditor relationship	-	0/+	8a, 8b
Type of auditor report issued in previous year(s)	-	++	8c
Financial Health	0	-	9
Strategic reasons (expected future growth)	N/A	+	10

Shareholder (owner) –manager relationship

Most previous empirical studies investigating the relationship between the shareholder (owner) – manager relation and the demand for audit used management-ownership share (or family-ownership - non family management) as variable to test this relation (Carey et al., 2000; Seow, 2001; Senkow et al., 2001; Collis et al., 2004; Collis, 2010) and have found mixed results. This study did find the expected negative association between the management-ownership share and the demand for audit. However, this association showed to be not significant.

Besides the management-ownership variable, two additional variables have been used in this study to investigate the relationship between shareholder – manager relation and the demand for audit:
- the number of shareholders (hypothesis 1a); and
- the existence of shareholders with no access to internal financial information (hypothesis 1b) .

It is reasoned that with the number of shareholders or with the dependency on presented financial information by management, instead of having direct access to internal financial information, the uncertainty of shareholders (principal) towards management (agent) acting in the best interests of the principal (Jensen and Meckling, 1976) increases. Following agency theory, it is expected that a positive association exists with the demand for audit. Both variables showed to have a positive significant association with the demand for audit.

Also, based on the literature review of chapter two, it is reasoned that the decision whether or not choosing an audit of financial statements in a non-mandatory environment is part of a 'bounded rationality' decision making process of management. Although Jensen and Meckling (1976) acknowledge that in the principal-agency relationship the 'agency problems' arise as a result of delegating some decision making authority, they ignore "all elements of the owner-manager decision problem involving portfolio considerations induced by the presence of uncertainty and the existence of diversifiable risk" (Jensen and Meckling, 1976: 314). Following 'bounded rationality' theory (Simon, 1982) it is expected that the decision also will be influenced by perceptions (see chapter 2.4.3). Therefore, a perception variable is used in this study to test the relationship between the shareholder – manager relation and the demand for audit also. Although other empirical studies regarding the demand for audit have taken into account management views (perception) in the decision making process on the benefits of auditing (Jensen and Payne, 2003; Collis et al., 2004; Niemi et al. 2009 and Collis, 2010) and the decision for the demand for audit. However, to my knowledge, no study investigated the perception of management of shareholder's need for audited financial statements and the demand for audit. The results of hypothesis 1e shows that the relationship between management perception of shareholder's need for auditing is positively associated with the demand for auditing.

It, therefore can be concluded that the difference in support found between this study and other previous studies (see table 5.11) is caused by the additional variables in this study regarding the relationship between the shareholder – manager relation and the demand for audit.

Leverage and Cost of debt capital

Based on agency theory it is argued that there is a potential agency conflict between the provider of debt capital and the company. Variable leverage has been used in a number of previous studies as a proxy to count for the severity of this potential conflict. Whereas some studies (e.g. Chow, 1982; Buijink, 1992; Carey et al., 2000) found a positive significant association between leverage and the demand for audit, other studies (e.g. Senkow et al., 2001; Seow, 2001) found no significant association. This study also did not find a significant association between leverage and the demand for audit.

It is also argued (e.g. Blackwell et al., 2008; Kim et al., 2007) that auditing reduces information uncertainty by lenders and as a result reduces the cost of debt. The results of previous empirical studies, using data of private companies also, regarding the relationship between the cost of debt capital and auditing showed mixed support. This study did not find a significant association between the cost of debt capital (lending conditions) and the demand for auditing.

However, a significant positive association was found between the existence of lender requirements and the demand for auditing. A possible explanation for the found mixed results in this study with regard to the variables explaining the relationship between providers of debt-capital and the demand for auditing is the existence of other 'monitoring tools' and 'bonding mechanism' for debt capital providers besides the external audit of financial statements. Looking more closely at the Dutch situation under investigation in this study, the debt capital providers are mainly banking institutions. To secure the loans provided to SME companies, banking institutions have the 'power' to demand pledges from the company, such as mortgages, personal liability, contractual agreements (see chapter 2.4.3). This could explain why this study did not find significant positive associations between leverage and the cost of debt capital and the demand for auditing.

Size

From the bivariate analyses in this study it can be concluded that size overall seems not to have a significant association with the demand for audit. As such, comparing these results with the results of previous studies initially would give no rise for further discussion. However, a point of interest we should take into account with size in this study is the population of companies of this study (see also chapter 4.3.2). The population consists of companies which as a result of deregulation in 2006 no longer are classified as medium-sized and subsequently may no longer met the mandatory requirement for an audit. Therefore, the population to some extent can be considered as homogenous with respect to the size criteria. Given the latter, we would expect on forehand (or postulate) that in this study the variables associated with size would not be significant for the decision whether or not to opt for a non-mandatory audit.

Substitute for internal control
This study found support for the relationship between the demand for audit and the perception of management that audit provides a check on internal accounting records and systems. This contributes to the view that external auditing may serve as a substitute for internal control. Based on previous empirical research (Jensen and Payne, 1993), it was also hypothesized that a 'lower' quality of the financial department is associated with a higher probability that the company demands an audit to mitigate the low level of accounting expertise within the company (substitute effect). However, based on the results, it turned out to be the opposite. The existence of a qualified financial department is associated with a higher probability that the company demands an audit. This leaves us with the question: Why would a company with a qualified financial department more likely demand an audit? An explanation could be that due to a more substantive knowledge of the benefits of an audit these companies are more willing to retain the audit? Collis et al. (2004) investigated whether the education of management (management of the company having a degree in business administration and therefore has general knowledge of the costs and benefits of the audit) is associated with a higher probability that the company would choose for a non-mandatory audit and found a significant positive relationship between education and the demand for audit. Reasoning that companies facing organizational complexity more likely to have a qualified financial department, the demand for audit can be related to possible existing organizational complexity (Abdel-khalik, 1993; Knechel et al., 2008). Given the available data in this study no clear explanation for this phenomenon can be provided.

Dependency on auditor relationship
The relation between the dependency on the auditor relationship and the demand for audit has been tested using two variables: audit tenure (hypothesis 8a) and number of other services provided by the auditor (hypothesis 8b). The results showed the expected positive association between audit tenure and the demand for audit. Although a clear explanation for the existence of this relationship cannot be given, a possible explanation could be found in the broad business education of auditors in the Netherlands, whereby findings and recommendations of the auditor to management regarding the improvement of the existing 'AAO-system' (see chapter 4.2.1.1) are viewed as an added value of audit by management for own purposes. The results for the number of other services and the demand for audit, however did not showed the expected positive association.

It was expected, following Senkow et al. (2001), that due to 'knowledge spillovers' the mean number of other services provided by the audit firm for companies which opt for an audit would be higher than for the companies which did not opt for an audit. However, the results turned out to be that the mean number of other services provides was lower. Although the difference show not to be significant, the question remains: why a negative association between the number of other services and the demand for audit in this study exists? Based on the data available, no clear answer can be given. A possible explanation for this can be the (recent) impeded restrictions on the nature of other services provided in combination with the audit. As a result of this companies which opt for the demand for audit do render less other services of the audit firm. Another possible explanation can be that companies which opt for an audit have more 'in house' financial quality and are capable to perform certain services provided by the auditor (e.g. preparing the financial statements).

Overall it can be concluded that the results of the individual hypotheses testing supports the claims made that the benefits of 'acquiring' an audit are indeed multi-faceted (Knechel et al., 2008) and that the audit of financial statements, besides the classical agency theory argument for auditing, may also be valuable for other reasons. However, in answering the research question of this study *'what are drivers for the demand for audit in a non-mandatory environment?'* we are also interested in the extent to which of these identified relationships are deemed to be important in the decision making process whether or not to opt for a non-mandatory audit.

The next chapter we will answer this part of the research question using the general logistic regression model presented in chapter 3.3.2. But as we have learned from 'bounded rationality theory' in chapter two, the decision maker is a 'satisficer' and probably will not take into account all existing possible relationships.

Chapter 6. Empirical Results II – Regression analyses

6.1   Introduction

The purpose of this study is to conduct a comprehensive research regarding the drivers for auditing in a non-mandatory setting. We know from the descriptive data that 62% of the companies choose to continue with the audit. We also know that there are multiple significant relationships. However, we still do not know what incremental influence is of each individual component over the other individual components. In other words: we still do not know which factors are the main drivers in the decision making process of management to opt for a non-mandatory audit. This chapter therefore presents multivariate regression analyses to investigate to which extent the demand for audit (DVA) can be explained by these variables.

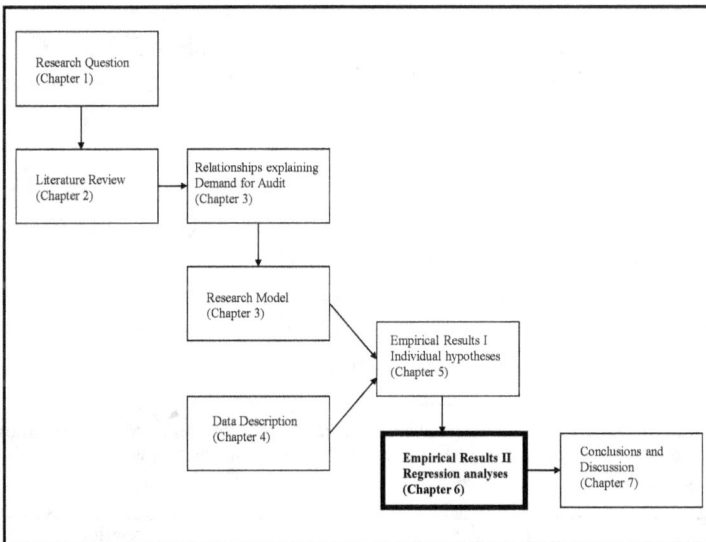

Figure 6.1: Overview of the structure of this study

As the outcome of our dependent variable can only be a 'yes' or 'no' whether the company has chosen for a voluntary audit or not, logistic regression analysis has to be performed to explain the influence of the identified independent variables. Based on the literature review the general regression model for this study (see chapter 3.3.2) has been formulated as:

DVA = f(external agency variables, internal agency variables, other variables)

In section 6.2 several preliminary analyses will be conducted. Section 6.3 presents the results of the multivariate regression analyses, followed by an additional analysis in section 6.4 of the relationship between variables used in this study regarding the shareholder – manager relationship. In section 6.5 a comparative analysis of some of the results of this study with the studies of Collis et al. (2004) and Niemi et al. (2009) is presented.

6.2   Preliminary analyses

6.2.1   Correlation and multi collinearity

Before starting with the multivariate regression analyses, a check on correlation and multi collinearity of the independent variables is performed. To check if the independent variables used in the logistic regression model are correlated both Pearson and Spearman correlation tests have been conducted. Table 6.1 shows that no strong or very strong correlation[85] between the 23 independent variables exist.

However, there appeared to be a clear relation between a number of independent variables, e.g. between CREDIBLY, CHECK and QUALITY, between LENDPLUS and COMPCRED and between CATOMZ and FINAFD for both Pearson and Spearman correlation. Besides this the correlation matrix also shows a clear relation between SHRH# and LVRG and between CATOMZ and FINAFD, but only for Pearson correlation[86].

---

[85] To determine to which extent correlation between independent variables is statistical significant the size of the correlation can be examined. In measuring the correlation the following valuation is used (den Boer et al., 1994).

Correlation coefficient	Classification	Strength of relation
< .20	Very low correlation	Negligible relation
> .20 < .40	Low correlation	Present but weak relation
> .40 < .70	Limited correlation	Clear relation
> .70 < .90	High correlation	Strong relation
> .90	Very high correlation	Very strong relation

[86] The outcome of Pearson correlation may be highly influenced by outliers. As the standard deviation of the mean of SHRH# (see table 4.5) indicates that outliers exist an additional Pearson correlation is conducted replacing the top 3 of outliers with the mean. Results shows that the correlation drops to 0.050 and is not significant anymore confirming that the outcome of the Pearson correlation is caused by not normal distribution. In this case Spearman correlation more appropriate. Results of the Spearman correlation showed that no clear correlation exists between SHRH# and LVRG.

Table 6.1 Correlation matrix of variables in this study. Pearson (Spearman) correlations below (above) the diagonal

	1	2	3	4	5	6	7	8	9	10	11	12
1. DVA	1	.092	.121	.079	-.051	.520**	.332**	.012	.213**	.125	.151	-.114
2. SHRH#	.116	1	.405**	.002	.183**	.039	.055	.182*	-.016	.065	.214**	.135
3. SHRHAC	.121	.227**	1	-.009	-.214**	.260**	.057	-.005	-.045	.061	.090	.007
4. STAKE#	.088	.266**	.006	1	-.092	.207*	-.051	.133	.120	.060	.108	.065
5. MOWN50	-.051	-.087	-.214**	-.084	1	-.273**	-.033	.061	.202*	.046	.128	-.104
6. SHRHND	.528**	.165	.269**	.198*	-.278**	1	.296**	.001	.043	.104	.203*	.038
7. CREDIBLY	.346**	.022	.083	-.053	-.029	.331**	1	-.034	.129	.295**	.278**	-.072
8. LVRG	.095	.660**	.150	.327**	-.045	.088	-.012	1	.217**	.118	.186*	.207*
9. LRQM	.213**	-.091	-.045	.104	.202*	.043	.109	.033	1	.351**	.156	-.060
10. LENDPLUS	.134	-.083	.052	.037	.052	.105	.248**	-.043	.342**	1	.443**	.077
11. COMPCRED	.155	.043	.092	.092	.123	.196*	.267**	.079	.155	.452**	1	.047
12. ASSETS	-.045	.236**	.018	.068	-.141	.104	-.048	-.148	-.110	.004	.007	1
13. CATOMZ	.094	.068	.122	.159*	-.031	.056	-.039	.098	.279**	.148	.235**	.072
14. CATEMPLS	.184*	-.108	-.012	-.042	.048	.056	.116	.002	.142	.032	.076	-.332**
15. OUTDIR	.137	.291**	.242**	.164*	-.071	.190*	.115	.094	.188*	.060	.024	.101
16. CHECK	.401**	.126	.070	.009	.072	.341**	.433**	.063	.101	.178*	.164*	-.148
17. FINAFD	.170*	.086	.160*	.161*	.045	.182*	.004	.076	.178*	.046	.076	.016
18. EDUFIN	.063	.005	.156	.095	-.175*	.124	-.045	.091	.000	.085	.082	-.071
19. QUALITY	.394**	.053	.006	-.067	.072	.304**	.509**	.031	.113	.211**	.183*	-.100
20. AUDTERM	.231**	-.029	-.022	.056	.046	.017	.055	-.016	.079	.021	-.111	-.081
21. AUDSERV	-.060	-.242**	-.155	-.001	.283**	-.217**	-.053	-.121	.223**	.014	-.015	-.148
22. AUDREP	.189*	.030	.012	.084	-.116	.185*	.140	-.076	.057	.022	-.004	.214**
23. HEALTH	.023	-.197*	.011	-.106	.036	.035	-.103	-.169*	.091	.023	.039	.147
24. STRAT	.232**	-.171	.073	.017	.038	.251**	.115	-.053	-.003	.211*	.199*	-.232**

For variable definitions, see table 5.10. **p<.001 and *p<.005 (2 tailed).

Table 6.1 Correlation matrix of variables in this study. Pearson (Spearman) correlations below (above) the diagonal (continued)

	13	14	15	16	17	18	19	20	21	22	23	24
1 DVA	.094	.184	.137	.405**	.170*	.063	.393**	.285**	-.040	.189*	.023	.228
2 SHRH#	.101	-.078	.166*	.206*	.194*	.102	.146	-.020	-.111	.006	-.060	-.034
3 SHRHAC	.122	-.012	.242**	.063	.160*	.156	-.011	.031	-.153	.012	.011	.054
4 STAKE#	.157	-.038	.128	.025	.165*	.086	-.056	.069	.056	.068	-.085	.018
5 MOWN50	-.031	.048	-.071	.070	.045	-.175*	.075	-.003	.285**	-.116	.036	.020
6 SHRHND	.066	.049	.186*	.359**	.178*	.118	.287**	.110	-.212*	.185*	.034	.241**
7 CREDIBLY	-.018	.114	.081	.386**	-.015	-.014	.490**	.054	-.040	.113	-.083	.074
8 LVRG	.146	.235**	-.061	.027	.188*	.077	.106	.030	-.075	.035	-.121	.042
9 LRQM	.279**	.142	.188*	.082	.178*	.000	.113	.088	.249**	.057	.091	-.008
10 LENDPLUS	.154	.021	.061	.185*	.034	.079	.232**	.080	.044	.023	.031	.192*
11 COMPCRED	.233**	.074	.017	.177*	.077	.076	.199*	-.110	-.022	-.008	.037	.198*
12 ASSETS	.116	-.476**	.061	-.091	-.010	-.036	-.079	-.112	-.090	.146	.105	-.226*
13 CATOMZ	1	-.075	.136	.061	.460**	.147	-.011	.089	-.020	.043	.070	.072
14 CATEMPLS	.012	1	.012	.012	.034	.155	.041	.116	-.070	.175*	-.009	.128
15 OUTDIR	.136	.012	1	.175*	.150	.078	.009	.190*	-.234**	.203*	-.141	.077
16 CHECK	.072	.043	.180*	1	.080	-.110	.680**	.097	.021	.145	-.078	.218*
17 FINAFD	.460**	.034	.150	.095	1	.352**	.068	.022	-.002	-.003	-.007	.086
18 EDUFIN	.147	.155	.078	-.116	.352**	1	-.080	.083	-.133	.022	-.027	.069
19 QUALITY	-.036	.030	.016	.696**	.048	-.101	1	.059	.073	.030	-.004	.240**
20 AUDTERM	.054	.139	.163	.111	.050	.070	.052	1	-.218*	.253**	-.130	.104
21 AUDSERV	-.031	-.071	-.211**	.024	.009	-.151	.075	-.110	1	-.276**	.098	.047
22 AUDREP	.043	.175*	.203*	.154	-.003	.022	.024	.236**	-.279**	1	.073	-.041
23 HEALTH	.070	-.009	-.141	-.095	-.007	-.027	-.027	-.086	.068	.073	1	-.018
24 STRAT	.083	.144	.074	.254**	.088	.063	.244**	.069	.062	-.042	-.004	1

For variable definitions, see table 5.10. **p<.001 and *p<.005 (2 tailed).

The existence of correlation between independent variables in a regression analysis raises the possibility of multi collinearity, the situation where two or more independent variables are highly linearly related. The existence of multi collinearity in a regression analysis increases the likelihood that the coefficient estimates of individual independent variables changes erratically in response to small changes. Although the existence of multi collinearity does not reduce the predictive power of the model as a whole, it affects the calculations (the estimated coefficient and significance) of the individual independent variables. As this study is interested in the drivers for the demand for auditing in a non-mandatory environment and we are therefore interested in the predictive power of identified individual independent variables, multi collinearity is not desirable. As the results of the correlation matrix indicate for a number of independent variables a risk of multi collinearity exists. Therefore, two additional statistical analyses to test for multi collinearity[87] are conducted. Both the results of the Tolerance (Tol) and Variance Inflated Factor (VIF) test (see appendix III) show no high multi collinearity between the independent variables. Therefore it can be concluded that it is expected that the coefficient estimates of the individual independent variables will not be strongly affected in response to small changes.

6.2.2   Parsimonious tests

So far 23 independent variables have been identified based on literature review and previous empirical studies. However, including a large number variables in a model creates the possibility that the model may be 'overfit' and therefore producing numerically unstable estimates (Hosmer and Lemeshow, 2000). The problem of 'overfitting' and producing problematic results in a multivariate regression model exists more profoundly in the situation where the number of variables is large relative to the number of outcome observations. A general rule for multivariate logistic regression models is a minimum of 10 observations for each independent variable (Hosmer and Lemeshow, 2000; Lambrecht and Verslype, 2009). Given the number of 154 observations in this study, a need for the development of the most parsimonious model exist. In selecting and reducing the number of variables several procedures are available, the following two procedures will be carried out:

   1.   Selection of variables based on the results of the conducted univariate analyses;

---

[87] As multi collinearity is a potential problem of the independent variables in regression models, this makes the detection of multi collinearity in logistic regression the same as in linear regression. Tolerance and VIF are two generally accepted and used statistical tests for multi collineairity (Mortelmans, 2010: 156).

2. Dimension reduction procedures.

Finally step-wise regression analyses is performed (chapter 6.3.2), which also reduces the large number of independent variables ('predictors') to a smaller number.

Selection of variables based on the results of the conducted univariate analyses

In selecting variables for the multivariate analyses it is recommended not to use a traditional accepted significance level (such as 0.05). Hosmer and Lemeshow (2000) recommend the use of a 0.25 significance level for selecting variables. Although a possible disadvantage of using a higher level is the risk of including variables based on the univariate analyses, namely "that it ignores the possibility that a collection of variables, each of which is weakly associated with the outcome, can become an important predictor of the outcome when taken together" (Hosmer and Lemeshow, 2000: 95). Using a 0.25 significance level showed that of the tested variables in chapter five only the variables MOWN50, ASSETS and HEALTH do not classify for inclusion in the logistic regression model. The variables FINAFD, EDUFIN and AUDSERV are also excluded. Although, the individual hypothesis testing for the variables show that they are significant (using the 0.25 significance level) the hypotheses are rejected. The reason for rejecting the hypotheses is that the expected direction of the relationship with the demand for audit was not confirmed (see chapter five).

Dimension reduction methods

There are several statistical available dimension reduction methods of which factor analysis is one of the most widely used linear dimension reduction methods. The main application of factor analysis is to reduce the number of variables and to detect structure in the relationship between variables, that is to classify them (Fodor, 2002).

The independent variables related to the added value of an audit were selected for the factor analysis. With regard to the added value of an audit, respondents were asked whether they agree or disagree with questions regarding the usefulness of the audit, using a rating scale where 1 = strong disagree and 5 = strong agree. Table 6.2 shows the results of these questions.

Table 6.2 Perceptions of added value of the audit (% of respondents)							
Perceptions of added value of the audit	**5**	**4**	**3**	**2**	**1**	**No response**	**Total**
Provides check on internal records (CHECK)	14	38	29	11	8	0	100
Improves credibility of information (CREDIBLY)	26	40	23	7	4	0	100
Improves quality of information (QUALITY)	8	22	40	14	15	1	100
Improves lending conditions (LENDPLUS)	21	27	24	17	11	0	100
Improves companies credit rating (COMPCRED)	11	20	33	18	17	1	100

N = 154

As these questions involved the perceptions held regarding the added value, it is expected that given the existing literature on perceptions, besides existing (economic) facts also beliefs & values and attitudes of the decision maker are of importance. Assuming that this beliefs & values and attitudes of the respondent are congruent, it is expected that the perceptions of added value of the audit for a number of the variables, included in table 6.2, are analogue. Varimax rotated factor analysis was used. The rotation converged in only three iterations and table 6.3 shows that two factors were extracted, which account for 72% of the variance.

Table 6.3 Factor analysis		
Variable	**Factor 1** **Improves reliability**	**Factor 2** **Improves lending abilities**
CHECK	**.871**	.047
QUALITY	**.894**	.091
CREDIBLY	**.713**	.267
LENDPLUS	.136	**.831**
COMPCRED	.110	**.846**

Notes: N = 153
Total variance explained
Factor 1: Eigenvalue 2.393; 47.851 of variance
Factor 2: Eigenvalue 1.191; 23.811 of variance

As shown in table 6.3 factor one groups together the first three variables, with loadings in excess of 0.7 and accounts for 48% of the variance. This factor has been labelled intuitively as 'improves reliability'. The second factor groups together the other two variables, with loadings in excess of 0.8 and accounts for 24% of the variance. This factor has been labelled intuitively as 'improves lending abilities'. Based on the factor scores the number of variables in the following logistic regression will be reduced, whereby:

- IMPRREL will replace the variables CHECK, QUALITY and CREDIBLY; and
- LENDAB will replace the variables LENDPLUS en COMPCRED.

6.2.3   Size as control variable

Whether or not companies are mandatorily obliged to have their financial statements audited is, within the European Union, currently based on size criteria. Legislators still consider the size variables to be the 'easiest and clearest' way to proxy for the 'wealth at risk' and the severity of the supposed existing agency conflicts, where government ('the state') interferes from a point of view of protecting the general public in society and making the economy more efficient[88]. Variable size is used in all previous empirical demand for audit studies (see table 3.2) as a control variable and this study will also use size as a control variable. To select which of the size variables will be used as control variable, logistic regression is executed to test if the likelihood of management retaining /choosing for a non-mandatory audit increases with the size of the firm ('wealth at risk'). Table 6.4 shows in the panels A – C the results for each individual measure of size as the explanatory variable. Panel D enters al the size measures into the logistic regression together. It shows that only CATEMPLS is significant. However, the use of the variable employees as 'size'-measure for the existence of 'external' agency conflicts is a fuzzy one. The number of employees as variable is also widely used in empirical research as a proxy to count for the loss of control of management within the company as a result of delegating authority to employees. However, the latter is also considered to be a potential agency conflict, although an internal agency conflict. In the relationship 'loss of control' management acts as principal and not as agent, as management in delegating authority to employees still holds the responsibility for the 'deeds' of these employees and bears the risk of employees not acting according to the delegated authority. The twofold function of the variable CATEMPLS may, therefore, explain that this variable is the only significant size variable in the logistic regression model and explaining 4,8% of the 'error reduction' (see panel C of table 6.4).

Also, based on the low pseudo R^2, it can be concluded that size criteria in this study for management do not seem to play a major role in their decision whether

---

[88] Public Interest Theory (PIT) assumes that regulatory bodies try to make an economy more efficient through intervention in the market.

or not to opt for a non-mandatory audit[89]. The low R^2 of 6,2% of this study is comparable to the study of Collis et al. (2004) of 5,6% , which also showed that size criteria alone have a low explanatory value for the demand for audit of SME companies. As CATEMPLS is the only size variable to be significant in this logistic regression model, it is decided to use only CATEMPLS as control variable for size in the subsequent analyses.

Table 6.4 Logistic regression model: size factors and demand for audit					
Label	B	SE	Wald	Sig.	Odds-ratio
Panel A					
INTERCEPT	1.972	2.665	0.548	0.459	7.186
ASSETS	-0.095	0.169	0.317	0.574	0.909
Panel B					
INTERCEPT	0.163	0.330	0.243	0.622	1.176
CATOMZ	0.441	0.383	1.329	0.249	1.555
Panel C					
INTERCEPT	0.283	0.184	2.376	0.123	1.327
CATEMPLS	1.029	0.464	4.927	0.026**	2.799
Panel D					
INTERCEPT	-0.472	2.879	0.027	0.870	0.624
ASSETS	0.023	0.181	0.016	0.899	1.023
CATOMZ	0.530	0.395	1.802	0.179	1.699
CATEMPLS	1.084	0.490	4.891	0.027**	2.956

Model summary
N = 154
Panel A : Chi-square 0.316 , df 1 , p-value 0.574, -2 Log likelihood 204.679; Pseudo R^2 0.003
Panel B : Chi-square 1.320 , df 1 , p-value 0.251, -2 Log likelihood 201.746; Pseudo R^2 0.012
Panel C : Chi-square 5.544 , df 1 , p-value 0.019**, -2 Log likelihood 199.451; Pseudo R^2 0.048
Panel D : Chi-square 7.152 , df 3 , p-value 0.067*, -2 Log likelihood 195.914; Pseudo R^2 0.062
For description of variables see Table 5.10

---

[89] As explained already in chapter 5 on forehand it was predicted that size criteria alone in this study would not have a significant influence on the decision whether or not to opt for a non mandatory audit. The sample used in this study was comprised from the population of companies which as a result of deregulation, by enlarging the size criteria, are not longer to be considered as medium-sized but as small (see chapter 4). Therefore to some extent the population can be considered homogeneous to size and as such it was expected that size would not be significant in the decision.

6.3 Logistic regression model

6.3.1 Introduction

Both literature and empirical research have identified relationships explaining the demand for audit (see also chapter three and five). To investigate the explanatory power of these relationship in the decision whether or not (dichotomous variable) to choose for a non-mandatory audit a logistic regression model is used. Chapter 3.3.2 presented the general research model for this study. The final model used in this chapter is slightly adapted as it is decided to use size as a control variable and to present size separately in the model. Also it is decided, based on the found significance of the hypotheses of chapter five which made use of perception variables (see table 5.10) and the discussion of the influence of perception on decision making (chapter 2.4.3), to present the perception variables separately in the model also. Therefore the final logistic regression model of this study is:

$$\text{DVA} = \beta_0 + \beta_1(\text{SIZE}) + \beta_2(\text{EXTERNAL AGENCY factors}) + \beta_2(\text{INTERNAL AGENCY factors}) + \beta_3(\text{OTHER factors}) + \beta_4(\text{PERCEPTIONS OF DECISIONMAKER}) + \varepsilon$$

The results of the conducted multivariate logistic regression will be presented in four stages, whereby size in all stages will be included as control variable. In the first stage, the model consists of the external agency factors. The second stage provides a model consisting of the internal agency factors and the other factors. To test the explanatory power of the impact of perceptions on the decision for the demand for audit, the perception-variables are presented separately in the third stage. The fourth stage consists of the stepwise logistic regression model.

6.3.2 Multivariate analyses

As 62% of the companies in the case of deregulation choose for a non-mandatory audit and this cannot be explained by size factors alone (see chapter 6.2.3), it is important to consider what other factors may contribute to the demand for audit in SME companies. However, due to the number of identified variables and the number of observations in this study, parsimonious methods have to be used to reduce the number of independent variables included in the regression model. Using univariate analysis and factor analysis the original number of 23 identified variables could be reduced to 14 variables (of which 2 are newly created variables as a result of the factor analysis). As a result of the analysis of the size variables as control variable another variable was removed and due to the number of missing values it is decided to leave also out the variable STRAT[90]. However, it was decided to put variable MOWN50 in the model, although MOWN50 showed to be non-significant even at the 0.25 level. The reason to include this variable is that from literature review and previous empirical research it is considered to be an important and significant proxy variable explaining the demand for audit (Hosmer and Lemeshow, 2000). A total of thirteen independent variables will be included in the multivariate analyses. Table 6.5 provides the variables included in the logistic regression model.

Table 6.6 presents the results of the logistic regression model. Panel A represents the external agency factors. Next to control variable SIZE the external agency variables SHRH#, SHRHAC, STAKE#, LVRG and LRQM are added to the model. Variables SHRH# , SHRHAC, STAKE# and MOWN50 represent the agency relationship between the shareholder and the manager whereas the variables LVRG and LRQM represent the relationship between the provider of debt capital and the company (shareholder/manager). The expected coefficients show all the expected sign, including the expected negative sign for variable MOWN50 (it is expected that the higher management's ownership share in the company, this would have a negative impact on the demand for audit). It only shows that SIZE and LRQM are significant in this model and all others are insignificant. However, the p-value of the model is 0.008 showing that explanatory power of the model with all added independent variables is significant compared to the intercept-only model. It can be concluded from the pseudo R^2 of 15.9% that the variables representing the external agency relationships counts for an 'error reduction' of 11.1%[91].

Panel B represents the internal agency factors and other factors. Adding the variables OUTDIR, AUDTERM and AUDREP together with control variable SIZE into the logistic regression model, it shows that only AUDTERM is significant. The estimated coefficients of the independent variables show all the expected sign. The pseudo R^2 of Panel B shows that the 'internal agency and other factors'-model counts for an 'error reduction' of 14.1% and that the model shows to have significantly more explanatory power than the INTERCEPT-only model (p-value 0.007).

---

[90] The variable STRAT counting for the strategic reasons for choosing/retaining a non-mandatory audit has a relatively large number of missing values (18%) and this would reduces the number of valid cases in the analyses substantially, which in turn would enhance the problem of 'overfitting' in the model (Hosmer and Lemeshow, 2000; Schafer and Graham, 2002).

[91] Panel A shows a pseudo R^2 of 15.9%. However, as the pseudo r-square of adding only the variable SIZE (represented by the variable CATOMZ, see table 6.4) to the model is 4.8%, the pseudo R^2 share of the external agency variables can be calculated as 15.9% minus 4.8%.

Table 6.5 demand for voluntary audit: variables in the logistic regression model

Label	Description	Predicted sign
DVA	Whether the company has chosen to opt for a non mandatory audit (1 = yes, 0 = no)	Dependent variable
SIZE	Size category, this is treated as a categorical variable coded "1" of the company is classified as medium sized or large by the category of employees and "0" if it is classified as small	+
SHRH#	The number of shareholders of the company	+
SHRHAC	The existence of shareholders who have no direct access to internal financial information (1 = yes, 0 = no)	+
STAKE#	The number of stakeholders, identified by management, of the company next to shareholders	+
MOWN50	The percentage of shares held by company's management (1 = >50%, 0 = < 50%)	-
LVRG	The proportion of debt as measured by debt-to-asset ratio	+
LRQM	The existence of a lender requirement for an audit at the time of change in legislation (1 = yes, 0 = no)	+
OUTDIR	The existence of outside directors (1 = yes, 0 = no)	+
AUDTERM	The number of years the current auditor has been engaged with the company	+
AUDREP	Whether an unqualified audit report has been issued in previous year(s) (1 = yes, 0 = no)	+
SHRHND	Perception of management of shareholder's need for audited financial statements (1 = strong disagree, 5 = strong agree)	+
IMPRREL	Perception of management that the audit improves reliability (1 = strong disagree, 5 = strong agree)	+
LENDAB	Perception of management that the audit improves lending abilities (1 = strong disagree, 5 = strong agree)	+

The influence of perceptions on the demand for audit is shown in Panel C of the logistic regression model. Besides the control variable SIZE the variables SHRHND, IMPREL and LENDAB are added to the model. The p-value of <.001 shows that the explanatory power of the model is significant, whereas the pseudo

R^2 shows that the 'perception-model' leads to an 'error-reduction' of 47.8%, which is substantially higher than both the 'external-agency'-model and the 'internal agency and other factors'-model. It shows that only the variable LENDAB is not significant.

Panel D presents the results of the total regression model. Using stepwise regression[92] (backward selection) all non-significant effects are excluded from the full model containing all independent variables (see table 6.5) and retaining only the factors that are significantly related to the demand for audit. The model summary shows, based on the Chi-square (67.330) and the p-value (<.001) that this model is the most significant of all. Also the explanatory power of this model is high (pseudo R^2 of 0.60). From this model it can be concluded that the external agency relationship between shareholders and (management of) the company, presented by the variables SHRHAC and SHRHND, in the context of SME companies is the main driver for the demand for audit. However, it is noticeable that the relationship with the auditor and the perceptions of the added value of audit for internal purposes also seems to be important drivers for management of SME companies to demand an audit. The latter relationships possibly indicate the need for 'personal' benefits of the company of both the relationship with the auditor as the audit. These results are remarkable given the installing by governments of additional requirements on external auditing and the audit profession in recent years to mitigate expected potential risks of the involvement of the auditor with the company audited.

In answering the research question of this study: *what are drivers for the demand for auditing in a non-mandatory environment?,* it can be concluded that, using backward stepwise regression, the demand can be explained by the SIZE, SHRHAC, LRQM, AUDTERM, AUDREP, SHRHND and IMPREL. Of the total of thirteen independent variables included in the full model these seven independent variables showed to have a significant contribution in explaining the demand for audit.

---

[92] With the use of stepwise logistic regression the choice of a probability level to judge the importance of variables to entry in the stepwise regression is important. Although most standard statistical packages use an entry level of 0.05, research have shown that this level for stepwise regression is to stringent and often results in excluding important variables of the model. If the goal of the analysis may be broader, to provide a more complete picture, the use of an entry level of 0.25 is a reasonable choice (Hosmer and Lemeshow, 2000). As the broader picture, the enrichment of our knowledge regarding the drivers for the demand for audit, is a goal of this study it is decided, following Hosmer and Lemeshow, to use an entry level (and removal level) of 0.25 for the stepwise regression.

Table 6.6 Demand for Audit: Multivariate analyses

Label	Predicted	Panel A		Panel B		Panel C		Panel D	
		coefficient	p-value	coefficient	p-value	coefficient	p-value	coefficient	p-value
INTERCEPT	?	-0.549	0.372	-0.585	0.180	-5.160	<.001***	-7.015	<.001***
SIZE	+	1.050	0.030**	0.896	0.081*	1.154	0.067*	1.425	0.080*
SHRH#	+	0.077	0.185						
SHRHAC	+	0.393	0.326					1.055	0.127
STAKE#	+	0.108	0.536						
MOWN50	-	-0.356	0.343						
LVRG	+	0.097	0.730						
LRQM	+	1.131	0.013**					0.997	0.130
OUTDIR	+			0.335	0.513				
AUDTERM	+			0.049	0.078*			0.078	0.023**
AUDREP	+			0.611	0.211			0.433	0.555
SHRHND	+					0.725	<.001***	0.679	0.001***
IMPREL	+					0.956	0.001***	1.148	0.001***
LENDAB	+					0.067	0.766		
Model summary									
N		154		129		138		117	
Wald chi-square		19.199 (df 7)		14.004 (df 4)		59.592 (df 4)		67.330 (df 7)	
p-value		0.008		0.007		<.001		<.001	
-2 Log likelihood		185.797		154.065		123.253		85.432	
Pseudo R²		0.159		0.141		0.478		0.600	

As with the use of backward stepwise regression the disadvantage occurs that it cannot properly work in the presence of too many variables relative to the number of outcome observations, some robustness checks are performed.

Using forward stepwise regression[93] instead of backward stepwise regression shows exactly the same results as the backward stepwise regression model. Therefore it can be concluded that the presented independent variables in Panel D showed to be robust as the results of the backward stepwise regression model are identical to the forward stepwise regression model.

As with the use of backward stepwise regression the disadvantage occurs that it cannot properly work in the presence of too many variables relative to the number of outcome observations, some robustness checks are performed.

Using forward stepwise regression[94] instead of backward stepwise regression shows exactly the same results as the backward stepwise regression model. Therefore it can be concluded that the presented independent variables in Panel D showed to be robust as the results of the backward stepwise regression model are identical to the forward stepwise regression model.

Finally, the result of the logistic regression of the full model are shown in table 6.7. The SPSS output of the full model is presented in Appendix V. The summary measures for the 'goodness-of-fit' of the model shows for the Chi-square test the significance of the overall model. Also the explanatory power of the model is to be considered high[95], with a pseudo R^2 of 0.604. It showed that in the full model there are four significant independent variables (predictors): SIZE, AUDTERM, SHRHND and IMPREL. Comparing the full model with the stepwise regression model (see panel D of table 6.6) it can be concluded that the explanatory power (pseudo R^2) of the full model is only slightly higher (0.604 vs. 0.600).

---

[93] Hosmer and Lemeshow (2000) indicates that when stepwise logistic regression is performed as check the backward-selection has to be followed with forward selection. With the use of forward stepwise regression only the variables are included with significant main effects and interactions between these main effects. A possible problem with logistic regression is that using different model building strategies may lead to different results, caused by existing correlation between the independent variables.

[94] Hosmer and Lemeshow (2000) indicates that when stepwise logistic regression is performed as check the backward-selection has to be followed with forward selection. With the use of forward stepwise regression only the variables are included with significant main effects and interactions between these main effects. A possible problem with logistic regression is that using different model building strategies may lead to different results, caused by existing correlation between the independent variables.

[95] Based on a comparison with the other presented models in this study and also compared to previous empirical studies using the demand for audit as a dependent variable (see table 2.1).

It can be questioned to which extent the independent variables SHRH#, STAKE#, MOWN50, LVRG, OUTDIR and LENDAB are drivers for the demand for audit. Should these independent variables be excluded, as they may be of no interest? It is decided to present the full model[96] as:

1. We know that a problem with adding to many independent variables in a model, the variance of estimated coefficients ('overfitting') increases. However, the results of the estimated coefficients (B) in the full model are not unrealistic large, indicating that the full model is not 'overfit';

2. We know that using different model building strategies (including and removing) of independent variables the coefficients of the other independent variables may be affected (Hosmer and Lemeshow, 2000). Comparing the coefficients of the full model with the stepwise regression model (see panel D of table 6.6) shows that, excluding the aforementioned independent variables does not affect the coefficients substantially;

3. The independent variables are originally selected, based on literature review and previous empirical research as potential drivers for the demand for audit. So small and non-significant results are therefore also of interest.

---

[96] This full model consists of all 13 independent variables of table 6.5. The number of observations is 117. As such, the number of independent variables related to the number of observations does not respects the 10:1-rule. The classification plot showed an U-shaped distribution. No outliers were detected, using casewise listing for outliers based on -3 < ZRESID > 3.

Table 6.7 Full logistic regression model

Label	B	SE	Wald	Sig.	Odds-ratio
INTERCEPT	-6.765	1.783	14.404	<.001***	0.001
SIZE	1.467	0.831	3.118	0.077*	4.337
SHRH#	0.024	0.075	0.103	0.748	1.025
SHRHAC	0.938	0.726	1.672	0.196	2.556
STAKE#	-0.045	0.269	0.028	0.867	0.956
MOWN50	-0.012	0.629	0.000	0.985	0.988
LVRG	0.150	0.359	0.176	0.675	1.162
LRQM	0.975	0.742	1.726	0.189	2.651
OUTDIR	0.158	0.859	0.034	0.854	1.171
AUDTERM	0.078	0.036	4.625	0.032**	1.081
AUDREP	0.415	0.748	0.308	0.579	1.514
SHRHND	0.696	0.222	9.867	0.002***	2.006
IMPREL	1.154	0.366	9.925	0.002***	3.170
LENDAB	-0.106	0.292	0.133	0.716	0.899

Model summary
N = 117
Chi-square 67.840 , df 13 , p-value < 0.001
-2 Log likelihood 84.921, Pseudo R^2 0.604 (Nagelkerke)

So far we have treated missing values based on a list wise deletion, removing all cases with one or more missing values. Although this is a common method and its main virtue is simplicity, this method has its shortcomings, as high rates of case deletion can result in serious implications for parameter bias and inefficiency (King et al., 2001; Schafer and Graham, 2002). Also "researchers become acutely aware of the inefficiency of case deletion in multivariate analyses involving many items, in which mild rates of missing values on each item may cause large portions of the sample to be discarded" (Schafer and Graham, 2002: 156). Indeed this is actually the case in this study, where due to missing values the original number of 154 observations is reduced to 117 observations in the final model (see table 6.7). To overcome this problem in the subsequently analysis we have dealt with the missing values in this study (see Appendix IV). The dataset used for the regression analyses consists of 13 independent variables and 154 observations, totalling in 2,002 individual items. Descriptive analysis of missing values shows that 44[97] items are missing, counting for 2.2 % of the total items. Of the 154 observations: 117 observations have no missing values, 33 observations have one missing value, 2 observations have two missing values and 2 observations have three missing values. The missing values are imputed by single imputation. The results of the 'reruns' of the multivariate tests table 6.7 after imputing for missing values are presented in Appendix IV. The results show that the presented results regarding the main drivers for the demand for audit, are robust.

Overall it can be concluded, based on the various multivariate analyses presented in this chapter, that the main drivers for the choosing/retaining an audit in a non-mandatory environment are:

- the shareholder – company relationship, expressed by the variables SHRHAC and SHRHND;
- the existence of lender requirements, expressed by the variable LRQM;
- the perception of added value of the audit held by management, expressed by the variable IMPREL;
- the relationship with the current auditor, expressed by the variables AUDTERM and AUDREP; and
- size of the company measured by the number of employees, expressed by the variable CATEMPLS.

6.4 Additional analysis on the relationship between (economic) facts and perception

This section presents the results of an additional analysis with the purpose of providing some insights in the relationship between proxy variables commonly used in empirical studies and the direct influence of perception on decision making.

In general previous studies have made use of variables, proxying for hypothesized relationships with the demand for audit, as it showed to be hard/difficult to gather data which can be used as direct variables to explain the demand for audit. A main advantage of this study is that besides the gathering of the usual factual data, proxying for a relation with the demand for audit also the actual choice of management is observed. The separation between ownership and management is to be seen as the most important potential existing agency conflict and therefore driving the demand for audit. However, the proxy variables used to measure this

---

[97] The number of 44 missing items can be broken down into: OUTDIR: 1; AUDTERM: 18; AUDREP: 9; SHRHND: 13; IMPREL: 1 and LENDAB: 2.

relationship in previous empirical studies did not always show to be significant. Therefore it is of interest to explore the relationship between the proxy variables on both the demand for audit and on the perception held (the direct variable)[98] in the decision making process. With regard to the decision made, a perception question (variable SHRHND, see table 5.10 for description) was added in the questionnaire, directly measuring the importance of the need for audited financial statements of the existing shareholder(s) in the decision making process for DVA (direct variable).

The literature review of chapter two emphasizes the importance of perceptions in the decision making process. Bounded rationality theory postulates that decision makers will not take all facts into consideration. Instead they will use a simplified model and their decision will be 'coloured' by the perception[99] held. It is assumed that existing (economic) facts, commonly used for proxying for the demand for audit, also underlie the perception decision makers have, as the existence of (economic) facts with a phenomenon are a prerequisite for the perception of that same phenomenon to be a part of the decision making process. This is illustrated by the following figure[100].

---

[98] To my knowledge no other previous study has investigated the relation between indirect proxy variables and the direct variable. However, Senkow et al. (2001) recognized the possible influence of proxy variables counting for an expected agency relationship and the ultimate decision as they carried out an additional analysis in their study regarding the conditions which might predispose a lender to negotiate a requirement for audited financial statements as a condition of obtaining a loan.

[99] Perception is defined in this study as the interpretation of 'reality' after information/stimuli is filtered out, selected, organized using existing knowledge, needs, beliefs, values, assumptions and attitudes.

[100] For purposes of this study this figure is simplified with regard to perception, as it does not take into account other 'drivers' of perception (i.e. needs, beliefs, values, assumptions and attitudes).

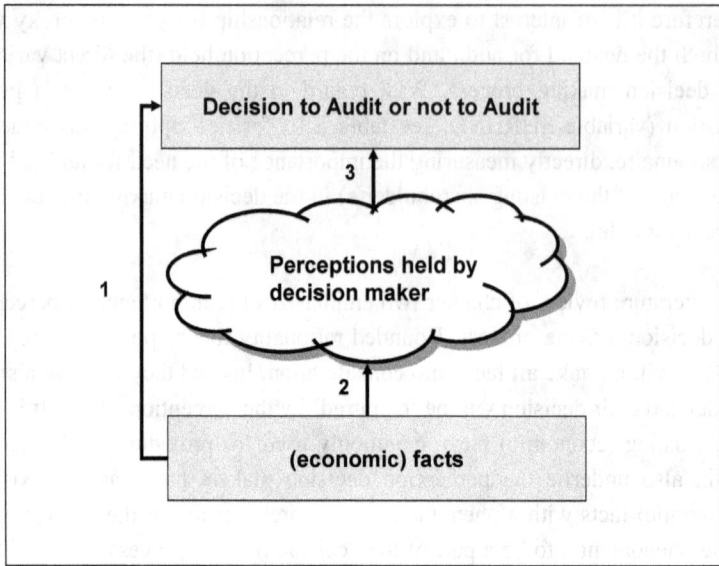

Figure 6.2: Influence of perception on decision making

Whereas commonly, and also in this study, the (economic) facts have been empirically tested for measuring the relationship of the shareholder-manager conflict on the demand for audit (relationship 1 of figure 6.2) this study also tested this relationship by asking management whether shareholders' need for financial statement plays a role in the actual choice (relationship 3 of figure 6.2). By assuming that perceptions held are also influenced by (economic) facts it is reasoned that a relationship will exist between the (economic) facts proxying for the demand for audit and the perceptions held by the decision maker (relationship 2 of figure 6.2). To test whether this predicted relationship 2 exists a regression analysis is conducted and the results will be compared to the results of the regression analysis of relationship 1.

The independent (factual) proxy variables in the regressions are: (a) the number of shareholders (SHRH#); (b) if shareholders have direct access to internal financial information (SHRHAC); and (c) management ownership share in the company (MOWN50). For an in detail explanation of these independent variables see also Table 5.10. As we know from the bivariate analysis of chapter 5.2.1.1 the proxy variables SHRH# and SHRHAC show to be significant and the proxy variable MOWN50 showed to be non-significant. Variable SHRHND counts for the perception of management. The individual test of the direct variable SHRHND, the perception of the need for audited financial statements by the existing shareholders, in the decision making process showed to be strongly significant (p < .001). From previously conducted tests (chapter 6.2.1) we know that checks for correlation and multi collinearity were satisfactory.

Table 6.8 shows the results of the logistic regression of DVA related to the (economic) factual variables (relationship 1) and table 6.9 shows the results of the logistic regression of the perception of shareholder's need related to the (economic) factual variables (relationship 2).

Table 6.8 Logistic regression model DVA and (economic) factual variables (relationship 1)					
Label	B	SE	Wald	Sig.	Odds-ratio
INTERCEPT	0.237	0.279	0.722	0.395	1.268
SHRH#	0.058	0.053	1.193	0.275	1.060
SHRHAC	0.396	0.380	1.085	0.297	1.486
MOWN50	-0.107	0.347	0.094	0.759	0.899

Model summary
N = 154
Chi-square 4.252 , df 3 , p-value 0.236
-2 Log likelihood 200.744, Pseudo R^2 0.037 (Nagelkerke)

The results of the logistic regression of DVA related to the (economic) facts regarding the shareholder – manager agency conflict (table 6.8) show that all independent variables are not significant in the model. The low pseudo R^2 of 3.7% also indicates that these variables have a low explanatory power in explaining the demand for audit. Only using these (traditional) variables in explaining the demand for audit from the perspective of the shareholder-manager agency conflict would lead to the conclusion that the shareholder-manager agency relationship is not a main driver for the demand for audit in this study.

Table 6.9 Logistic regression model of the Perception of shareholder's need and (economic) factual variables (relationship 2)

Label	B	SE	Wald	Sig.	Odds-ratio
INTERCEPT	-0.185	0.291	0.403	0.526	0.831
SHRH#	0.044	0.045	0.954	0.329	1.045
SHRHAC	0.853	0.395	4.655	0.031**	2.347
MOWN50	-1.000	0.372	7.229	0.007***	0.368

Model summary
N = 141
Chi-square 18.762 , df 3 , p-value <.000***
-2 Log likelihood 175.505, Pseudo R^2 0.167 (Nagelkerke)

However, using the same independent variables in a logistic regression of the perception of shareholder's need for the demand for audit, shows that these independent variables, with the exception of SHRH#, are significant. This illustrates that although (economic) facts, proxying a relationship with the demand for voluntary audit alone appears not to play an important role in explaining the demand for audit, an indirect influence exists, as these (economic) facts are significant in explaining the perception. The pseudo R^2 of 16.7% also indicates that, although the (economic) facts have a more pronounced influence on the perception of shareholder's need than on the demand for audit decision indirectly, the perception is likely to be influenced to a greater extent by other factors (e.g. other (economic) facts, beliefs & values)[101]. From this additional test it can be concluded that existing (economic) facts related to the shareholder-manager relationship explain the demand for audit and also explain to some extent the perceptions held, but that in the final decision it is expected that sociological and psychological factors appear to play a strong role also.

6.5   Comparative analysis

The empirical results of this study (see section 6.3) have revealed what the main drivers are for the demand for audit in a non-mandatory environment. Also this study contributes to the existing literature by filling in the calls for a greater integration of literature, by integrating elements of other theories   such as stakeholder theory and bounded rationality theory (see chapter two), in order to

---

[101] Also a logistic regression was conducted of DVA and the perception of shareholders' need. The variable SHRHND was strong significant in this model. The chi-square of the model is 42.354 and the pseudo R^2 is 0.354.

effectively predict and explain the demand for audit as well as this study did observe choices of management facing a non-mandatory audit requirement (see chapter 1.3). However, using data of Dutch private companies and given the acknowledgment that cultural differences may cause other factors to be main drivers for the demand for audit in other setting (see also chapter 4.2.1.2) the question remains: Are the presented results to some extent generalizable? To gather some insights into this questions this chapter provides a comparative analysis of this study by extending the comparative analysis of Niemi et al. (2009) of their study with the study of Collis et al. (2004).

The main difference between this study and both the studies of Collis and Niemi, is that this study uses data of a population of companies which are, as a result of deregulation, facing a renewed audit decision. Whereas both other studies use data of a sample of private SME companies which at the time of inquiry were subject to a mandatory audit regime. However, although given this difference and most likely existing other differences (e.g. culture, median size of companies) it is still of interest to explore for potential similarities. The conducted comparative analysis follows the logistic regression model used by Niemi et al. (2009) in their comparative analysis with the study of Collis et al. (2004). Due to number of, and differences in, variables used, this comparative analysis does not encompass all identified significant variables used in the logistic regression model of this study. First the description of the variables used in this comparative analysis are presented in table 6.10, subsequently the results of the logistic regressions (see table 6.12) are presented and discussed.

When we look at the results of the logistic regression in table 6.11 it shows that pseudo R^2 in all studies is more or less similar, ranging between the 31.3% and 34.8%. This indicates that the presented comparative model in all countries more or less has the same explanatory power to explain the demand for audit. A closer look at the individual significance of the independent variables shows that in general the variables in the Dutch sample show to be less significant than in the other studies. Whereas variables SIZE, CHECK and QUALITY show to be significant at the $p < 0.001$ level in the UK and Finland it only shows to be significant at the $p < 0.05$ or $p < 0.10$ level in the Netherlands. This difference for the variable SIZE can be explained by the more or less homogenous population in the Netherlands from which the sample is drawn (see also chapter 5.2.3), whereas for the variables CHECK and QUALITY it is not clear at first glance.

Table 6.10 Comparative analysis: Description of variables

	This study	Collis et al. (2004)	Niemi et al. (2009)
SIZE	Number of employees. This is treated as a categorical variable coded "1" of the company is classified as medium sized or large by the category of employees and "0" if it is classified as small	Turnover in £	The natural logarithm of turnover in €
BANK	The existence of a lender requirement for an audit at the time of change in legislation (1 = yes, 0 = no)	Whether the statutory accounts of the company are given to the bank (1 = yes, 0 = no)	Whether the company uses outside (bank) financing (1 = yes, 0 = no)
OWNERSHIP	The percentage of shares held by management in the company (1 = 50% or more, 0 < 50%)	Whether the company is wholly family-owned (1 = yes, 0 = no)	Whether the company is family-owned (1 = yes, 0 = no)
CHECK	Extent of agreement that the audit provides a check on the accounting records and systems (1 = strong disagree, 5 = strong agree)	Extent of agreement that the audit provides a check on the accounting records and systems (1 = strong disagree, 5 = strong agree)	Extent of agreement that the audit provides a check on the accounting records and systems (1 = strong disagree, 5 = strong agree)
QUALITY	Extent of agreement that the audit improves the quality of the prepared financial statements (1 = strong disagree, 5 = strong agree)	Extent of agreement that the audit improves the quality of the prepared financial statements (1 = strong disagree, 5 = strong agree)	Extent of agreement that the audit improves the quality of the prepared financial statements (1 = strong disagree, 5 = strong agree)
FINEDUCATION[102]	Whether the company has a qualified head of the financial department, proxying for the awareness of the cost and benefit of an audit (1 = yes, 0 = no)	Whether the respondent has a degree in business management, proxying for the awareness of the cost and benefit of an audit (1 = yes, 0 = no)	Awareness of the cost and benefit of an audit (1 = strong disagree, 5 = strong agree)

The data of the variables CHECK and QUALITY are in all studies collected by likert-scale questions and present the perception of the extent of agreement that the audit provides a check on the accounting records and systems (CHECK) or improves the quality of the prepared financial statements (QUALITY). Table 6.11 provides the medians of these two variables from the different studies and the percentages of companies which (would) opt for a non-mandatory audit.

---

[102] Following Collis et al. (2004) variable FINEDUCATION is been used as a proxy to express the knowledge of the costs and benefits of an audit. It is therefore that Niemi et al. (2009) in their comparative analysis use a likert scale variable (measuring the awareness of the cost and benefit of an audit). In this study the variable FINEDUCATION originally was used to hypothesize the relationship that companies with low levels of accounting expertise more likely would demand an audit (see chapter 5). However, the results show to be significant in the opposite direction, which possibly could be explained by a more substantive knowledge of the benefits of an audit (see chapter 5.6). Given this direction and given the comparative analysis it is decided to use this variable as a 'more or less'

Table 6.11 Comparative analysis: Means of variables in analysis						
	This study		Collis et al.		Niemi et al.	
	N	*Mean*	*N*	*Mean*	*N*	*Mean*
CHECK	154	3.360	366	4.150	311	2.257
QUALITY	153	2.930	364	3.150	311	3.841
% DVA 'Yes'	62.2%		63%		79.7%	

It shows that the percentage of companies that choose (or is willing to) a non-mandatory audit in both this study and the study of Collis et al. is 62/63%. Whereas the % of companies willing to continue with a voluntary audit in the eventual absence of a mandatory audit regime in Finland is around 80%. A possible explanation for the higher percentage in Finland may be the existing mandatory audit regime. As shown in table 4.2 of chapter 4, unlike the Netherlands and the United Kingdom, currently almost all Finnish companies are mandatory required by national law to have their financial statements audited (Niemi et al., 2009). From a sociological point of view of 'isomorphism'[103] this may explain why management of companies are more willing to continue with the audit. Another explanation may be the existence of cultural differences between the Netherlands, the United Kingdom and Finland. In table 4.1 of chapter 4.2.1.2 an overview is presented of the cultural differences between these countries (Hofstede, 2001). The level of uncertainty avoidance in Finland compared to the Netherlands and the United Kingdom might be an explanation for the difference in the mean of the variable QUALITY (see table 6.12), whereas the masculinity and short term orientation of the United Kingdom might explain the difference in the mean for the variable CHECK of the United Kingdom compared to the Netherlands and Finland.

The variable OWNERSHIP showed to be not significant in the Dutch and Finnish sample whereas this variable showed to be significant in the UK sample. A clear explanation for this difference is not eligible, although it should be noticed that the direction of the sign in all studies is in line with the predicted sign. Furthermore, the difference in significance of the individual independent

---

similar variable to the variables used in the studies of Collis et al. (2004) and Niemi et al. (2009) to proxy for the cost and benefit of an audit.
[103] Dimaggio and Powell (1983) in their paper "The Iron Cage Revisited: Institutional Isomorphism and Collective Rationality in Organizational Fields" describe the phenomenon of isomorphism. They identify three types of isomorphism: coercive isomorphism, mimetic isomorphism and normative isomorphism. It is argued that as a result of isomorphism organizations become more homogeneous. Isomorphism can be described as a constraining process that forces an individual company in a population to resemble other companies that face the same set of environmental conditions. Given the fact that almost all companies in Finland are audited both coercive isomorphism and mimetic isomorphism could possible force companies to continue with the audit.

variables in this study compared to Collis et al. and Niemi et al. is also expressed in the relative low Wald chi-square of 43.35 of the logistic regression model. Although this chi-square is significant at the p < .001 level, which indicates that the model fits the data, it suggests that in the Dutch situation other more powerful explanatory variables may exist. As we know from section 6.3.2 this is indeed the case. Nevertheless this comparative analysis showed that, although differences exist which to some extent can be attributed to historical and cultural differences in the development of auditing between the different countries, it can be concluded that it appears that many drivers for the demand for audit in SME companies seem to be similar across the different countries.

Table 6.12 Comparative analysis of the Dutch model versus Collis et al. (2004) and Niemi et al. (2009)

Label	Predicted	This study		Collis et al. (2004)		Niemi et al. (2009)	
		coefficient	p-value	coefficient	p-value	coefficient	p-value
INTERCEPT	?	-3.196	<.001***	-4.550	<.001***	-12.268	<.001***
SIZE	+	1.034	0.052*	0.333	0.026**	0.550	<.001***
BANK	+	1.058	0.031**	0.592	0.049**	0.680	0.057*
OWNERSHIP	-	-0.627	0.132	-0.632	0.042**	-0.361	0.597
CHECK	+	0.550	0.024**	0.579	<.001***	0.708	<.001***
QUALITY	+	0.490	0.042**	0.626	<.001***	1.079	<.001***
FINEDUCATION	+	0.386	0.370	1.140	0.001**	0.523	0.020**

Model summary

N		153		332		311	
Wald chi-square		43.35***		93.50***		65.72***	
p-value		<.001		<.001		<.001	
-2 Log likelihood		160.675		311.09		349.27	
Pseudo R^2		0.335		0.348		0.313	

For variable definition, see Table 6.11 The reference category of dependent variables is "no" which indicated that the respective company has not opt for a voluntary audit (the Dutch setting) or is not willing to incur non-mandatory audit (UK and Finland). ***p <0.001, ** p < 0.05, * p <0.10; p-values are two-tailed.

Chapter 7.   Conclusions and discussion

7.1   Introduction

Do financial statements audits have added value? Economic scandals, an ongoing proceduralization[104] of the audit profession are examples of events that negatively affects public perception of the value of auditing. Nonetheless, legislators still consider auditing as a cornerstone in the 'trust-mechanisms' of financial economic markets, particular referring to the audit of large public entities. But do audits also have added value for private companies? It showed that a lack of scientific research exists with regard to the demand for audit for private (SME) companies (Willekens, 2008). Whereas the results of the studies which previously focussed on private companies suggest that the value of auditing for SME companies may be valuable for other reasons than the 'classic agency theory argument' underlying the demand for audit in general (Knechel et al., 2008).

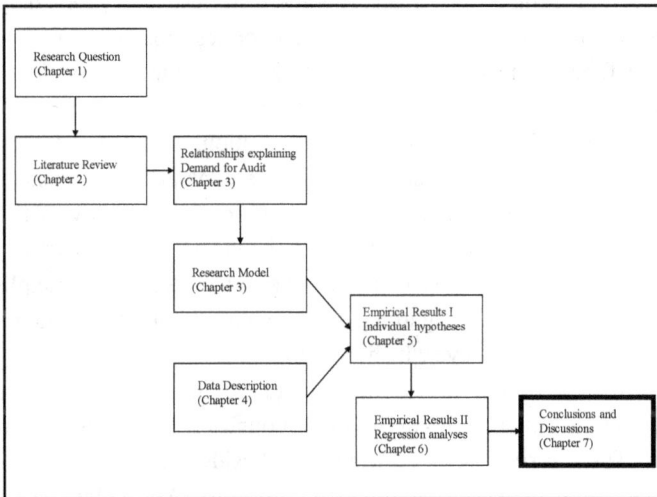

Figure 7.1: Overview of the structure of this study

The objective of this study is to contribute to the existing literature on the value of auditing for private SME companies and the research question of this study has been formulated as: *What are drivers for the demand for audit in a non-*

---

[104] The concept of proceduralization is a result of the (risks encountered in the) reflexive modernity as described by scholars as Giddens (1990) and Beck (1992, 1999). Proceduralization is the transformation of a social context of legal freedom (e.g. the audit profession as standard setter) in a system of justification, standardization and codification of the new social context. In other words: proceduralization of the audit profession includes among others the process of development and implementation of standards, procedures and laws.

mandatory environment? A literature review and empirical research have been conducted to find answers for this question. This chapter will summarize the results, discuss possible implications and provide some suggestions for future research in the area of the demand for audit in general and for SME companies more specifically. In section 7.2 the results of this study are summarized and the overall conclusions are presented. Followed, in section 7.3, by a discussion of possible implications for the demand for audit based on the derived conclusions of this study. Section 7.4 discusses the limitations of this study. This chapter is concluded with suggestions for further research in section 7.5.

7.2   Summary and overall conclusions

To answer the research question of this study, first the question is asked: why is there a demand for audit in contemporary society? In chapter 2 it is described that with the rise of modern corporations and the subsequently rise of financial capital markets ('the market place for large corporations to raise (new) capital'), auditing emerged as a control mechanism to make economies more efficient. To protect the effective functioning of capital markets in economic society, legislators in most countries have impeded mandatory audit regimes. As modern auditing arose as a result of the rise of the modern corporation, the demand for auditing generally is also explained by economic theories explaining the existence of the those corporations. Agency theory, and more specific the theory of the firm of Jensen and Meckling (1976), is considered to be the paradigm to explain the demand for audit. Various scholars in the audit research discipline have conducted empirical studies regarding the demand for audit to validate agency theory (chapter 2.2.3). However, it showed that only a relative limited number of empirical studies were able to use the demand for audit as a variable, probably caused by the fact that auditing in most countries for public companies is mandatory. Their results also indicate that besides the theoretical expected relationships the demand for audit, especially for SME companies, may be valuable for other reasons than the 'classical agency theory argument'. Furthermore, it is noticed that the paradigm, i.e agency theory, is being criticized by other scholars in other disciplines (e.g. organization theory). An analysis of the main criticism brought forward against agency theory has been conducted, to see if this criticism could have possible consequences for the demand for audit and could contribute to our understanding of the drivers for the demand for audit. The analysis revealed two themes which could have consequences for theory development and the identification of the existence of additional drivers for the demand for audit: the view of the firm as an institution in society and the 'bounded rationality' of decision makers. Variables testing for hypothesized relationships, based on these themes, are included in the empirical part of this study. Chapter three discussed more in detail the relationships explaining the demand for audit in previous empirical research and the variables used. Given the aim of this study to include as many as possible relationships in the research model, a total of 22 relationships, new and already known from previous studies, were identified as possible drivers for the demand for audit.

Chapter four, five and six empirically investigated the drivers for the demand for audit in a Dutch private SME setting. First, a brief sketch was provided of the historical development of auditing in the Netherlands and audit regulation. As Dutch data is used and it is postulated that auditing is a social control mechanism, the possibility exists that the empirically results of this study may differ from the results of other studies which can be contributed to specific economic, historical and cultural factors. The descriptive results show that 62% of the companies chooses to have their financial statements audited, even if it is no longer mandatory. This finding is comparable with the results of a study done in the UK (Collis et al., 2004), but between the 10-15% lower than the results of the studies in Canada (Senkow et al., 2001) and Finland (Niemi et al., 2009). This could be explained by size and the corresponding risks (large private Canadian companies) and sociological/cultural factors (almost all Finnish companies are currently mandatory obliged by national law to have their financial statements audited).

The results of individual hypothesis testing of identified relationships with the demand for audit in chapter five showed that perceptions held by decision makers do have a strong significant relationship with the demand for audit. The perception held by management that shareholder's desire an audit influences their decision whether or not to have the financial statements audited. Whereas, the commonly used proxy variables such as management ownership share, showed to be moderately significant or even not significant. Using bounded rationality theory, it is reasoned that (economic) facts do play a role in the perception people have. As such the variables 'proxying' the shareholder relationship are to be expected to influence the perception. The additional analysis in chapter 6.4 showed that a relationship exists between the perception and the proxy variables. A comparative analysis in chapter 6.5 of the results of this study with the study of Collis et al. (2004) and Niemi et al. (2009) showed that the main drivers for the demand for audit in SME companies seem to be similar.

From the results the multivariate regression analysis in chapter 6.3, the following observations can be made regarding the (main) drivers for the demand for audit:

The classical shareholder – manager relationship is the most important driver for the demand for audit

The results of this study implicate, that in a private SME setting the relationship between shareholder and manager is the most important driver for the demand for audit. This supports the explanatory power of the theory of the firm, as set out by Jensen and Meckling (1976). With respect to this relationship it can be observed that when the company has shareholders without access to internal financial information audit demand increases. In other words, not the existence (number of, or % shares) of the shareholder-manager relationship is important, but the nature of the relationship between the shareholder and the manager (company). The latter could be further supported by the observation of the significance of another shareholder-manager relationship variable used, management's ownership share. In general, it is hypothesized that the higher management's ownership share, the lower the probability the company demands an audit. However, the results showed that this is not a main driver. The existence of shareholders without access to internal financial information can be a driver for the demand for audit both from the perspective of the shareholder as of management. As without access to internal financial information, the shareholder is dependent on the financial information provided by management. The existence of shareholders without access also has a significant influence on the perceptions held by management regarding shareholder's need for audited financial statements as is shown the additional analysis of chapter 6.4.

The existence of a lender requirement is another main driver for the demand for audit

The relationship between the providers of debt capital and the company is considered to be another important driver for the demand for audit. With respect to this relationship, it is hypothesized that the higher the proportion of debt in the company's capital structure, the higher the probability the company demands an audit. It is also hypothesized that auditing reduces the cost of debt capital. The existence of a lender requirement is another variable, considered to be a driver for the demand for audit. It is hypothesized that providers of debt capital uses lender requirements to limit the potential conflict of interest with the shareholder/manager. Whereas, the results of this study, as presented in chapter 5.2.2 (individual hypotheses) and chapter 6.3 (logistic regression model), showed that leverage and the cost of debt are no drivers for the demand for audit, the existence of a lender requirement showed to be a main driver. The existence of a lender requirement can be considered to be part of the outcome of negotiations between the bank and the company. To mitigate their risks the bank demands an audit as condition under which they are willing to provide the loan. This latter could indicate that other 'risk' considerations, than for example leverage, are of more importance for lenders of debt capital in their need for a demand for audit. A suggestion for future research is to investigate which determinants are driving lenders of debt capital to negotiate a lender requirement in which an audit is demanded.

On the use of size criteria explaining the demand for audit
To determine whether or not a company classified for a mandatory audit, the following size criteria are used: total assets, turnover and number of employees. This study uses data of a population which, as a result of deregulation, no longer are classified as medium sized companies in 2006. As such, the population of this study to some extent can be considered as homogenous regarding their size. From the results of the bivariate analyses in chapter 5.2.3 it can be concluded that only the number of employees has a significant positive relationship with the demand for audit. However, the number of employees does not only proxy for the wealth at risk for external stakeholders, but can also proxy the loss of control (and subsequently the complexity) within the company (Abdel-khalik, 1993). In chapter 6.2.3 a multivariate analysis of the combined size factors and the demand for audit is conducted. Based on the pseudo R^2 of 0.062 (see panel D of table 6.4) it can be concluded that the size factors in this study have a low explanatory power to predict the demand for audit and of the size factors only the number of employees showed to be significant. This low explanatory power of the size-criteria in this study is to be expected given the population of SME companies. However, as we know from the descriptive statistics (chapter 4.3.5), the percentage of companies which opt for a non-mandatory audit in this study is 62%. Given this percentage it can be questioned if (current levels of) size criteria are appropriate to determine whether or not a SME company should have its financial statements mandatorily audited.

Perceptions held by management
Similar to the studies of Collis et al. (2004), Niemi et al. (2009) and Collis (2010), this study also found a significant positive relationship between the perceptions held by management that the audit has added value as a check on internal controls and the improvement of the quality of the prepared financial statements and the demand for audit. From other empirical studies (using the demand for audit as a variable or using a proxy as audit fee or audit choice) it is known that the relationship between the demand for audit and internal control sometimes showed mixed results (chapter 3.2.2). As these studies used other variables to proxy for this relationship, e.g. the relation between the audit fee and the internal audit budget, it can be questioned if a relationship between these variables and the perceptions held by management exists. This study added an additional perception variable to the commonly used proxy variables measuring

the relationship between the shareholder-manager relation and the demand for audit (see chapter 3.3.1). The results of the individual hypothesis testing in chapter 5.2.1.3 showed a positive significant association between the perception held by management that an audit of financial statements is desired by existing shareholders and the demand for audit. Besides this variable, this study also used variables based on factual data, such as management-ownership share, the number of shareholders and the existence of shareholders without access to internal financial information for testing the association between the shareholder (owner) – manager relationship and the demand for audit. Although the results in chapter 5.2.1, with the exception of the management ownership share, showed to have a positive significant relationship, they have less predictive power in the multivariate regression model of chapter 6.3 than the perception held by management that an audit is desired by existing shareholders on the demand for audit. To explore the existence and influence of factual data on the perceptions held, using bounded rationality theory, an additional analysis has been conducted in chapter 6.4. The results of this test showed a significant positive association, indicating that the perception held to some extent can be explained by existing factual data.

7.3   Discussion

The results of this study can serve as a basis for further discussion about the theory of the demand for auditing and can contribute to the search for a more richer picture of the drivers for the demand for audit. The results can also be used for a discussion about the current practical implications of a mandatory audit regime for private companies, for example the usability of the current used criteria for the mandatory audit regime.

7.3.1   Implications for research regarding the demand for audit

What do the results of this study tell us? First and most important it can be concluded that, even in absence of a mandatory obligation, the demand for audit to a large extent can be explained by the current paradigm, agency theory. The results of this study also shows that other drivers for the demand for audit in private companies exist. As such this study supports the claim made by a number of scholars (e.g. Knechel et al., 2008) that an audit for private companies may be valuable for other reasons. Although, using only the agency theory and the theory of the firm (Jensen and Meckling, 1976) to explain the demand for audit produces just satisfactory results. A too narrow focus on this theory increases the risk that other possible drivers for the demand for audit will be overlooked and are excluded. Also sticking to the assumptions underlying these theories, bears the risk of underestimating the considerations made in real life.

The results of this study suggest that perceptions held play a profound role in the decision whether or not to opt for a non-mandatory audit (e.g. the perceptions that shareholder's need an audit and the perception that an audit provides a check on internal controls and improves the quality of the financial information). This study does not reveal the building blocks for the emergence of the perceptions held. However, the conducted additional analyses showed that present factual circumstances (e.g. the existence of shareholders without access to internal financial information) have a significant association with the perceptions held. Besides, anecdotic evidence showed that holding a negative perception leads to a view on auditing which subsequently could negatively impacts the demand for audit[105]. Thus, decision makers do not only make the theoretically expected rational economic cost-benefit analysis, but as the results of this study showed the decision is also influenced by perceptions. For researchers in the field of psychology and organizational theory, the role and influence of perceptions on the decision making process is nothing new and already has been the subject of a large number of studies for many years (e.g. Simon, 1982; Kahneman and Tversky, 1982). The influence of these perceptions has, to my knowledge, not yet received much attention in the demand for audit research. However it is noticeable that studies looking at the effect of audited financial statements on loan officers decision (e.g. Wright and Davidson, 2000) explicitly takes into account the perceptions held by loan officers. Whereas several studies noticed the role of perceptions or used perceptions as variable (Jensen and Payne, 1993; Collis et al., 2004; Niemi et al., 2009; Collis, 2010) to explain the demand for audit, no calls have yet been made to explore the drivers for the perceptions held in more detail. A possible explanation for this lack may be the focus on quantitative empirical research in the studies explaining the demand for audit. However, as the results of this study showed the robustness of some of the perceptions held by management and the demand for audit in different institutional settings, it gives rise for researchers to gain further insights into the conditions (including the microeconomic determinants) that might predispose the perceptions held by management (supposing that they are the ultimate decision maker) regarding the

---

[105] An example of these negative perceptions is the view 'auditing is mandatory' combined with the Dutch culture of aversion to detailed rules and regulation to ensure compliance. Also the qualitative responses of a number of respondents (see chapter 4.3.3.1) indicate the importance of (whether or not irrational) negative perceptions regarding the audit in the decision making process: "An audit is not very effective to detect fraud and also does not contribute to an improvement of our business operations, therefore it is too costly", "The current audit is redundant and time and cost consuming as the auditors do not have industry knowledge. As a result our relation with the audit firm deteriorated".

need for audited financial statements by stakeholders and the added value of an audit for their own purposes. We will discuss some opportunities for future research in this area in further detail in section 7.5.

Although the results of this study showed that agency theory is capable to predict the demand for audit to a large extent, these findings should not serve as a justification not to explore for rivalling theories or other drivers to enable us to find a more comprehensive predictive theory (Wallace, 2004). In a time where the concept of auditing and the audit profession becomes more and more scrutinized, a call is made for exploring to which extent theoretical progress in neighbouring disciplines may have implications for our theory development regarding the demand for audit? By relaxing some of the assumptions underlying agency theory, this study shows that this is fruitful. A way of gaining further insight in the demand for audit may be (a reconsidering of the) the validation of the current theory explaining the demand for audit. Should the audit research discipline in its attempt to increase knowledge of the demand for audit also "reinventing the wheel" of years ago as Fukuyama (2004) signals in other economic disciplines? Looking into history, it is clear that modern auditing serves as a mechanism to reduce uncertainty between participants in (economic) society. Economic exchanges between participants has much to do with 'trust' participants place in each other and in 'the market'. The rise of modern auditing therefore can be attributed to societal changes and technology development. With the separation of capital/ownership and management, the risk of providers of capital increased as they became dependent on the acts and information provided by management. But as we know the world has become more complex and interdependent, resulting that also the interests of other actors in society can be at risk. Therefore actors within society (including actors within the company) who are facing uncertainty related to this risk may have a need to mitigate this risk. As it is clear that these risks are more profoundly apparent with large companies, this also could be the case in the situation of private SME companies. For scholars researching the demand for audit it might be of interest to take notice of attempts made by scholars in neighbouring disciplines (e.g. transaction cost economics) to incorporate other lenses (Möllering, 2006) into the demand for audit theory to relax the behavioural assumptions underlying the current paradigm and increase realism into the model. Suggestions for research possibilities in this area will be presented in section 7.5.

7.3.2 Implications for current audit practice

Is it necessary to have mandatory audit regime for private SME companies? Is size to be considered a sufficient criteria to 'proxy' for the mandatory audit? Whereas in the United States only public listed companies are required to have their financial statements audited, all member states of the European Union have a mandatory audit regime for private SME companies. EU legislation requires member states to install at least the size criteria as set by the European Union (see chapter 4.3.1), although a more stringent regime is allowed. As a result all companies that meet those size criteria are mandatory obliged to have their financial statements audited. This mandatory audit regime for private SME companies combined with recent developments such as several corporate scandals and more stringent oversight on the audit profession 'fuels' a growing public discussion regarding the added value of auditing, whereby some criticasters even suggest to abolish the audit. Besides this, the European Commission is currently evaluating existing audit policies (European Commission, 2010). The results of this study contribute to this discussion as it confirms that, given the existence of certain drivers, the audit does have added value.

However, the question remains: Is it necessary to have a mandatory audit regime for SME companies? Is size still to be considered the only variable to 'proxy' for the mandatory audit? The findings of this study showed that in absence of a mandatory requirement almost two third of the companies opt for an audit. Also the results of this study showed that the demand for audit to a large extent can be explained by the identified drivers for the demand for audit, whereby the shareholder – manager relationship showed to be the most significant driver for the demand for audit. However, the results of the size criteria showed to be not significant, with the exception of the number of employees, and only to a small amount contributed to the explanatory power of the demand for audit model. The latter could be explained as the population of this study, based on the size criteria, to some extent could be considered as homogenous (see chapter 6.2.3).

Based on the findings of this study it can be concluded that other criteria than size are potentially more capable to predict the demand for audit. It is therefore suggested that legislators reconsider the usefulness of the current size criteria to require companies to have their financial statements audited. Besides this, legislators could also reconsider the usefulness of the current mandatory audit regime taking into account the protection of stakeholders who do not have the (economic) power[106] to negotiate a demand for audit. Replacing the current mandatory audit regime with for example incorporating in company law that minority shareholders have the possibility to demand an audit and giving this possibility also to the works council may be alternatives to consider[107]. This study contributes to the enrichment of our knowledge of the drivers for the demand for audit (in other words: who is demanding an audit and why?) and as such offers legislators the opportunity to install more effective legislation and at the same time lessen the administrative burden of companies.

For auditors and audit firms the findings of this study may be beneficial as it contributes to the enrichment of the knowledge that the added value of an audit is indeed multifaceted (Knechel et al., 2008) and that the existence of a mix of different drivers may the inducement for the demand for audit. In the absence of a mandatory audit regime, auditors have to 'sell' (and in a broader context: (re)convincing (economic) society of the benefits of the audit in general) the added value of an audit. Combined with the recognition that decision makers are ultimately 'satisficers', which only include those elements which they think that are of importance in their decision making process, the findings of this study may support auditors and audit firms to discuss potential existing drivers not included. Broadening the view of possible existing other potential benefits of the audit increases the subjective environment of the decision maker regarding the audit and subsequently could have an influence on the ultimate decision made.

7.4   Limitations of this study

This study has investigated what the drivers are for the demand for audit in a non-mandatory environment. As with most research this study is susceptible to a number of limitations. Although many potential drivers are included in this study, due to difficulties in data collection not all drivers for the demand for audit are included in the multivariate regression analysis. As a result of the literature review of chapter two and three a total of 22 relationships have been identified as potential drivers for the demand for audit. However, due to the initial number of 154 returned questionnaires (chapter 4.3.3.2) not all relationships could be included in the multivariate regression analysis. To reduce the risk of 'overfit', parsimonious methods had to be carried out to reduce the number of relationships

---

[106] It is expected that for instance banking institutions and large creditors have the (economic) power to demand an audit (see chapter 5.6).

[107] In the United Kingdom it is incorporated in company law that if 10% of the shareholders demands an audit, the company is obliged to have their financial statements audited. In the Netherlands a law on works councils ('wet op de ondernemingsraden') exists which requires companies with a certain number of employees to install a working council.

(chapter 6.2.2). Theoretically, including all relationships in a larger sample could lead to other results. Also, due to difficulties in data collection, it was not always possible to use more refined measures to predict relationships. For example for the degree of loss of control/complexity, earnings management and financial health more refined measures exists than those used in this study.

Another limitation is related to the selection of the population. Due to the fact that the population consists of all companies, which as a result of deregulation no longer classify as medium sized, the sample spans a limited range in size, which potentially limits the generalizing ability of this study. However, the comparative analysis performed with other studies (see chapter 6.5) indicates that a number of drivers for the demand for audit seems to be similar. Also the use of questionnaires introduces several limitations, already noticed in chapter four. For example, with the use of any survey study the concern of potential non response bias exists. These limitations has been addressed in chapter 4.3.3.2.

Finally, for a number of identified relationships in this study, variables are used involving the perceptions held by management at the time of decision making. However, due to the 'time-gap', between the actual decision to (dis) continue the audit and the perceptions held at the time of responding to the questionnaire, the perceptions may be 'coloured' by latter events. Also, perceptions held are, besides the existence of factual knowledge, the result of personal characteristics of the decision maker. Therefore the risk exists that social desirable answers have been given by the respondents. The underlying conditions for the perceptions held have not been investigated in this study, but offers avenues for future research.

7.5   Further research

Based on the discussion and implications of the findings of this study some suggestions for future research already have been addressed. Also the discussion of the limitations of this study raised suggestions for future research. In this chapter we will explore a few, at first glance other avenues for future research regarding the demand for audit, which could be of interest in enriching our understanding of the drivers for the demand for audit.

The complexity of the environment in which a private SME company operates may be a possible driver for the demand for audit. Although in general it is assumed that private SME companies are less complex (Abdel-khalik, 1993; Knechel et al., 2008), empirical research shows that with an increase of complexity the demand for audit or the demand for high quality audits increases.

Most of these studies have focused on the complexity within the organization (organizational control) to determine whether there is a relationship between complexity and the demand for audit and in general found a positive significant relationship. However, due to changes in society (e.g. globalization, technological developments), the way companies (entities) are organized are also subject to changes. The evolution of a 'network economy' and the existence of independent suppliers in a supply chain are examples of these changes. Even if private SME companies in itself do not have to be complex, they may be an essential part of a larger complex economic structure. This latter phenomenon could be a driver for the demand for audit also, as the other participants in the network of supply chain are interdependent on the continuing existence and reliability of network or the supply chain as a whole[108]. Future research, viewing the private SME company as an institution in society and exploring the complexity of the 'web' the company is operating in, may contribute to the enrichment of our knowledge for the drivers for the demand for audit[109].

In absence of a mandatory audit regime, the results of this study indicates that a 'mix' of factors[110] influences the decision. It can also be concluded that in the absence of a mandatory audit regime the role of perceptions held by management becomes more profoundly apparent in their decision making process whether or not to opt for an audit. As this study has followed a quantitative research approach, the necessary data regarding the perceptions has been gathered using likert-scale questions in a questionnaire. However, perceptions are built on the subjective interpretation of perceived factual circumstances that are to be considered relevant and are taken into account in the decision making process. As such the followed research approach does not reveal the determinants which underlie the perceptions, and the ultimate influence in the decision making process of management. To explore these determinants, the use of a qualitative research approach may be more appropriate. Although qualitative research have some obvious shortcomings as a research technique (e.g. whether the observed verbal protocol reflects the true thought processes of management in an actual

---

[108] To mitigate the risk associated with these interdependence 'outsiders' may have also demand other monitoring mechanism. The existence of outside directors in private SME companies (which is not mandatory for private SME companies in the Netherlands) may be to some extent also the result of the existence of 'outside complexity'. This study did take into account the existence of outside directors, but did not investigate the reasons why companies voluntarily installed a committee of outside directors.

[109] It should be noticed that besides the demand for financial statement audit, this phenomenon may also give rise to a demand for other types of audits, such as an audit of systems and/or processes.

[110] The results of the full logistic regression model (see table 6.7) showed to be strong significant (p<0.001) indicating the model as a whole is significant. Also the explanatory power of the model can be considered to be high (pseudo R^2 of 0.604).

decision making process), qualitative research offers unique insights which cannot be obtained using a quantitative research approach.

Also a point of interest to investigate in future research, may be the incorporation of a 'social-context variable' into the demand for audit model. A call for introducing such a variable has already been made in the context of transaction cost economics (Chiles and McMackin, 1996). Whereas this study postulates that auditing is a social control mechanism and recognizes that historical and cultural factors can possibly influence the demand for audit. Adding a 'social-context variable' in the demand for audit creates the possibility to explore whether this parameter adds to our knowledge in understanding whether or not an audit in different settings is demanded and the factors driving this demand.

Furthermore, the results of this study showed that even in absence of a mandatory regime, a demand for audit in private SME companies exists. Knowing that we are living in a globalizing world and knowing that private companies in for example the USA and Canada (Senkow et al., 2001) are not subject to a mandatory audit regime. Also knowing that the existence of mandatory audit regime bears the disadvantage to exclude other potential benefits of the audit (see also chapter 2.4.3). Therefore it might of interest to investigate whether current (European) mandatory audit regime for private companies still is the most desirable and to investigate the 'pros and cons' of a further alleviation of existing mandatory audit regime for (large and medium-sized) private companies.

Finally, a lack of insight why contemporary society demands an audit accommodates the risk of not meeting the needs and expectations of society and as a result auditing may be perceived to have no added value and become redundant, a call is made to continue this study into a longitudinal study regarding the factors driving the demand for audit. Within Europe, conducting such a longitudinal study can contribute to the ongoing harmonisation process.

Appendix I   Questionnaire

This appendix contains an extract of the questionnaire showing variables analysed, the cover letter and the reminder. As the questionnaire and the accompanied cover letters were sent to Dutch companies, the remainder of this appendix is Dutch.

UNIVERSITEIT VAN AMSTERDAM

Amsterdam Business School

Bijlage bij brief 18 januari 2010

VRAGENLIJST ONDERZOEK TOEGEVOEGDE WAARDE ACCOUNTANTSCONTROLE

Aan welke groottecriteria voldoet de onderneming (inclusief eventueel te consolideren dochterondernemingen) volgens de laatste jaarrekening?:
Kruis aan wat van toepassing is

Netto-omzet in €

< 8,8 mln	8,8 - 35 mln	> 35 mln

Balanstotaal in €

< 4,4 mln	4,4 - 17,5 mln	> 17,5 mln

Aantal werknemers

< 50	50 - 250	> 250

Hoeveel aandeelhouders (eigenaren) heeft de onderneming?

Aantal aandeelhouders

Aantal aandeelhouders met toegang tot de interne financiële administratie

Aantal aandeelhouders zonder toegang tot de interne financiële administratie

Bezit het management aandelen in de onderneming?

JA

NEE

Zo ja, bezit het management meer dan 50% van van het aandelenkapitaal van de onderneming?

JA

NEE

Beschikt de onderneming over een Raad van Commissarissen?

JA

NEE

Beschikt de onderneming over een afdeling financiële administratie?

JA

NEE

HBD/2010/TWA/<UNIEK IDENTIFICATIENUMMER>

Wat is de hoogst genoten opleiding van het hoofd van de afdeling financiële administratie?

MBO

HBO

WO

Specifieke beroepsopleiding: ....

Welke partijen ontvangen een exemplaar van de jaarrekening?
Kruis aan wat van toepassing is, meerdere antwoorden mogelijk

Aandeelhouders

Bank(-en) en andere financieringsverstrekkers

Directeuren / managers die geen aandeelhouder zijn

Werknemers

Belastingdienst

(Grote) leveranciers

(Grote) afnemers / klanten

Anderen, namelijk: ....

Accountantscontrole op de jaarekening wordt uitgevoerd op verzoek van:
Bank(-en) en andere financieringsverstrekkers, het is als verplichting
opgenomen in de financieringsvoorwaarden

Hoeveel jaar wordt/werd op de jaarrekening reeds accountantscontrole toegepast?

Aantal jaren

Hoeveel jaar wordt door de **huidige accountant** de controle uitgevoerd?

Aantal jaren

Maakt de onderneming gebruik van een externe accountant om de jaarrekening op te stellen of samen te stellen? (dit betreft geen accountantscontrole)

JA

NEE

Welke diensten zijn de afgelopen 3 jaar afgenomen bij de externe accountant naast de controle van de jaarrekening (indien van toepassing)?
Kruis aan wat van toepassing is, meerdere antwoorden mogelijk

Opstellen periodieke financiële informatie (bijv. maandrapportages)

Verzorging van belastingaangiften / belastingadvies

Privé-belastingaangiften

Salarisadminstratie

Advies op het gebied van aantrekken financiering

Advies op gebied van inrichten administratieve organisatie

Overig, namelijk: ....

171

Wat is uw visie betreffende de volgende stellingen over accountantscontrole?

Omcirkel het getal dat het meest overeenkomt met uw mening:

5 = belangrijk, 1 = minst belangrijk

Verhoogt de kwaliteit van de financiële afdeling en interne controle	5	4	3	2	1
Verbetert de kwaliteit van de financiële informatie	5	4	3	2	1
Verhoogt de betrouwbaarheid van de opgestelde jaarrekening	5	4	3	2	1
Heeft positief effect op leningsvoorwaarden bij aantrekken financiering	5	4	3	2	1
Heeft een positief effect op de kredietwaardigheidsbeoordeling door credit company's zoals bijvoorbeeld Graydon of Dun and Bradstreet	5	4	3	2	1
Anders, namelijk:	5	4	3	2	1

Zou u een accountantscontrole laten uitvoeren, zelfs wanneer de onderneming hiertoe niet wettelijk verplicht is?

Kruis aan wat van toepassing is, één antwoord mogelijk:

JA, er vindt nu al vrijwillige accountantscontrole plaats ☐

JA ☐

NEE ☐

Hoe belangrijk zijn/waren de volgende factoren in de beslissing om wel / niet accountantscontrole te laten uitvoeren?

Omcirkel het getal dat het meest overeenkomt met uw mening:

5 = belangrijk, 1 = minst belangrijk

Aandeelhouders hebben behoefte aan een jaarrekening met accountantsverklaring	5	4	3	2	1
Verwachte groei van onderneming, waardoor onderneming op termijn weer onder wettelijke verplichting zal vallen	5	4	3	2	1
Anders, namelijk:	5	4	3	2	1

Ruimte voor opmerkingen:

....

....

....

....

Vriendelijk bedankt voor uw medewerking!
Voor het terugsturen van de vragenlijst kunt u gebruik maken van de bijgevoegde antwoordenveloppe

172

Amsterdam Business School

Amsterdam, 18 januari 2010

Betreft: onderzoek naar de toegevoegde waarde van accountantscontrole

Geachte heer/mevrouw,

In Nederland is door de wetgever bepaald dat ondernemingen van een bepaalde omvang jaarlijks verplicht accountantscontrole moeten laten uitvoeren.

Vraag is echter: zou een onderneming ook accountantscontrole laten uitvoeren indien zij hiertoe niet wettelijk is verplicht?

Momenteel wordt o.a. in Nederland gediscussieerd over vragen zoals:
- Moeten de wettelijke verplichtingen ten aanzien van accountantscontrole verder worden versoepeld?
- Wat is de toegevoegde waarde van accountantscontrole voor niet-beursgenoteerde ondernemingen?

In deze discussie is de visie van ondernemers ten aanzien van accountantscontrole van belang. Zij zijn immers degene die met deze regelgeving hebben te maken. Om inzicht te krijgen in de visie en behoeften van ondernemers voeren wij een onderzoek uit onder een specifieke groep ondernemingen naar de toegevoegde waarde van accountantscontrole. Uw onderneming behoort tot de geselecteerde groep van ondernemingen.

Wij willen u dan ook vriendelijk verzoeken om aan dit onderzoek mee te werken door het invullen van bijgevoegde vragenlijst. De vragenlijst is zodanig opgezet, zodat u deze in een tijdsbestek van maximaal 10 minuten kunt invullen. De ingevulde vragenlijst kunt u aan ons retourneren middels bijgevoegde retourenveloppe.

Het spreekt voor zich dat wij vertrouwelijk met uw antwoorden omgaan. Uw antwoorden worden uitsluitend gebruikt ten behoeve van ons onderzoek en worden niet gerapporteerd noch ter beschikking gesteld aan welke instantie dan ook.

Alvast hartelijk dank voor uw bijdrage aan ons onderzoek. Met de resultaten van ons onderzoek willen wij een bijdrage leveren aan het ondernemersklimaat en de dienstverlening van accountantskantoren in Nederland.

Met vriendelijke groet,

Drs. Hans B. Duits

cc. Prof. Dr. Ph. Wallage

Amsterdam Business School

Amsterdam, 2 maart 2010

Betreft: uw medewerking in het kader van een onderzoek naar de toegevoegde waarde van accountantscontrole

Geachte heer/mevrouw,

Medio januari hebben wij u bijgevoegde brief gestuurd met daarin het verzoek om deel te nemen aan ons onderzoek naar de toegevoegde waarde van accountantscontrole in Nederland.

Uw medewerking is belangrijk voor het welslagen van ons onderzoek!

Vandaar dat wij u middels deze brief nogmaals willen vragen om uw medewerking, door bijgevoegde vragenlijst in te vullen (dit kost u maximaal 10 minuten van uw tijd) en te retourneren middels de eveneens bijgevoegde retourenveloppe.

Alvast heel hartelijk dank en wij zien uit naar uw reactie.

Met vriendelijke groeten,

Drs. Hans B. Duits

cc. Prof. Dr. Ph. Wallage

Bijlagen: brief d.d. 18 januari 2010 / vragenlijst

Appendix II Results of Mann-Whithney Test for non-response bias[111]

Hypothesis Test Summary

	Null Hypothesis	Test	Sig.	Decision
1	The distribution of ASSETS is the same across categories of non response.	Independent-Samples Mann-Whitney U Test	.857	Retain the null hypothesis.
2	The distribution of SHRH# is the same across categories of non response.	Independent-Samples Mann-Whitney U Test	.116	Retain the null hypothesis.
3	The distribution of STAKE# is the same across categories of non response.	Independent-Samples Mann-Whitney U Test	.674	Retain the null hypothesis.
4	The distribution of LVRG is the same across categories of non response.	Independent-Samples Mann-Whitney U Test	.685	Retain the null hypothesis.
5	The distribution of CHECK is the same across categories of non response.	Independent-Samples Mann-Whitney U Test	.155	Retain the null hypothesis.
6	The distribution of QUALITY is the same across categories of non response.	Independent-Samples Mann-Whitney U Test	.533	Retain the null hypothesis.
7	The distribution of CREDIBLY is the same across categories of non response.	Independent-Samples Mann-Whitney U Test	.514	Retain the null hypothesis.
8	The distribution of LENDPLUS is the same across categories of non response.	Independent-Samples Mann-Whitney U Test	.435	Retain the null hypothesis.
9	The distribution of COMPCRED is the same across categories of non response.	Independent-Samples Mann-Whitney U Test	.732	Retain the null hypothesis.
10	The distribution of AUDTERM is the same across categories of non response.	Independent-Samples Mann-Whitney U Test	.070	Retain the null hypothesis.
11	The distribution of AUDSERV is the same across categories of non response.	Independent-Samples Mann-Whitney U Test	.276	Retain the null hypothesis.

Asymptotic significances are displayed. The significance level is .05.

---

[111]For the Mann-Whitney test the variables CHECK, QUALITY, CREDIBLY, LENDPLUS and COMPCRED are treated as 'interval-variables'.

Appendix III Multi collinearity: Tolerance and VIF tests

As the correlation matrix of Chapter six (see table 6.1) showed that there are some signs of correlation between independent variables, it is tested whether this correlation could result in the existence of multi collinearity. Multi collinearity exists when independent variables correlate linear with each other. Multi collinearity can increase estimates of coefficient variance, yield models in which no variable is statistically significant even though de explanatory power (R^2) of the model is large, create situations in which small changes in the data produce wide swings in the coefficients of estimates (Hosmer and Lemeshow, 2000; O'Brien, 2007; Mortelmans, 2010).

As multi collinearity is related to independent variables this makes the detection of multi collinearity in logistic regression models the same as in linear regression models. Two general accepted and commonly used statistic tests in linear regression to detect multi collinearity are: Tolerance and Variance Inflation Factor (VIF) (Hosmer and Lemeshow, 2000; Mortelmans, 2010).

Tolerance and Variance Inflation Fator (VIF):
De Tolerance of an independent variable is defined as: $TOL_j = 1 - R^2$independent variable. The Tolerance is a measure to test the proportion of variance, which an independent variable shares with the other independent variables. The R^2 shows to which extent the variance in this independent variable can be explained by the other independent variables. $1 - R^2$ indicates the portion unexplained variance. The outcome of the tolerance measure is between 0 and 1, whereby low tolerance values indicating a strong existence of multi collinearity.

The Variance Inflation Factor (VIF) is the reciprocal of tolerance: $1/(1 - R^2$independent variable). The VIF has an intuitive and clear interpretation in the terms of the effects of collinearity on the estimated variance of the estimated regression coefficient for the tested independent variable. "A VIF of 10 for an independent variable indicates that the variance of the regression coefficient is 10 times greater than it would have been if the tested independent variable had been linearly independent of the other variables in the analysis. Thus, it tells us how much the variance has been inflated by this lack of independence" (O'Brien, 2007: 684).

When do levels of measurement for Tolerance and VIF casting doubts on the existence of multi collinearity? Within the statistical literature several levels are proposed. Mortelmans (2010) notes that in general a level of 0.10 for tolerance (and 10 for VIF) is used. O'Brien refers to various authors proposing levels to be used: "Menard (1995:66) states "A tolerance of less than 0.20 is cause for concern; a tolerance of less than 0.10 almost certainly indicates a serious collinearity problem ... Neter et al. (1989: 409 state a maximum VIF value in excess of 10 is often taken as an indication that multi-collinearity may be unduly influencing the least square estimates. Hair et al. (1995) suggest that a VIF of less than 10 are indicative of inconsequential collinearity" (O'Brien, 2007: 688). Based on the levels suggested this study follows the rule of 10 for analyzing the results of the Tolerance and VIF tests.

If multi collinearity exists, there are several ways to deal with this problem. A commonly used practice is to remove one of the independent variables creating multi collinearity of the model. Removing of an independent variable can be justified as with the existence of high multi collinearity the other independent variable still controls for the removed independent variable. An alternative is to use ridge regression methods. However, the results of the Tolerance and VIF tests (see below) indicates that no serious multi collinearity problem exists for the independent variables used in this study.

Multi collinearity test : Tolerance (TOL)

	1	2	3	4	5	6	7	8	9	10	11	12
1. SHRH#		0.546	0.531	0.527	0.527	0.533	0.532	0.527	0.535	0.531	0.645	0.530
2. SHRHAC	0.687		0.665	0.669	0.735	0.680	0.701	0.665	0.678	0.672	0.664	0.665
3. STAKE#	0.835	0.830		0.830	0.857	0.860	0.833	0.829	0.830	0.852	0.830	0.829
4. MOWN50	0.733	0.738	0.734		0.805	0.733	0.733	0.766	0.747	0.756	0.735	0.736
5. SHRHND	0.492	0.545	0.509	0.540		0.494	0.494	0.497	0.509	0.506	0.509	0.496
6. CREDIBLY	0.534	0.541	0.548	0.528	0.530		0.547	0.531	0.528	0.561	0.528	0.529
7. LVRG	0.714	0.747	0.712	0.708	0.711	0.734		0.727	0.719	0.724	0.796	0.709
8. LRQM	0.603	0.604	0.603	0.630	0.609	0.607	0.619		0.676	0.606	0.607	0.626
9. LENDPLUS	0.580	0.583	0.572	0.582	0.591	0.571	0.580	0.640		0.705	0.577	0.570
10. COMPCRED	0.565	0.567	0.577	0.578	0.578	0.596	0.574	0.564	0.693		0.564	0.605
11. ASSETS	0.545	0.446	0.446	0.447	0.461	0.446	0.501	0.449	0.451	0.448		0.453
12. CATOMZ	0.620	0.617	0.617	0.619	0.622	0.618	0.618	0.640	0.616	0.665	0.626	
13. CATEMPLS	0.721	0.718	0.718	0.721	0.718	0.718	0.727	0.726	0.718	0.720	0.800	0.741
14. OUTDIR	0.671	0.654	0.633	0.634	0.637	0.633	0.657	0.709	0.638	0.633	0.633	0.638
15. CHECK	0.351	0.340	0.341	0.340	0.341	0.350	0.340	0.341	0.343	0.340	0.357	0.340
16. FINAFD	0.593	0.591	0.603	0.593	0.591	0.597	0.596	0.594	0.599	0.591	0.598	0.680
17. EDUFIN	0.692	0.694	0.699	0.697	0.700	0.697	0.693	0.693	0.705	0.692	0.712	0.692
18. QUALITY	0.344	0.352	0.344	0.343	0.358	0.372	0.344	0.344	0.348	0.347	0.343	0.343
19. AUDTERM	0.815	0.815	0.826	0.826	0.818	0.814	0.817	0.815	0.819	0.835	0.819	0.818
20. AUDSERV	0.643	0.638	0.613	0.614	0.644	0.612	0.632	0.690	0.653	0.613	0.612	0.619
21. AUDREP	0.608	0.604	0.591	0.595	0.601	0.599	0.596	0.609	0.596	0.591	0.654	0.594
22. HEALTH	0.842	0.811	0.821	0.806	0.805	0.829	0.805	0.811	0.808	0.812	0.850	0.805
23. STRAT	0.725	0.706	0.704	0.717	0.760	0.706	0.704	0.720	0.718	0.705	0.719	0.709

For variable definitions, see chapter 5 table 5.10

Multi collinearity test : Tolerance (TOL)

	13	14	15	16	17	18	19	20	21	22	23
1. SHRH#	0.529	0.558	0.544	0.528	0.527	0.529	0.527	0.554	0.542	0.552	0.542
2. SHRHAC	0.664	0.686	0.664	0.664	0.666	0.681	0.665	0.692	0.678	0.669	0.665
3. STAKE#	0.829	0.828	0.829	0.845	0.836	0.832	0.841	0.829	0.829	0.845	0.828
4. MOWN50	0.736	0.734	0.733	0.735	0.738	0.734	0.743	0.735	0.738	0.734	0.746
5. SHRHND	0.492	0.495	0.492	0.492	0.497	0.513	0.494	0.517	0.500	0.492	0.531
6. CREDIBLY	0.528	0.528	0.542	0.533	0.531	0.572	0.528	0.528	0.535	0.544	0.529
7. LVRG	0.716	0.734	0.707	0.713	0.709	0.711	0.710	0.730	0.714	0.708	0.707
8. LRQM	0.609	0.675	0.604	0.606	0.603	0.605	0.603	0.679	0.621	0.607	0.616
9. LENDPLUS	0.571	0.575	0.575	0.578	0.582	0.580	0.574	0.608	0.576	0.573	0.581
10. COMPCRED	0.562	0.561	0.561	0.561	0.561	0.568	0.575	0.561	0.561	0.566	0.561
11. ASSETS	0.497	0.445	0.467	0.451	0.459	0.445	0.448	0.445	0.493	0.471	0.455
12. CATOMZ	0.637	0.622	0.617	0.710	0.617	0.617	0.619	0.623	0.620	0.617	0.620
13. CATEMPLS		0.718	0.730	0.720	0.721	0.718	0.718	0.721	0.790	0.718	0.731
14. OUTDIR	0.633		0.649	0.638	0.634	0.647	0.635	0.665	0.636	0.645	0.645
15. CHECK	0.346	0.349		0.341	0.344	0.522	0.345	0.344	0.355	0.341	0.341
16. FINAFD	0.592	0.595	0.592		0.694	0.591	0.591	0.591	0.618	0.591	0.591
17. EDUFIN	0.695	0.693	0.699	0.812		0.694	0.694	0.693	0.692	0.692	0.693
18. QUALITY	0.343	0.351	0.525	0.343	0.344		0.345	0.343	0.348	0.347	0.343
19. AUDTERM	0.814	0.817	0.825	0.815	0.817	0.818		0.820	0.861	0.817	0.815
20. AUDSERV	0.614	0.643	0.618	0.613	0.613	0.612	0.617		0.631	0.612	0.613
21. AUDREP	0.650	0.594	0.617	0.618	0.591	0.600	0.625	0.609		0.591	0.599
22. HEALTH	0.804	0.819	0.805	0.804	0.805	0.814	0.808	0.805	0.805		0.805
23. STRAT	0.717	0.718	0.706	0.704	0.705	0.705	0.705	0.705	0.713	0.704	

For variable definitions, see chapter 5 table 5.10

Multi collinearity test : Variance Inflating Factor (VIF)

	1	2	3	4	5	6	7	8	9	10	11	12
1. SHRH#		1.833	1.882	1.899	1.898	1.875	1.880	1.896	1.868	1.883	1.551	1.888
2. SHRHAC	1.455		1.503	1.495	1.360	1.470	1.428	1.503	1.474	1.489	1.505	1.504
3. STAKE#	1.197	1.205		1.205	1.167	1.163	1.200	1.206	1.205	1.173	1.205	1.206
4. MOWN50	1.365	1.355	1.362		1.242	1.364	1.365	1.306	1.338	1.323	1.360	1.358
5. SHRHND	2.035	1.836	1.966	1.851		2.026	2.025	2.012	1.965	1.975	1.965	2.017
6. CREDIBLY	1.872	1.850	1.825	1.894	1.888		1.827	1.882	1.893	1.783	1.894	1.891
7. LVRG	1.400	1.340	1.405	1.413	1.407	1.363		1.376	1.391	1.381	1.256	1.410
8. LRQM	1.658	1.657	1.658	1.588	1.642	1.649	1.615		1.479	1.650	1.647	1.598
9. LENDPLUS	1.725	1.715	1.748	1.718	1.693	1.751	1.725	1.561		1.418	1.733	1.753
10. COMPCRED	1.769	1.763	1.733	1.730	1.731	1.678	1.743	1.774	1.443		1.774	1.652
11. ASSETS	1.833	2.243	2.240	2.237	2.169	2.244	1.995	2.227	2.219	2.233		2.210
12. CATOMZ	1.613	1.620	1.620	1.614	1.608	1.619	1.618	1.562	1.623	1.503	1.597	
13. CATEMPLS	1.387	1.393	1.392	1.387	1.392	1.392	1.375	1.378	1.393	1.389	1.250	1.349
14. OUTDIR	1.491	1.530	1.580	1.576	1.569	1.580	1.522	1.410	1.567	1.579	1.580	1.566
15. CHECK	2.847	2.937	2.936	2.938	2.935	2.860	2.939	2.933	2.914	2.938	2.803	2.938
16. FINAFD	1.688	1.692	1.660	1.688	1.692	1.676	1.679	1.683	1.670	1.693	1.674	1.470
17. EDUFIN	1.446	1.442	1.432	1.435	1.429	1.435	1.443	1.444	1.418	1.445	1.404	1.444
18. QUALITY	2.906	2.843	2.905	2.913	2.793	2.689	2.904	2.904	2.871	2.880	2.917	2.913
19. AUDTERM	1.227	1.226	1.210	1.211	1.223	1.228	1.225	1.227	1.222	1.198	1.220	1.223
20. AUDSERV	1.555	1.567	1.632	1.628	1.552	1.634	1.583	1.450	1.532	1.632	1.634	1.615
21. AUDREP	1.645	1.656	1.691	1.681	1.665	1.671	1.677	1.641	1.677	1.691	1.529	1.684
22. HEALTH	1.187	1.233	1.219	1.241	1.242	1.206	1.243	1.233	1.237	1.232	1.177	1.243
23. STRAT	1.380	1.417	1.420	1.395	1.315	1.416	1.420	1.389	1.394	1.419	1.392	1.411

For variable definitions, see chapter 5 table 5.10

Multi collinearity test : Variance Inflating Factor (VIF)

	13	14	15	16	17	18	19	20	21	22	23
1. SHRH#	1.891	1.791	1.839	1.893	1.898	1.891	1.897	1.807	1.845	1.813	1.844
2. SHRHAC	1.506	1.459	1.506	1.505	1.502	1.468	1.504	1.444	1.474	1.494	1.503
3. STAKE#	1.207	1.208	1.206	1.184	1.196	1.202	1.189	1.206	1.207	1.184	1.207
4. MOWN50	1.359	1.362	1.364	1.361	1.355	1.363	1.345	1.360	1.355	1.362	1.341
5. SHRHND	2.033	2.020	2.032	2.033	2.011	1.948	2.025	1.933	2.001	2.032	1.884
6. CREDIBLY	1.894	1.895	1.845	1.876	1.882	1.747	1.895	1.895	1.870	1.839	1.889
7. LVRG	1.396	1.362	1.414	1.402	1.411	1.407	1.409	1.369	1.400	1.413	1.414
8. LRQM	1.642	1.481	1.657	1.651	1.658	1.653	1.658	1.473	1.609	1.647	1.624
9. LENDPLUS	1.753	1.739	1.738	1.729	1.719	1.725	1.743	1.644	1.737	1.744	1.720
10. COMPCRED	1.779	1.783	1.783	1.784	1.783	1.761	1.740	1.782	1.782	1.768	1.782
11. ASSETS	2.014	2.245	2.141	2.220	2.181	2.245	2.230	2.245	2.027	2.125	2.200
12. CATOMZ	1.571	1.608	1.622	1.409	1.621	1.620	1.615	1.604	1.614	1.622	1.612
13. CATEMPLS		1.392	1.369	1.389	1.386	1.393	1.393	1.388	1.266	1.393	1.369
14. OUTDIR	1.579		1.540	1.568	1.577	1.545	1.575	1.503	1.572	1.551	1.550
15. CHECK	2.888	2.864		2.935	2.908	1.917	2.901	2.908	2.815	2.936	2.931
16. FINAFD	1.688	1.680	1.691		1.441	1.692	1.692	1.691	1.619	1.693	1.692
17. EDUFIN	1.439	1.443	1.431	1.231		1.440	1.440	1.442	1.446	1.444	1.443
18. QUALITY	2.917	2.852	1.903	2.916	2.906		2.902	2.917	2.873	2.885	2.913
19. AUDTERM	1.228	1.225	1.213	1.228	1.224	1.222		1.219	1.161	1.223	1.227
20. AUDSERV	1.628	1.554	1.617	1.632	1.630	1.634	1.622		1.585	1.633	1.631
21. AUDREP	1.539	1.684	1.621	1.619	1.693	1.667	1.601	1.642		1.692	1.671
22. HEALTH	1.243	1.221	1.242	1.243	1.242	1.229	1.238	1.243	1.243		1.243
23. STRAT	1.395	1.394	1.416	1.420	1.417	1.418	1.419	1.418	1.402	1.420	

For variable definitions, see chapter 5 table 5.10

Appendix IV Treatment of missing values

Missing data are unfortunately an unwanted reality in most forms of research and missing data are usually a nuisance, not the main focus of inquiry. Threats to a study's internal and external validity are primary problems associated with missing data. Even the use of appropriate strategies for coping with missing data may, as a result of different approaches[112], lead to different conclusions. (Croninger and Douglas, 2005).

Initially we have treated missing values based in this study on a list wise deletion. List wise deletion is a more extreme case of exclusion removing any case from the sample that has missing values for the variables, resulting that every case in the sample provides full information for the analysis. Although this is a common method and its main virtue is simplicity this method has its shortcomings. The primary drawback of list wise deletion is the possibility of biased conclusions, as high rates of case deletion can result in serious implications for parameter bias and inefficiency (King et al., 2011; Schafer and Graham, 2002). Another disadvantage of list wise deletion is the risk of "inefficiency of list wise deletion in multivariate analyses involving many items, in which mild rates of missing values on each item may cause large portions of the sample to be discarded" (Schafer and Graham, 2002: 156). Using list wise deletion in this study (see table 6.7) results in a decrease of the original number of 154 observations to 117 observations when all independent variables are added to the logistic regression model. To which extent does the dataset suffer from the risk that mild rates of missing values on different variables have lead to the large portion of cases being discarded using list wise deletion? Originally, the dataset used for the regression analyses consists of 13 independent variables and 154 observations, totalling in 2,002 individual values. Descriptive analysis of missing values shows:

---

[112] A number of different approaches to cope with missing values exist. Examples of these approaches are: list wise deletion of cases, pair wise deletion, excluding variables with a high item non-response, mean plugging, estimation of conditional means, hot deck imputation, reweighting, regression-based imputation, imputing using the EM algorithm and multiple imputation.

Overall Summary of Missing Values

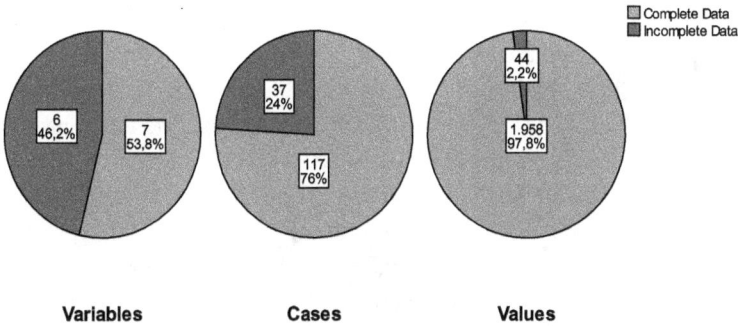

Complete Data
Incomplete Data

| Variables | Cases | Values |

It showed that only a very small amount of values is missing (2.2% of the total values), but that these missing values occurred in 6 of the 13 independent variables leading to a reduction of 24% of the total cases. The distribution of the missing values across the independent variables is as follows:

Variable	Number of missing values
OUTDIR	1
AUDTERM	18
AUDREP	9
SHRHND	13
IMPREL	1
LENDAB	2

Of the 37 cases, 33 cases missing 1 value, 2 cases missing 2 values and 2 cases missing 3 values.

As the aim of this study is to answer the question: what are the (main) drivers for the demand for audit, we are interested in the regression analysis of the demand for audit and valid coefficients for the identified independent variables. Although a possible disadvantage of using list wise deletion is that it may generate biased parameters (valid coefficients) it does not always have to have such harmful effects. "Sometimes the fraction of missing observations is small or the assumptions hold sufficiently well so that the bias is not large" (King et al, 2001: 51). To investigate whether the assumptions hold sufficiently, we have conducted a number of additional analyses. As we know from the descriptive data of the missing values the number of missing values for the variables OUTDIR, IMPREL and LENDAB are very small. Therefore it was decided to use single imputation (mean substitution) for the missing values for these variables, this results that the number of valid cases increases from 117 to 121. Subsequently two additional regression analysis (see results presented in table below) were conducted, by excluding the variables AUDTERM and AUDREP, to investigate the impact on the remaining variables. Excluding the variable AUDTERM results in an increase of 13 cases in the number of valid cases, excluding the variable AUDREP results in an increase of 8 cases[113]. Given the results of these additional regression analyses, it was concluded to impute the missing values for these two variables, using single imputation (mean substitution). With regard to the variable SHRHND it is decided not to use an imputation method to deal with the missing values of this variable. As both the individual hypothesis testing (see chapter 5.2.1.3) as the correlation matrix (table 6.1 of chapter six) show that SHRHND does have a strong significant relationship with the demand for audit, using strategies for imputing missing values it is expected that the risks on a distortion of the distributions and relationships between the independent variables increases seriously. In the end, imputation methods (even if they are statistically sophisticated) are still nothing more than 'guessing' the answers for non-item response. The pros and cons of using list wise deletion for variable SHRHND are, therefore, outweighing the pros and cons of using a missing value imputation method. As a result the final number of valid cases increases to 141 and the results of the full logistic regression model after imputing for missing values are presented in the last two columns of the following table. After imputing for missing values, the results for both the full model as the significant independent variables in the model show similar results. Based on this analysis it can be concluded that even with the use of list wise deletion the assumptions in the model holds sufficiently well, which contributes to the robustness of the results.

---

[113] The increase of the number of valid cases after excluding either the variables AUDTERM (+13) or AUDREP (+7) is not equal to the number of missing values for the variables (AUDTERM: 18; AUDREP: 9). This difference is caused by the cases missing more than one variable.

Demand for Audit: Multivariate analyses after imputing missing values

Label	Predicted	Result full logistic regression model (table 6.7)		Results excluding variable AUDTERM		Results excluding variable AUDREP		Results full model after imputing missing values	
		coefficient	p-value	coefficient	p-value	coefficient	p-value	coefficient	p-value
INTERCEPT	?	-6.765	<.001***	-6.150	<.001***	-6.346	<.001***	-6.802	<.001***
SIZE	+	1.467	0.077*	0.992	0.152	1.049	0.138	0.963	0.181
SHRH#	+	0.024	0.748	0.029	0.707	0.061	0.445	0.055	0.484
SHRHAC	+	0.938	0.196	0.209	0.713	0.484	0.421	0.128	0.824
STAKE#	+	-0.045	0.867	0.018	0.944	-0.048	0.844	0.012	0.959
MOWN50	-	-0.012	0.985	0.340	0.543	0.254	0.663	0.324	0.567
LVRG	+	0.150	0.675	0.181	0.588	0.173	0.607	0.282	0.424
LRQM	+	0.975	0.189	0.980	0.121	1.012	0.124	0.973	0.126
OUTDIR	+	0.158	0.854	0.776	0.327	-0.257	0.732	-0.078	0.913
AUDTERM	+	0.078	0.032**			0.091	0.009**	0.087	0.014**
AUDREP	+	0.415	0.579	0.516	0.425			0.312	0.645
SHRHND	+	0.696	0.002***	0.753	<.001***	0.723	<.001***	0.807	<.001***
IMPREL	+	1.154	0.002***	1.013	0.001***	1.004	0.002***	0.992	0.002***
LENDAB	+	-0.106	0.716	-0.062	0.808	-0.058	0.836	-0.090	0.741
Model summary									
N		117		134		127		141	
Wald chi-square		67.840 (df 13)		66.834 (df 12)		67.003 (df 12)		76.009 (df 13)	
p-value		<.001		<.001		<.001		<.001	
-2 Log likelihood		84.921		109.138		100.382		110.679	
Pseudo R²		0.604		0.537		0.560		0.568	

Appendix V SPSS output of the full logistic regression model (table 6.7)

This appendix shows the SPSS output of the full logistic regression presented in table 6.7 of chapter 6.3. First the case processing summary is presented.

Case Processing Summary

Unweighted Cases[a]		N	Percent
Selected Cases	Included in Analysis	117	76,0
	Missing Cases	37	24,0
	Total	154	100,0
Unselected Cases		0	,0
Total		154	100,0

a. If weight is in effect, see classification table for the total number of cases.

The beginning block 0 shows the results of the classification table and the logistic regression of the Intercept-model only.

Classification Table[a,b]

Observed			Predicted		
			demand voluntary audit		Percentage Correct
			nee	ja	
Step 0	demand voluntary audit	nee	0	42	,0
		ja	0	75	100,0
	Overall Percentage				64,1

a. Constant is included in the model.

b. The cut value is ,500

Variables in the Equation

		B	S.E.	Wald	df	Sig.	Exp(B)
Step 0	Constant	,580	,193	9,051	1	,003	1,786

Including the independent variables in block I shows the omnibus test of model coefficients, the model summary, the classification table, variables in the equitation and the casewise list.

Omnibus Tests of Model Coefficients

		Chi-square	df	Sig.
Step 1	Step	67,840	13	,000
	Block	67,840	13	,000
	Model	67,840	13	,000

186

Model Summary

Step	-2 Log likelihood	Cox & Snell R Square	Nagelkerke R Square
1	84,921[a]	,440	,604

a. Estimation terminated at iteration number 6 because parameter estimates changed by less than ,001.

Classification Table[a]

Observed			Predicted		
			demand voluntary audit		
			nee	ja	Percentage Correct
Step 1	demand voluntary audit	nee	31	11	73,8
		ja	8	67	89,3
	Overall Percentage				83,8

a. The cut value is ,500

Variables in the Equation

		B	S.E.	Wald	df	Sig.	Exp(B)
Step 1[a]	SIZE	1,467	,831	3,118	1	,077	4,337
	SHRH#	,024	,075	,103	1	,748	1,025
	SHRHAC	,938	,726	1,672	1	,196	2,556
	STAKE#	-,045	,269	,028	1	,867	,956
	MOWN50	-,012	,629	,000	1	,985	,988
	LVRG	,150	,359	,176	1	,675	1,162
	LRQM	,975	,742	1,726	1	,189	2,651
	OUTDIR	,158	,859	,034	1	,854	1,171
	AUDTERMC	,078	,036	4,625	1	,032	1,081
	AUDREP	,415	,748	,308	1	,579	1,514
	SHRHND	,696	,222	9,867	1	,002	2,006
	IMPREL	1,154	,366	9,925	1	,002	3,170
	LENDAB	-,106	,292	,133	1	,716	,899
	Constant	-6,765	1,783	14,404	1	,000	,001

a. Variable(s) entered on step 1: SIZE, SHRH#, SHRHAC, STAKE#, MOWN50, LVRG, LRQM, OUTDIR, AUDTERMC, AUDREP, SHRHND, IMPREL, LENDAB.

Casewise List[a]

a. The casewise plot is not produced because no outliers were found.

Appendix VI Results of Mann-Whithney Test for filing classification bias[114]

Hypothesis Test Summary

	Null Hypothesis	Test	Sig.	Decision
1	The distribution of ASSETS is the same across categories of filing classification.	Independent-Samples Mann-Whitney U Test	.227	Retain the null hypothesis.
2	The distribution of SHRH# is the same across categories of filing classification.	Independent-Samples Mann-Whitney U Test	.625	Retain the null hypothesis.
3	The distribution of STAKE# is the same across categories of filing classification.	Independent-Samples Mann-Whitney U Test	.540	Retain the null hypothesis.
4	The distribution of LVRG is the same across categories of filing classification.	Independent-Samples Mann-Whitney U Test	.127	Retain the null hypothesis.
5	The distribution of CHECK is the same across categories of filing classification.	Independent-Samples Mann-Whitney U Test	.716	Retain the null hypothesis.
6	The distribution of QUALITY is the same across categories of filing classification.	Independent-Samples Mann-Whitney U Test	.253	Retain the null hypothesis.
7	The distribution of CREDIBLY is the same across categories of filing classification.	Independent-Samples Mann-Whitney U Test	.200	Retain the null hypothesis.
8	The distribution of LENDPLUS is the same across categories of filing classification.	Independent-Samples Mann-Whitney U Test	.953	Retain the null hypothesis.
9	The distribution of COMPCRED is the same across categories of filing classification.	Independent-Samples Mann-Whitney U Test	.620	Retain the null hypothesis.
10	The distribution of AUDTERM is the same across categories of filing classification.	Independent-Samples Mann-Whitney U Test	.278	Retain the null hypothesis.
11	The distribution of AUDSERV is the same across categories of filing classification.	Independent-Samples Mann-Whitney U Test	.057	Retain the null hypothesis.

Asymptotic significances are displayed. The significance level is .05.

---

[114] The similar variables are used in this Mann-Whitney test as are used in the Mann-Whitney test of Appendix II.

References[115]

Abdel-khalik, A.R. (1993). Why Do Private Companies Demand Auditing? A Case for Organization Loss of Control. *Journal of Accounting, Auditing & Finance*, 8(1), 31-52.

ACCA (2011). *The value of audit: views from retail (private) investors*. The Association of Chartered Certified Accountants.

Alchain, A.A. & Demsetz, H. (1972). Production, Information Costs, and Economic Organization. *The American Economic Review, 62(December),* 777-795.

Anderson, D., Francis, J.R. & Stokes, D. (1993). Auditing, Directorships and the Demand for Monitoring. *Journal of Accounting and Public Policy, 12*, 353-375.

Aristotle: translated and edited by Roger Crisp (2000). *Nicomachean Ethics*. Cambridge: Cambridge University Press.

Augier, M. & Marsh, J.G. (Eds.). (2004). *Models of Man; Essays in Memory of Herbert A. Simon*. Cambridge, MA: The MIT Press.

Bachmann, R. (2001). Trust, Power and Control in Trans-Organizational Relations. *Organization Studies*, 22(2), 337-365.

Bachmann, R. (2003) Trust and Power as Means of Co-ordinating the Internal Relations of the Organization – A Conceptual Framework. Working Paper, University of Groningen.

Bamber, E.M. & Stratton, R.A. (1997). The Information Content of the Uncertainty-Modified Audit Report: Evidence from Bank Loan Officers. *Accounting Horizons, 11(2),* 1-11.

Bandyopadhyah, S. & Francis, J. (1995). The economic effect of differing levels of auditor assurance on bankers' lending decisions. *Canadian Journal of Administrative Sciences, 12,* 238-249.

Barefield, R.M., Graver, J.J. & O'Keefe, T.B. (1993). Additional Evidence on the Economics of Attest: Extending Results from the Audit Market to the Market for Compilations and Reviews. *Auditing: A Journal of Practice & Theory, 12(1),* 74-87.

Beck, U. (1992). *Risk Society: Towards a New Modernity*. London: Sage.

Beck, U. (1999). *World Risk Society*. Oxford: Blackwell Publishers Ltd.

Benston, G.J. (1985). The market for public accounting services: demand, supply and regulation. *Journal of Accounting and Public Policy*, 4: 33-79.

---

[115] This list of references also includes literature used during the writing of the dissertation, but not necessarily referenced to in the main text.

Berle, AA., & Means G.C. (1932). *The Modern Corporation and Private Property* (revised edition 1968). New York: Harcourt, Brace & World Inc.

Berry, A.J., Faulkner, S., Hughes, M. & Jarvis, R. (1993). Financial information, the banker and the small business. *British Accounting Review,* 25, 131-150.

Blackwell, D.W., Noland, T.R. & Winters, D.B. (1998). The Value of Auditor Assurance: Evidence from Loan Pricing. *Journal of Accounting Research,* 36(1), 57-70.

Blair, M.M. (1995). Ownership and Control: Rethinking Corporate Governance for the 21st Century. In Clarke, T. (Ed.) (2004), *Theories of Corporate Governance* (pp.78-92). New York NY: Routledge.

Blokdijk, H., Drieënhuizen, F. & Wallage, Ph. (1995). *Reflections on Auditing Theory: A contribution from the Netherlands.* Deventer: Bohn Stafleu Van Loghum.

Boer, D-J. den, Bouwman, H., Frissen, V. & Houben, M. (1994). *Methodologie en statistiek voor communicatie-onderzoek.* Houten: Kluwer Bedrijfswetenschappen.

Bollen, L.L.H. (1996). *Financial Reporting Regulation for Small and Medium Sized Private Firms.* PhD thesis. Maastricht: University of Maastricht.

Bradbury, M.E. (1990). The Incentives for Voluntary Audit Committee Formation. *Journal of Accounting and Public Policy, 9,* 19-36.

Brousseau, E. & Glanchant, J-M. (Eds.) (2008). *New institutional economics: a guidebook.* Cambridge, UK: Cambridge University Press.

Buijink, W.F.J. (1992). *Empirical financial accounting research, compliance with regulation, distributional properties of financial ratios and demand for external auditing.* PhD thesis. Maastricht: University of Maastricht.

Carey, P., Simnett, R. & Tanewski, G. (2000). Voluntary Demand for Internal and External Auditing by Family Businesses. *Auditing: A Journal of Practice and Theory, 19,* 37-51.

Child, J. & Rodrigues, S.B. (2004). Repairing the Breach of Trust in Corporate Governance. *Corporate Governance,12, April,* 143-152.

Chiles, T.H., McMackin, J.F. (1996). Integrating variable risk preferences, trust and transaction cost economics. *Academy of Management Review, 21(1),* 73-99.

Chow, C.W. (1982). The Demand for External Auditing: Size, Debt and Ownership Influences. *The Accounting Review,* 57(2), 272-291.

Clarke, T. (1998). The Stakeholder Corporation: A Business Philosophy for The Information Age. *Long Range Planning,* 31(2), 182-194.

Clarke, T. (2004). *Theories of Corporate Governance* (pp.78-92). New York NY: Routledge.

Coase, R.H. (1937). The Nature of the Firm. *Economica, 4(16),* 386-405.

Collis, J. (2003). *The Utility of the Statutory Accounts to the Directors of Small Private Companies in the UK,* PhD thesis, Kingston University.

Collis, J., Jarvis, R. & Skerratt, L. (2004). The demand for the audit in small companies in the UK. *Accounting and Business Research,* 34(2), 87-100.

Collis, J. (2010). Audit Exemption and the Demand for Voluntary Audit: A Comparative Study of the UK and Denmark. *International Journal of Auditing, 14,* 211-231.

Cools, K. (2005). *Controle is goed vertrouwen nog beter – Over bestuurders en corporate governance.* Assen: Koninklijke Van Gorcum B.V.

Costouros, G.J. (1978). Auditing in the Athenian state of the golden age (500-300 BC). *Accounting Historians Journal, 5(1),* 41-50.

Croninger, R.G. & Douglas, K.M. (2005). Missing Data and Institutional Research. In Umbach, P.D. (Ed.), *Survey research: Emerging Issues* (pp. 33-50). San Fransisco: Jossey-Bass.

Daily, C.M., Dalton, D.R. & Cannella, A.C. (2003). Corporate Governance: Decades of Dialogue and Data. *Academy of Management Review, 28(3),* 371-382.

Dassen, R.J.M. (1989). De Leer van het Gewekte Vertrouwen: Agency avant la letter? *Maandblad voor Accountancy en Bedrijfshuishoudkunde, September,* 341-352.

Davis, J.H., Schoorman, F.D. & Donaldson, L. (1997). Towards a Stewardship Theory of Management. In Clarke, T. (Ed.) (2004), *Theories of Corporate Governance* (pp.78-92). New York NY: Routledge.

DeAngelo, L. (1981). Auditor Size and Audit Quality. *Journal of Accounting & Economics, 3(3),* 183-199.

Deegan, C. (2002). The legitimizing effect of social and environmental disclosures – a theoretical foundation. *Accounting, Auditing & Accountability Journal, 15(3),* 282-311.

Dharan, B. (1992). Auditing as a Signal in small Business Lending. *Journal of Small Business Finance,* 2: 1-11.

DiMaggio, P.J. & Powell, W.W. (1983). The iron cage revisited: institutional isomorphism and collective rationality in organizational field. *American Sociological Review,* 48, 147-160.

Dobbin, F. (Editor). (2004). *The new economic sociology: a reader,* Princeton: Princeton University Press.

Donaldson, L. & Davis, J.H. (1991). Stewardship or Agency Theory: CEO Governance and Shareholder Returns. *Australian Journal of Management, 16(June),* 49-64.

Donaldson, L. & Davis, J.H. (1994). Boards and company performance – Research challenges the conventional wisdom. *Corporate Governance: An International Review, 2,* 151-160.

Douma, S.W. (1987). Op weg naar een economische organisatietheorie: agency theorie. *Maandblad voor Accountancy en Bedrijfshoudkunde,* 11, 420-432.

Eichenseher, J.W. & Shields, D. (1985). Corporate Director Liability and Monitoring Preferences. *Journal of Accounting and Public Policy, 4*, 13-31.

Eisenhardt, K.M. (1989). Agency Theory: An Assessment and Review. In Clarke, T. (Ed.) (2004), *Theories of Corporate Governance* (pp.78-92). New York NY: Routledge.

Eilifsen, A, Knechel, W.R. & Wallage, Ph. (2001). Application of the business risk audit model: A field study. *Accounting Horizons, 15(3),* 193-208.

Engels, F. (1884). The Origin of the State. In Hechter, M. & Horne, C. (Eds.). (2003). *Theories of Social Order* (pp. 179-182). Stanford: Stanford University Press.

Ettredge, M., Simon, D., Smith, D. & Stone, M. (1994). Why do companies purchase timely quarterly reviews? *Journal of Accounting and Economics, 18,* 131-155.

Ettredge, M., Reed, M. & Stone, M. (2000). An Examination of Substitution among Monitoring Devices: The Case of Internal and External Audit Expenditures. *Review of Quantitative Finance and Accounting, 15*, 57-79.

European Commission (1996). *Green Paper: The Role, the Position and the Liability of the Statutory Auditor within the European Union.* Brussels: Commission of the European Communities.

European Commission (1998). *Communication from the Commission: The Statutory Audit in the European Union: the Way Forward.* Brussels: Commission of the European Communities.

European Commission (2000). *Commission Recommendations: Quality Assurance for the Statutory Audit in the EU: Minimum Requirement.* Brussels: Commission of the European Communities.

European Commission (2003). *Communication from the Commission: Reinforcing the statutory audit in the European Union.* Brussels: Commission of the European Communities.

European Commission (2007a). *Communication from the Commission on a simplified business environment for companies in the areas of company law, accounting and auditing.* Brussels: Commission of the European Communities.

European Commission (2007b). *Synthesis of the reactions received to the Commission communication on a simplified business environment for companies in the areas of company law, accounting and auditing.* Brussels: Commission of the European Communities.

European Commission (2010). *Greenbook – Audit Policy: Lessons of the crisis.* Brussels: Commission of the European Communities.

Fama, E.F. (1980). Agency problems and the theory of the firm. *Journal of Political Economy*, 88(2): 299-307.

Fama, E.F. & Jensen, M.C. (1983). Agency problems and residual claims. *Journal of Law & Economics, 26 (June), 327*-349.

Feyeraband, P. (1975). *Tegen de methode* (3td ed., Dutch translation). Rotterdam: Lemniscaat B.V.

Flint, D. (1985). Professor Limperg's Audit Philosophy – The theory of Inspired Confidence. *The Social Responsibility of the Auditor*. Amsterdam: Limperg Instituut.

Flint, D. (1988). *Philosophy and principles of auditing, an introduction.* London: Macmillan Education Ltd.

Fodor, I.K. (2002). A survey of dimension reduction techniques. Working Paper, University of California.

Folmer, H. & Lindenberg, S.M. (2011). Economen moeten meer duelleren. *ESB*, 96(4612), 378-380.

Fortin, S. & Pittman, J.A. (2007). The Role of Auditor Choice in Debt Pricing in Private Firms. *Contemporary Accounting Research, 24(3),* 859-896.

Foss, N.J. (1994). The Theory of the Firm: The Austrians as Precursors and Critics of Contemporary Theory. *The Review of Austrian Economics, 7(1)*, 31-65.

Foss, N.J. & Knudsen, C (Eds.). (1996). *Towards a Competence Theory of the Firm*. New York NY: Routledge.

Foss, N.J. & Klein, P.G. (2006). The Emergence of the Modern Theory of the Firm. Working Paper. Retrieved from http://ssrn.com/abstract=982094.

Foss, N.J. & Klein, P.G. (2008). The Theory of the Firm and Its Critics: A Stocktaking and Assessment. In E. Brousseau & J-M. Glachant (Eds.), *New institutional economics: a guidebook* (pp. 425-442). Cambridge, UK: Cambridge University Press.

Francis, J.R. & Wilson, E.R. (1988). Auditor Changes: A Joint Test of Theories Relating to Agency Costs and Auditor Differentiation. *The Accounting Review, 63(4),* 663-682.

Frank, R.H. (1994). *Microeconomics and behaviour.* New York NY: McGraw-Hill Publishing Company.

Freeman, R.E. (1984). *Strategic Management – A Stakeholders Approach* (2010, reissue). Cambridge: Cambridge University Press.

Friedman, M. (1962). *Capitalism and Freedom* (2nd ed.). Chicago: The University of Chicago Press.

Fukuyama, F. (2005). *State Building – Governance and world order in the twenty-first century* (paperback edition). London: Profile Books Ltd.

Giddens, A. (1984). *The Constitution of Society*. Berkeley and Los Angeles: University of California Press.

Giddens, A. (1990). *The Consequences of Modernity*. Stanford: Stanford University Press.

Giddens, A. (1991). *Modernity and Self-identity – Self and Society in the Late Modern Age*. Stanford: Stanford University Press.

Giddens, A. (2003). *Runaway world: how globalization is reshaping our lives*. New York NY: Routledge.

Gigerenzer, G. & Goldstein, D.G. (1996). Reasoning the Fast and Frugal Way: Models of Bounded Rationality. *Psychological Review, 103(4),* 650-669.

Granovetter, M. (1985). Economic Action and Social Structure; The Problem of Embeddedness. *American Journal of Sociology*, 91(3), 481-510.

Haw, I, Qi, D. & Wu, W. (2008). The Economic Consequence of Voluntary Audit. *Journal of Accounting, Auditing & Finance*, 63-93.

Hay, D.C & Davis, D. (2004). The Voluntary Choice of an Auditor of Any Level of Quality. Auditing: *A Journal of Practice & Theory, 23(2),* 37-53.

Hay, D.C., Knechel W.R. & Wong, N. (2006). Audit Fees: A Meta-Analysis of the Effect of Supply and Demand Attributes. *Contemporary Accounting Research, 23(1),* 141-191.

Hayek, F.A. (1979). *Law, Legislation and Liberty – Volume 3 The Political Order of a Free People*. London: Routledge & Kegan Paul Ltd.

Hayes, R., Schilder, A., Dassen, R.J.M. & Wallage, Ph. (1999). *Principles of Auditing: An International Perspective*. London: McGraw-Hill Publishing Company.

Hechter, M. & Horne, C. (Eds.). (2003). *Theories of Social Order*. Stanford: Stanford University Press.

Henn, M., Weinstein, M. & Foard, N. (2006). *A short introduction to Social Research*. London: SAGE Publications Ltd.

Helsland, T.A.M.F.E. van & Bollen, L.H.H. (1998). Vrijwillige accountantscontrole bij kleine vennootschappen. *De Accountant, 1,* 43-49.

Hofstede, G.H. (2001). *Culture's consequences: Comparing values, behaviors, institutions, and organizations across nations* (2nd ed.). London: Sage Publications Ltd.

Hogewind, S.N., Hoppe, R., Ridder, W.J. de (2005). *Zekerheden in de toekomst: metamorfose van de accountant*. Den Haag: Stichting Maatschappij en Onderneming.

Hosmer, D.W. & Lemeshow, S. (2000). *Applied Logistic Regression* (2nd ed.). New York NY: John Wiley & Sons Inc.

Humphrey, C. & Turley, S. (1986). The Nature of the Audit in Small Companies - An Empirical Investigation. *Research Supplement to The Accountants Magazine, 2*, 25-42.

Humphrey, C. (2001), Audit research – looking beyond North America. *Critical Perspectives on Accounting, 12*, 339-368.

Humphrey, C. & Owen, D. (2000). Debating the 'Power' of Audit. *International Journal of Auditing, 4*, 29-50.

Jensen, K.L. & Payne, J.L. (2003). Management Trade-Offs of Internal Control and External Auditor Expertise. *Auditing: A Journal of Practice & Theory, 22(2)*, 90-119.

Jensen, M.C. & Meckling, W.H. (1976). Theory of the firm: Managerial behaviour, agency costs, and ownership structure. *Journal of Financial Economics* 3, 305-360.

Jensen, M.C. (1983). Organization theory and methodology. *Accounting Review,56*, 319-338.

Jensen, M.C. & Meckling, W.H. (1994). The Nature of Man. *Journal of Applied Corporate Finance, 7(2)*, 4-19.

Jensen, M.C. (2001). Value Maximization, Stakeholder Theory, and the Corporate Objective Function. *Journal of Applied Corporate Finance, 14(3)*, 8-22.

Johnson, D., Pany, K. & White, R. (1983). Audit reports and the loan decision: Actions and perceptions. *Auditing: A Journal of Practice & Theory, 2(1)*, 38-51.

Kahneman, D., Slovic, P. & Tversky, A. (Eds.). (1982). *Judgment under uncertainty: Heuristics and biases*. Cambridge MA, Cambridge University Press.

Kahneman, D. (2011). *Thinking, Fast and Slow*. London: Allen Lane an imprint of Penguin Books.

Kant, I. (1781). *Kritiek van de zuivere rede*. Translated and edited by Veenbaas, J. & Visser, W. (2004). Amsterdam: Uitgeverij Boom.

Kim, J.B., Simunic, D.A., Stein, M.T. & Yi, C.H. (2007). Voluntary Audits and the Cost of Debt Capital for Privately Held Firms: Korean Evidence. Working Paper, University of British Colombia.

Kimman, E.J.J.M. (1991), Accountants: standvastig in de eer van uw stand. *De Accountant, september*, 10-14.

King, G., Honaker, J., Joseph, A. & Scheve, K. (2001). Analyzing Incomplete Political Science Data: An Alternative Algorithm for Multiple Imputation. *American Political Science Review, 95(1)*, 49-69.

Kiser, E. (1999). Comparing varieties of agency theory in economics, political science, and sociology; an illustration from state policy implementation. *Sociological Theory, 17*: 146-170.

Koster, P. (2005, September 16). Accountants leven bij de gratie van de wetgever. *NRC Handelsblad*. Retrieved from http://www.archief.nrc.nl.

Knechel, W.R., Wallage, Ph., Eilifsen, A. & Praag, B. van (2006). The Demand Attributes of Assurance Service Providers and the Role of Independent Accountants. *International Journal of Auditing, 10(2)*, 143-162.

Knechel, W.R., Niemi, L. & Sundgren, S. (2008). Determinants of Auditor Choice: Evidence from a Small Client Market. *International Journal of Auditing, 12*, 65-88.

Knight, F.H. (1921). *Risk, Uncertainty and profit*. Boston: Houghton Mifflin.

Kuhn, T.S. (1962). *The Structure of Scientific Revolutions* (3th ed.). Chicago: The University of Chicago Press.

Lambrecht, P. & Verslype (2009). Het adequate gebruik van Multivariabele Logistische Regressie Analyse in de Intensieve Zorg literatuur anno 2006. Paper. University of Gent.

Lennox, C.S. (2005). Management ownership and audit firm size. *Contemporary Accounting Research, 22(1)*, 205-227.

Lennox, C.S. & Pittman, J. (2011). Voluntary Audits versus Mandatory Audits. Working Paper. Nanyang Technological University.

Limperg Jr., Th. (1932/1933). De Functie van de Accountant en de Leer van het Gewekte Vertrouwen. *Maandblad voor Accountancy en Bedrijfshuishoudkunde*, verzameld in: Vijftig Jaar MAB, Muusses Purmerend, 1974.

Luft Mobus, J. (2005). Mandatory environmental disclosures in a legitimacy context. *Accounting, Auditing & Accountability Journal, 18(4)*, 492-517.

Luhmann, N, (1979), *Trust and power*, New York: John Wiley.

Luhmann, N. (1968,). *Vertrauen: ein Mechanismus der Reduktion Sozialer Komplexität (4e auflage 2000)*, Stuttgart: Lucius und Lucius.

Luhmann, N. (2005), *Risk: A Sociological Theory*, London: Aldine Transaction.

Mahoney, J.T. (2005). *Economic Foundations of Strategy*. London: Sage Publications Ltd.

Maijoor, S. (1991). *The Economics of Accounting Regulation: Effects of Dutch accounting regulation for public accountants and firms*. PhD thesis. Maastricht, University of Maastricht.

Maijoor, S. (2000). The Internal Control Explosion. *International Journal of Auditing, 4*, 101-109.

Mannheim, K. (Ed.): Translated, edited and with an introduction by Gerth, H.H. & Wrighte Mills, C. (1947). *From Max Weber: Essays in Sociology*. London: Kegan Paul, Trench, Trubner & Co. Ltd.

MARC (2010). *The Value of Audit*. Maastricht: Maastricht University.

March, J.G. & Simon, H.A. (1958). *Organizations* (2nd ed.). Oxford: Blackwell Publishers.

Mautz, R.K. &Sharaf, H.A. (1961). *The Philosophy of Auditing*. American Accounting Association.

Meuwissen, R. & Wallage, Ph. (2008). The auditing profession in the Netherlands: from Limperg's principles to detailed rules. In R. Quick, S. Turley & M. Willekens (Eds.), *Auditing, Trust and Governance – Developing regulation in Europe* (pp. 168-185). New York NY: Routledge.

Michel-Kerjan, E. & Slovic, P. (Eds.). (2010). *The Irrational Economist – Making Decisions in a Dangerous World*. New York NY: Public Affairs.

Möllering, G. (2001). The Nature of Trust: From Georg Simmel to a Theory of Expectation, Interpretation and Suspension. *Sociology*, 15(2), 402-420.

Möllering, G. (2005). The trust/control duality: An integrative perspective on positive expectations of others. *International Sociology, 20(3)*, 283-305.

Möllering, G. (2006). *Trust: Reason, Routine, Reflexivity*, Oxford: Elsevier Ltd.

Morgan, G. (1998). Accounting as reality construction: Towards a new epistemology for accounting practice. *Accounting Organizations and Society*, 13(5), 477-485.

Mortelmans, D. & Dehertogh, B. (2007). *Uni- en bivariate analyse*. Leuven: Uitgeverij Acco.

Mortelmans, D. (2010). *Logistische Regressie*. Leuven: Uitgeverij Acco.

Mosch, R.H.J., and I. Verhoeven (2003), *Blauwe ogen of zwart op wit: Een contigentiebenadering van vertrouwensmechanismen*, Den Haag: Wetenschappelijke Raad voor het Regeringsbeleid (WRR-discussionpaper nr. 1).

Mundry, R. & Nunn, C.L. (2009). Stepwise Model Fitting and Statistical Inference: Turning Noise into Signal Pollution. *The American Naturalist, 173(1)*, 119-123.

Neu, D., Warsame, H. & Pedwell, K. (1998). Managing Public Impressions: Environmental Disclosures in Annual Reports. *Accounting, Organizations and Society, 23(3)*, 265-282.

Niemi, L., Kinnunen, J., Ojala, H. & Troberg, P. (2009). To Audit or Not to Audit? Further evidence of the drivers of the demand for the audit among SMEs under non-mandatory auditing, Working Paper. Helsinki School of Economics

Niskanen,, M., Karjalainen, J. & and Niskanen, J. (2009), Demand for Audit Quality in Small Private Firms: Evidence on Ownership Effects. Working Paper, University of Kuopi.

Noreen, E. (1988). The economics of ethics: a new perspective on agency theory. *Accounting, Organizations and Society, 13(4),* 359-369.

O'Brien, R.M. (2007). A caution regarding rules of thumb for variance inflation factors. *Quality & Quantity, 41,* 673-690.

O'Dwyer, B. (2003). Conceptions of corporate social responsibility: the nature of managerial capture. *Accounting, Auditing & Accountability Journal, 16(4),* 523-557.

Padilla, A. (2007). Property Economics of Agency Problems. Working Paper, University of Aix-Marseille.

Palmrose, Z. (1986a). Audit Fees and Auditor Size: Further Evidence. *Journal of Accounting Research, 24(1),* 97-110.

Palmrose, Z. (1986b). The Effect of Nonaudit Services on the Pricing of Audit Services: Further Evidence. *Journal of Accounting Research, 24(2),* 405-410.

Perrow, C. (1986). *Complex Organizations* (3th ed.). New York NY: Random House.

Pfeijffer, M. (2011). De zuivere accountant: terug naar de kern. *FD Outlook, June,* 38-44.

Pigott, T.D. (2001). A Review of Methods for Missing Data. *Educational Research and Evaluation, 7(4),* 353-383.

Popper, K. (1959). *The Logic of Scientific Discovery* (6th ed.). New York NY: Routledge.

Popper, K. (1970). Normal Science and its dangers. In L. Lakatos & A. Musgrave (Eds.), *Criticism and the growth of knowledge* (pp. 51-58). Cambridge, UK: Cambridge University Press.

Power, M. (1994). *The Audit Explosion.* London: Demos.

Power, M. (1997). *The Audit Society: rituals of verification* (2nd ed.). Oxford: Oxford University Press.

Power, M. (2000) The Audit Society – Second Thoughts. *International Journal of Auditing,* 4, 111-119.

Power, M. (2003). Evaluating the Audit Explosion. *Law & Policy, 25(3),* 185-202.

Power, M. (2004). *The Risk Management of Everything: rethinking the politics of uncertainty.* London: Demos.

Prast, H., Mosch, R. & Raaij, F. van (2005). *Vertrouwen, Cement van de Samenleving en Aanjager van de Economie.* Amsterdam: De Nederlandsche Bank.

Quick, R., Turley, S. & Willekens, M. (Eds.) (2008). *Auditing, Trust and Governance – Developing regulation in Europe.* New York NY: Routledge.

Rennie, M.D, Senkow, D.W., Rennie, R.D. & Wong, J.W. (2003). Deregulation of the Private Corporation Audit in Canada: Justification, Lobbying and Outcomes. *Research in Accounting Regulation,* 16: 227-241.

Rietschoten, P. van (2007). Van verplichting naar marktwerking. *De Accountant, June,* 46-50.

Robbins, L. (1935). *An essay on the nature and significance of economic science* (2th edition, revised and extended). London: MacMillan.

Schafer, J.L. & Graham, J.W. (2002). Missing Data: Our View of the State of the Art. *Psychological Methods, 7(2),* 147-177.

Schaik, F. van (2009). Het openbaar accountantsberoep in kaart gebracht. *Accountant Adviseur, September,* 35-37.

Schipper, F. (1991), Over de grondslagen van de audit, enkele kanttekeningen bij Flint en Limperg. *De Accountant, november,* 125-128.

Schipper, F. (1993) Rationaliteit en normativiteit, een discussiebijdrage. *De Accountant, november,* 35-355.

Senkow, D.W., Rennie, M.D., Rennie, R.D. & Wong, J.W. (2001). The Audit Retention Decision in the Face of Deregulation: Evidence from Large Private Canadian Corporations. *Auditing: A Journal of Practice & Theory, 20 (2),* 101-113.

Seow, J.L. (2001). The Demand for the UK Small Company Audit – An Agency Perspective. *International Small Business Journal, 19,* 61-79.

Shapiro, S. (1987). The social control of impersonal trust. *American Journal of Sociology, 93,* 623-658.

Shapiro, S. (2005). Agency Theory. *Annual Review Sociology, 31,* 263-284.

Simmel, G. (1903). *Philosophie des geldes.* Berlin: Dunker & Humblot.

Simon, H. (1982). *Models of Bounded Rationality – Behavioral Economics and Business Organization Volume 2.* Cambridge MA: The MIT Press.

Simon, H. (1997). *Administrative Behavior* (4th ed., revised version of the original 1947 edition). New York NY: The Free Press.

Simunic, D. (1980). The pricing of audit services: Theory and evidence. *Journal of Accounting Research, 18,* 161-190.

Simunic, D. (1984). Auditing, Consulting, and Auditor Independence. *Journal of Accounting Research, Autumn,* 769-702.

Simunic, D. & Stein, M. (1987). *Product differentiation in auditing: Auditor choice in the market for unseasoned new issues.* Research Monograph 13. Vancouver, BC: The Canadian Certified General Accountants' Research Foundation.

Smelser, N.J., & Swedberg, R. (Eds.). (2005). *The Handbook of Economic Sociology* (2nd ed.). Princeton: Princeton University Press.

Smith, M. (2003). *Research methods in accounting*. London: SAGE Publications Ltd.

Solomon, R.C. & Flores, F. (2001). *Building trust in business, politics, relationships and life*. Oxford: Oxford University Press.

Soros, G. (2009). *De crash van financiële markten (2nd ed.)*. Amsterdam/Antwerpen: Uitgeverij Contact.

Strikwerda, J. (2007).Het vraagstuk van de assurancefunctie in de 21^e eeuw. In W. Verhoog, P. van der Zanden & R. Schouten (Eds.), *Assurance voor de 21^e eeuw* (pp. 25-41). Amsterdam: NIVRA-VERA.

Trigilia, C. (1998), *Economic Sociology – State, Market, and Society in Modern Capitalism*, Oxford: Blackwell Publishing.

Vries, J. de (1985). *Geschiedenis der Accountancy in Nederland*. Assen/Maastricht: Van Gorcum.

Vocht, A. de (2010). *Basishandboek SPSS 18*. Utrecht: Bijleveld Press.

Wallace, W. (1981). The Economic Role of Auditing in Free and Regulated Markets. Retrieved from http://raw.rutgers.edu/raw/wallace/homepage.

Wallace, W. (1987). The Economic Role of the Audit in Free and Regulated Markets: A Review. *Research in Accounting Regulation, 1*, 1–34.

Wallace, W. (2004). The Economic Role of the Audit in Free and Regulated Market: A Look Back and a Look Forward. *Research in Accounting Regulation, 17*, 267-298.

Wallage, Ph. (1991). *Methodiek en mate van structuur: een beschouwing over het proces van accountantscontrole*. PhD thesis. Apeldoorn: Casparie Apeldoorn B.V.

Wallage, Ph., Blokdijk, J.H.. & Drieënhuizen, F. (1993). Historical factors affecting auditing in the Netherlands. *De Accountant, 3*, 182-186.

Watts, R.L., & Zimmerman, J.L. (1983). Agency Problems, Auditing, and the Theory of the Firm: Some Evidence. *Journal of Accounting & Economics, 26*(3), 613-634.

Watts, R.L. & Zimmerman, J.L. (1986). *Positive Accounting Theory*. Englewood Cliffs NJ, Prentice-Hall.

Watts, R.L. & Zimmerman, J.L. (1990). Positive Accounting Theory: A Ten Year Perspective. *The Accounting Review, 65(1),* 131-156.

Willekens, M., (2008). *De toegevoegde waarde van de audit*. die Keure, Belgium.

Williamson, O.E. (1975). *Markets and hierarchies: analysis and antitrust implications*. New York NY: The Free Press.

Williamson, O.E. (1996). *The mechanisms of governance*. New York NY: Oxford University Press.

Williamson, O.E. (2002). The theory of the firm as a governance structure: From choice to contract. *Journal of Economic Perspectives*, 16(3), 171-195.

Wright, M.E. & Davidson, R.A. (2000). The Effect of Auditor Attestation and Tolerance for Ambiguity on Commercial Lending Decisions. *Auditing: A Journal of Practice & Theory, 19(2),* 67-81.

Summary in Dutch (Nederlandse samenvatting)

De toegevoegde waarde van accountantscontrole in een niet-wettelijke omgeving

Waarom laten ondernemingen hun jaarrekeningen controleren door een accountant? Als we teruggaan in de geschiedenis blijkt dat de behoefte aan accountantscontrole vooral is ontstaan als gevolg van de ontwikkeling van de moderne onderneming. De moderne onderneming kenmerkt zich door een scheiding tussen eigendom (kapitaal) en leiding. Als gevolg hiervan ontstonden in landen actieve financiële markten voor ondernemingen om kapitaal aan te trekken. Hoewel er tekenen zijn dat het begrip accountantscontrole al veel langer bestaat, is het vooral de ontwikkeling van de moderne onderneming en de hiermee gepaard gaande problemen die mede aanleiding zijn geweest voor het ontstaan van het accountantsberoep zoals wij deze vandaag de dag kennen. Waar in het begin van het ontstaan van de moderne onderneming het laten uitvoeren van accountantscontrole nog op vrijwillige basis geschiedde, is in de loop van de tijd in veel landen de accountantscontrole voor groepen van ondernemingen door overheden wettelijk verplicht gesteld. De voornaamste reden voor wetgevers om de accountantscontrole verplicht te stellen, is dat accountantscontrole als één van de belangrijke controle mechanismen wordt gezien om het vertrouwen van het publiek in financiële markten te behouden. Het bestaan van deze wettelijke plicht bemoeilijkt het zicht op mogelijke andere aanwezige factoren die de vraag naar accountantscontrole beïnvloeden. Mogelijkerwijs heeft deze wettelijke plicht bijgedragen aan enerzijds het ontstaan van een 'beeld' in de hedendaagse samenleving dat 'accountants slechts bestaan bij de gratie van de wetgever' en dat er beperkt wetenschappelijk onderzoek is uitgevoerd naar de mogelijke andere factoren die de vraag naar accountantscontrole bepalen. Daarnaast blijkt dat overheden, in reactie op ondernemingsschandalen, in de afgelopen decennia vaak aanvullende wettelijke eisen aan de accountantscontrole van ondernemingen opleggen om het vertrouwen van het publiek te herstellen. Tegelijkertijd worden overheden ook geconfronteerd met 'druk' vanuit de samenleving om met name voor MKB-ondernemingen en burgers de vanuit de overheid opgelegde administratieve lasten te verlichten. Eén van de mogelijkheden die de overheid heeft om de administratieve lasten te verlichten, is om meer ondernemingen (gedeeltelijk) vrij te stellen van bestaande wettelijke verslaggevingseisen, waaronder de verplichting tot accountantscontrole. Wanneer zich een dergelijke situatie voordoet, biedt het een mogelijkheid om onderzoek uit te voeren naar de factoren die een rol spelen bij het besluit van de onderneming om op vrijwillige basis de accountantscontrole van de jaarrekening al dan niet voort te zetten. In Nederland heeft een dergelijke situatie zich in 2006 voorgedaan.

De onderzoeksvraag van deze studie is dan ook: *Wat zijn de factoren die de vraag naar accountantscontrole in een niet-wettelijke omgeving bepalen?*

De uitgangspunten van wetenschappelijk onderzoek ten aanzien van de vraag naar accountantscontrole in deze studie zijn tweeledig. Ten eerste wordt accountantscontrole als een 'sociaal controle mechanisme' beschouwd. Accountantscontrole draagt bij aan het vertrouwen tussen participanten in een samenleving. Als zodanig wordt de inhoud, plaats en positie van accountantscontrole mede bepaald door veranderingen in de samenleving door de tijd heen, hetgeen periodiek en vergelijkend onderzoek naar de vraag naar accountantscontrole rechtvaardigt. Ten tweede volgt deze studie een 'Kuhniaanse zienswijze' op het beoefenen van wetenschap. Beoefening van wetenschap wordt hierbij gezien als een organisch en sociale gelegenheid. Het onderzoek wordt uitgevoerd als een 'puzzel-oplossende activiteit' waarmee vooruitgang en groei in wetenschappelijke kennis wordt bereikt.

Dit proefschrift bestaat uit twee delen, een literatuurstudie en een empirische studie. In de literatuurstudie (hoofdstuk twee en drie) wordt eerst de evolutie van de ontwikkeling van de theorie naar de vraag van accountantscontrole behandeld. Vervolgens wordt eerder empirisch onderzoek geanalyseerd om factoren die de vraag naar accountantscontrole bepalen te identificeren, waarna het conceptueel kader voor de uit te voeren empirische studie uiteen wordt gezet. Het empirisch gedeelte (hoofdstuk vier, vijf en zes) bestaat uit een beschrijving van de dataset, het uitvoeren van uni- en bivariate analyses en de presentatie van de resultaten van de logistische regressie van het onderzoeksmodel. Hoofdstuk zeven bevat de conclusie van het onderzoek alsmede aanbevelingen voor verder onderzoek.

Waarom is er een vraag naar accountantscontrole? Deze vraag wordt door ondermeer de agency theorie beantwoord. Agency theorie, en in het bijzonder de theorie van de onderneming ('the theory of the firm', Jensen and Meckling (1976)), wordt gezien als het heersende paradigma voor de verklaring van het bestaan van de vraag naar accountantscontrole. Agency theorie is voortgekomen uit het ontstaan van moderne ondernemingen en geeft een theoretische verklaring voor de principaal-agent verhouding binnen moderne ondernemingen die het gevolg is van de scheiding tussen eigendom (de principalen) en de leiding (de agent). Hierdoor delegeert de principaal verantwoordelijkheid naar de agent om namens hem te handelen. Echter, omdat de principaal geen toegang heeft tot alle beschikbare informatie op het tijdstip dat de agent namens hem een beslissing neemt (informatie asymmetrie) is hij niet in staat om vast te stellen of de handelingen van de agent in het belang van de onderneming (en dus in het belang van de principaal) zijn. Om het ontstaan van mogelijke tegengestelde belangen tussen de belangen van de agent en de principaal te verkleinen, kan de principaal de agent beloningsprikkels toekennen en/of toezicht instellen. Accountantscontrole wordt gezien als een voorbeeld van de laatste. Agency theorie gaat uit van de vooronderstelling dat zowel de principaal als de agent maximaal nut nastreven, rationeel handelen en door eigen belang gemotiveerd worden. Daarnaast wordt in de theorie van de onderneming ervan uitgegaan dat de onderneming niets meer is dan een juridische fictie, een bundeling van contracten waar uitsluitend aandeelhouders zijn gerechtigd tot de winsten en de resterende vorderingen van de onderneming. Tegen deze vooronderstellingen zijn door wetenschappers uit andere (aanpalende) disciplines kritieken ingebracht, waarbij met name wordt aangegeven dat door het gebruik van deze vooronderstellingen de complexiteit van de verschijnselen onderschat wordt en voorbij gaat aan de werkelijkheid. Vanuit de "Kuhniaanse zienswijze' is van belang om na te gaan in hoeverre deze kritieken kunnen bijdragen aan de vooruitgang in wetenschappelijke kennis met betrekking tot de vraag naar accountantscontrole en of deze andere zienswijze nieuwe factoren aan het licht brengt die de vraag naar accountantscontrole mogelijk beïnvloeden. Vanuit onder meer 'stewardship' theorie, 'stakeholder' theorie en de theorie van beperkte rationaliteit worden met betrekking tot deze kritieken argumenten aangedragen die kunnen bijdragen tot een verrijking van het inzicht in zowel de theorie van de onderneming als de theorie naar de vraag naar accountantscontrole. Uit analyse van de kritieken kan een ander gezichtspunt ten aanzien van de onderneming worden gehanteerd, waarbij de onderneming niet slechts een juridische fictie is, maar een zelfstandig instituut in de samenleving. Ook het onderkennen dat beslissingen niet altijd op uitsluitend rationele gronden worden genomen door de agent, maar dat perceptie een belangrijke rol speelt in de besluitvorming is een ander gezichtspunt. Het hanteren van verschillende gezichtspunten kan ertoe leiden dat de factoren die de vraag naar accountantscontrole beïnvloeden worden uitgebreid, dan wel dat hierdoor een beter zicht ontstaat op het belang van reeds onderkende relaties met de vraag naar accountantscontrole.

Mogelijk mede veroorzaakt door bestaande wettelijke verplichtingen tot het uitvoeren van accountantscontrole in veel landen, is in de afgelopen decennia slechts beperkt empirisch onderzoek uitgevoerd waarbij de vraag naar accountantscontrole als variabele gebruikt is. Om meer inzicht te verkrijgen in de factoren die de vraag naar accountantscontrole beïnvloeden hebben wetenschappers dan ook gebruik gemaakt van surrogaat variabelen voor de vraag naar accountantscontrole, zoals de hoogte van de betaalde vergoeding voor accountantscontrole en/of de keuze voor de accountant. Uit het beperkte empirische onderzoek, waarbij de vraag naar accountantscontrole als variabele is gebruikt, blijkt dat al deze studies agency theorie als kader gebruiken voor het bestaan van de vraag naar accountantscontrole. Consistent met de theorie van de onderneming zijn de eerste studies met name gericht op de factoren met betrekking tot de agency relatie tussen de aandeelhouder en management en de agency relatie tussen de verstrekkers van vreemd vermogen en de onderneming en de vraag naar accountantscontrole, de zogenaamde externe agency theorie relaties. In de tijd is echter een uitbreiding in het aantal factoren waar te nemen. Bestaande interne agency relaties binnen de onderneming, zoals een verminderde mogelijkheid om direct toezicht uit te voeren door management, de complexiteit en de vervanging voor het gebrek aan interne controle zijn factoren waarvan de relatie met de vraag naar accountantscontrole empirisch onderzocht wordt. De aandacht voor de vraag naar accountantscontrole in middelgrote- en kleine ondernemingen leert dat mogelijk ook andere factoren, welke niet ontleend kunnen worden aan de agency theorie, een rol spelen bij de vraag naar accountantscontrole. Vanuit voorgaande studies zijn in totaal negentien factoren geïdentificeerd die de vraag naar accountantscontrole mogelijk beïnvloeden en vanuit de analyse van de kritieken tegen de vooronderstellingen van agency theorie is voor deze studie additioneel nog een drietal mogelijke factoren toegevoegd. In totaal zijn vanuit de literatuurstudie 22 factoren geïdentificeerd. Deze factoren zijn vervolgens geclassificeerd, waardoor het onderzoeksmodel voor het empirisch deel van het proefschrift kan worden geschreven als:

De vraag naar accountantscontrole = functie van (externe agency factoren, interne agency factoren, overige factoren)

Deel twee van het proefschrift bestaat uit het empirisch onderzoek. Voor het onderzoek wordt gebruik gemaakt van een populatie van Nederlandse ondernemingen die, als gevolg van een deregulatie in 2006, niet meer voldoen aan de wettelijke omvangcriteria voor middelgrote ondernemingen. Een gevolg van deze deregulatie is dat deze ondernemingen worden geconfronteerd met de mogelijkheid om in aanmerking komen voor een aantal wettelijke vrijstellingen, waaronder de verplichting tot het laten uitvoeren van accountantscontrole. Ter duiding van de context van de in deze studie gebruikte populatie van ondernemingen wordt in het begin van hoofdstuk vier een korte schets gegeven van de historische ontwikkeling van het accountantsberoep, culturele aspecten en het ontstaan van de wettelijke verplichting tot het laten uitvoeren van accountantscontrole in Nederland. Accountantscontrole wordt gezien als een 'sociaal controle mechanisme', waardoor de mogelijkheid aanwezig is dat culturele en historische ontwikkelingen invloed hebben op de mate waarin bepaalde factoren gekoppeld zijn aan de vraag naar accountantscontrole. De steekproef bestaat in totaal uit 154 ondernemingen. De benodigde gegevens zijn verzameld middels publiek beschikbare gegevens en middels privé gegevens van de onderneming. De privé gegevens van de onderneming zijn verzameld door middel van het uitsturen van vragenlijsten. In hoofdstuk vijf zijn, op basis van de geïdentificeerde factoren vanuit de literatuurstudie, variabelen geselecteerd en individuele hypotheses geformuleerd. Middels bivariate analyse is nagegaan in welke statistische mate deze variabelen geassocieerd zijn met de vraag naar accountantscontrole. Om vast te stellen welke variabelen het meest bijdragen aan de beslissing naar accountantscontrole in een niet wettelijke omgeving is gebruik gemaakt van multivariate (logistische) regressie analyse. Door het beperkte aantal beschikbare observaties dient het aantal verklarende variabelen dienovereenkomstig te worden aangepast. Door middel van variabele selectie en factor analyse is het aantal verklarende variabelen in de uiteindelijke multivariate (logistische) regressie analyse aldus teruggebracht tot dertien verklarende variabelen.

De resultaten laten zien dat bij afwezigheid van een wettelijke controleplicht 62% van de ondernemingen alsnog een accountantscontrole laat uitvoeren. Deze beslissing wordt met name beïnvloed door de relatie tussen de aandeelhouder en het management, het bestaan van een vereiste tot het laten uitvoeren van accountantscontrole in leningsovereenkomsten, de perceptie van management dat accountantscontrole toegevoegde waarde heeft op de kwaliteit van de interne administratie en de financiële rapportage, de omvang van het personeelsbestand van de onderneming en de relatie tussen de onderneming en de accountant. Consistent met agency theorie kan op basis van de resultaten worden geconcludeerd dat het bestaan van externe agency factoren de belangrijkste drijvende kracht is voor de vraag naar accountantscontrole. Ook blijkt uit de resultaten dat de aard van de aandeelhouder-management relatie van meer invloed is dan het feitelijke aandelenbelang. De situatie waarin het voorkomt dat de ondernemer aandeelhouders heeft die geen directe toegang tot de financiële administratie hebben, weegt zwaarder in de besluitvorming dan het aantal aandeelhouders of het percentage aandelenbezit wat door management wordt gehouden. Echter, de resultaten laten ook zien dat met name de perceptie van de 'agent' dat bestaande aandeelhouders behoefte hebben aan accountantscontrole sterk geassocieerd is met de vraag naar accountantscontrole. Dit laatste is consistent met de theorie van beperkte rationaliteit. De theorie van beperkte rationaliteit gaat uit dat de beslissing wordt genomen, gebruik maken van een gesimplificeerd model van de werkelijkheid en waarbij perceptie een rol speelt. Daar deze studie gebruik maakt van Nederlandse data, kunnen de gepresenteerde resultaten beïnvloed worden door bestaande historische en culturele ontwikkelingen in Nederland. Om een indruk te krijgen van de generaliseerbaarheid van de resultaten, is voor een aantal factoren een vergelijkende analyse gemaakt met twee eerdere empirische studies. Op basis van deze analyse blijkt, dat hoewel verschillen bestaan die mogelijk kunnen worden verklaard door bestaande historische en culturele verschillen, dat er een zekere mate van gelijkheid bestaat tussen de factoren die de vraag naar accountantscontrole beïnvloeden.

In hoofdstuk zeven wordt geconcludeerd dat in een niet wettelijke omgeving, de vraag naar accountantscontrole in belangrijke mate kan worden verklaard aan de hand van het huidige paradigma: agency theorie. Echter de resultaten bevestigen ook de bewering vanuit eerder empirisch onderzoek, dat ook andere factoren voor MKB-ondernemingen van waarde zijn om te kiezen voor accountantscontrole. In de beslissing om wel of niet te kiezen voor een niet-wettelijke controle speelt de door de besluitvormer gehouden perceptie een belangrijke rol. De aan deze perceptie ten grondslag liggende determinanten zijn niet onderzocht in deze studie. Toekomstig onderzoek naar deze determinanten kan bijdragen aan het verkrijgen van verder inzicht. De resultaten van deze studie laten ook zien dat een te enge focus op uitsluitend agency theorie het risico in zich herbergt dat mogelijk andere factoren die de vraag naar accountantscontrole bepalen over het hoofd worden gezien en door wetenschappers daardoor mogelijk worden uitgesloten in onderzoek. Rekening houdend met een verhoogde complexiteit van de context waarin de onderneming opereert (denk bijvoorbeeld aan het ontstaan van netwerkeconomieën) en het incorporeren van een 'sociale-context' variabele zijn elementen die kunnen worden meegenomen in toekomstig onderzoek. Aangezien (alsnog) bijna twee derde van de ondernemingen in deze studie kiest voor een niet-wettelijke accountantscontrole kan worden afgevraagd of een verdere verlichting van het huidige wettelijke controleregime voor een grotere groep van private ondernemingen aan de orde kan zijn. Aanbevolen wordt om toekomstig onderzoek hier naar uit te voeren. Tenslotte wordt de aanbeveling gedaan om deze studie naar de factoren die de vraag (lees: toegevoegde waarde) naar accountantscontrole bepalen door te zetten in een longitudinaal onderzoek om de invloed van de ontwikkeling in de maatschappij (context) op de vraag naar accountantscontrole.

Curriculum Vitae

Hans Duits (1969) studied business economics at the University of Amsterdam and followed the postgraduate education for registered auditor at the VU University Amsterdam. In 1995 he became a registered auditor. With over more than twenty years working experience as a public accountant in practice, he is currently employed both as SME Advisor at KPMG Accountants N.V. and as professor at the Faculty of Business and Management at the University of Applied Sciences Utrecht (HU) in the Netherlands. His research interests include the market for audit (assurance) services and governance for SME companies.

Hans Duits (1969) studeerde bedrijfseconomie aan de Universiteit van Amsterdam en volgde de postdoctorale opleiding tot registeraccountant aan de Vrije Universiteit van Amsterdam. Sinds 1995 is hij ingeschreven als registeraccountant. Met meer dan twintig jaar werkervaring als openbaar accountant, werkt hij momenteel zowel als MKB Adviseur bij KPMG Accountants N.V. en als lector aan de Faculteit Economie en Management van de Hogeschool Utrecht. Zijn onderzoeksinteresse behelst de markt voor accountants (assurance) diensten en governance ten behoeve van MKB ondernemingen.